Blurring Boundaries: Human Security and Forced Migration

Blurring Boundaries: Human Security and Forced Migration

Edited by

Stefan Salomon, Lisa Heschl,
Gerd Oberleitner and Wolfgang Benedek

BRILL
NIJHOFF

LEIDEN | BOSTON

Library of Congress Control Number: 2017942194

Typeface for the Latin, Greek, and Cyrillic scripts: "Brill". See and download: brill.com/brill-typeface.

ISBN 978-90-04-32686-6 (hardback)
ISBN 978-90-04-32687-3 (e-book)

This book is printed on acid-free paper and produced in a sustainable manner.

Open letter to the Australian government of 600 refugees detained in the Australian detention center on Manus Island in the course of the Operation Sovereign Borders of the Australian Government

As the refugees and asylum seekers trapped in Manus Island detention we would like to request you something different this time.

As previously we wrote and asked for help and there was no response to our request to be freed out of detention, we realized that there are no differences between us and rubbish. We are but a bunch of slaves that helped to stop the boats by living in hellish condition. The only difference is that we are very costly for the Australian tax payers and the Politicians, as our job to "stop the boats" is done.

We would like to give you some recommendations to stop the waste of this huge amount of money ruining Australian's reputation and to keep the Australian borders safe forever:

1. A navy ship that can put us all on board and dump us all in the ocean. (HMAS is always available)
2. A gas chamber (DECMIL will do it with a new contract)
3. Injection of a poison. (IHMS will help for this)

This is not a joke or a satire [...]. Please take it serious.

We are dying in Manus gradually, every single day we are literally tortured and traumatized and there is no safe country to offer us protection as DIBP says.

Best regards

Merry Christmas in advance

Contents

PART IV
Climate Change, Environmental Degradation and People on the Move

PART V
Human trafficking

Preface

The present volume results from a workshop on human security and migration that was held in November 2015 at the University of Graz. The idea behind the workshop was to take a step back and reflect on structural problems related to forced migration and the security driven "management" approaches surrounding it. The preparation and planning of the workshop started already well before the numbers of asylum seekers spiked in Europe in summer 2015. The wave of hospitality and empathy towards people seeking protection that prevailed in many EU Member States has dwindled since. Its place has been occupied, again, by a politics of short-termism, focusing on territorial borders, deterrence and prohibition. The failures to deal with the increasing number of people arriving at Europe's shores and the human and humanitarian tragedies stemming from that failure tragically illustrate the underlying structural issues of the state centred migration control approach. For decades, these policies of territoriality, deterrence and prohibition have been upheld at any cost, including human costs.

Blurring Boundaries, the title of this book, has a twofold meaning. The first meaning is descriptive. Formerly clear-cut boundaries between political, legal and social categories and practices increasingly evaporate. Questions on what is domestic and international and what is local and global are increasingly hard to answer, as boundaries have become diffuse and blurred. The second meaning of 'blurring' refers to an action, to engage in blurring boundaries. The contributions in this volume decisively engage in arguing for change of the prevailing state centred approach in migration law and policies. The contributions go beyond the immediate, pointing to things to come and reveal shortcomings of existing paradigms; they go beyond the local, setting things in a global perspective. Inherent to all contributions is thereby the aim to blur boundaries: Boundaries between prevailing doctrines and disciplines, dominant actors in the field of migration and their subordinates, boundaries of the well-established and its radical re-thinking. We chose a human security approach as expression of blurring these boundaries. By shifting the traditional notion of security from a state's to an individual's perspective, predominant approaches to migration are challenged on principled grounds. Apart from merely challenging established approaches, the volume aims to ignite debates on the way forward and on possible reconciliations of different interests in the field of forced migration.

This volume would of course have not been possible without the work of innumerable others whose names do not appear in this volume. As their number exceeds the space available, we would like to mention a few in gratitude here: Bernhard Wetschko for invaluable research assistance and editing; Gregor Fischer and Sarah Micheuz for their patient assistance in the preparation of the workshop; the dean's office at the Law Faculty of the University of Graz and the Austrian Federal Ministry for Integration, Europe and Foreign Affairs for the financial assistance without which the realisation of the workshop would not have been possible.

Wolfgang Benedek, Gerd Oberleitner, Lisa Heschl, Stefan Salomon

About the Contributors

Wolfgang Benedek
is the head of the Institute of International Law and International Relations and director of the European Training and Research Centre of Human Rights and Democracy of the University of Graz. He has published widely in the field human security, in particular with regard to terrorism, peace operations, multi-stakeholder partnerships and human rights.

Marco Borraccetti
holds a PhD in EU Law from the University of Bologna. He is Assistant Professor of European Union Law of the Alma Mater Studiorum – Università di Bologna, School of Political Science, where he teaches EU Institutional Law and EU Immigration Law (Jean Monnet Module with the financial support of the European Union). His current main research interests include: Migration and Mobility in the EU; the judicial protection of fundamental rights in the EU; THB and access to victims' rights.

Bríd Ní Ghráinne
is a lecturer in Refugee and International Law at the University of Sheffield, UK. She completed her doctorate in law at the University of Oxford, where her work was supervised by Prof. Guy S. Goodwin-Gill. Bríd also holds an LL.M in Public International Law from Leiden University, and a BCL (International) from the National University of Ireland, Galway. Previously, she worked as a legal researcher in the Irish Department of Foreign Affairs and Trade.

Lisa Heschl
holds a Dr. iur. degree from the University of Graz and an E.MA degree from the Inter-European University Centre in Venice. She is currently employed as a Post-Doc at the European Training and Research Centre for Human Rights and Democracy at the University of Graz. Her research and teaching focuses on European asylum and migration law and policy.

Maximilian Lakitsch
is currently a postdoc at the University of Graz. Prior to joining academia, he has worked for research and development NGOs in Austria and in Lebanon. His theoretical work covers conflict theory, peace building, religious conflicts and the Middle East. Maximilian studied Theology, Philos-

ophy and International Relations. He received his PhD about modernity and violence from the University of Graz and the American University of Beirut.

Mehrnaz Mostafavi

is the Chief of the Human Security Unit (HSU) at the United Nations (UN). She has been responsible for the advancement and promotion of human security and its translation into UN funded activities under the United Nations Trust Fund for Human Security. She has been instrumental, inter alia, in establishing the strategic vision of the HSU and its operational activities. She was actively engaged in advancing the recommendations of the Commission on Human Security at the Secretariat of the Advisory Board on Human Security (ABHS). Before joining the Secretariat of the ABHS, she worked at the Bureau for Development Policy at the UNDP. In addition to her contributions at the UN, Ms. Mostafavi has worked in the corporate multinational sector, as well as in academia.

Gerd Oberleitner

is Associate Professor of International Law and UNESCO Chair in Human Rights and Human Security at the University of Graz and Director of the European Training and Research Centre for Human Rights and Democracy at the University of Graz. He served as legal adviser in the Human Rights Department of the Austrian Ministry of Foreign Affairs and was Lecturer at the London School of Economics and Political Science (LSE) and Visiting Fellow at the LSE's Centre for the Study of Human Rights. His publications include *Global Human Rights Institutions: between Remedy and Ritual* (Polity, 2007) and *Human Rights in Armed Conflict – Law, Practice, Policy* (Cambridge University Press, 2015).

Daniel Petz

is currently a PhD student with the FWF-DK Climate Change at University of Graz, working on issues of climate change and intergenerational justice. Previously, he worked as an independent consultant on disaster risk management and human rights issues, completing research projects for the Brookings Institution, UNICEF, UNESCO and the Internal Displacement Monitoring Centre. He also worked as research assistant for the Brookings Institution's Project on Internal Displacement (Washington D.C., USA) and as lecturer and researcher for European Studies and Peace and Conflict Studies at Gadjah Mada University (Indonesia).

Stefan Salomon
currently heads the Refugee Law Clinic at the University of Graz. Stefan is specialized in refugee and asylum law and has extensive research experience in Sub-Sahara Africa. Prior to joining academia, Stefan worked at the Ministry of Foreign Affairs in Vienna, as a freelance journalist and as a trainee at Frontex.

Dana Schmalz
has been a research fellow at the Max Planck Institute for Comparative Public Law and International Law in Heidelberg/Berlin, writing her PhD on questions of refugee law as reflecting central challenges in contemporary democratic theory. Dana currently works as a postdoctoral fellow at the Max Planck Institute for the Study of Religious and Ethnic Diversity in Göttingen.

Vassilis P. Tzevelekos
is a Senior Lecturer in Law at the Liverpool School of Law and Social Justice, a member of the McCoubrey Centre for International Law and an Athens qualified lawyer. He is specialising in the theory of public international law and human rights law. He holds a PhD from the European University Institute and worked at Columbia Law School as well as the University of Michigan Law School. He is, inter alia, the co-editor of *The EU Accession to the ECHR* (V. Kosta, N. Skoutaris and V.P. Tzevelekos (eds.), Hart, 2014). and *Beyond Responsibility to Protect: Generating Change in International Law* (R.A. Barnes, V.P. Tzevelekos (eds.), Intersentia, forthcoming).

Susanna Villani
is currently a PhD candidate in EU law at the University of Bologna and UNED (Madrid). Her research topic relates to the European Union's response to disasters, with particular attention to state consent and the application of the solidarity clause. Moreover, Susanna has a particular interest in International Human Rights Law and International Environmental Law. She holds an MA in International Relations from the University of Florence and previously worked at the Ministry of Foreign Affairs.

Foreword

In recent years, multiple crises from conflicts to natural disasters have resulted in human displacement at a level unknown since World War II. According to the United Nations High Commissioner for Refugees, by the end of 2014, 59.5 million people all over the world were forcibly displaced. Up 16 per cent over the previous year, this was the highest number ever recorded.

The sheer scale of forced migration has spurred growing recognition that Governments, international organizations and others need to orchestrate better-planned responses. These need to not only meet the most basic, immediate needs, but also respond to the many risks and vulnerabilities that displaced people face.

Viewing migration through the human security lens highlights the social, political and economic dimensions of those on the move. This provides a comprehensive, nuanced basis for advancing the benefits of migration, while mitigating and preventing its risks. Within a framework of protection and empowerment, a focus on human security helps strengthen institutional mechanisms that protect and empower migrants and the communities that host them to live free from fear, want and indignity.

Four principles underpin the human security approach. First, it is people-centered, geared towards ensuring the survival, livelihood and dignity of all people, including migrants, displaced individuals and host communities. Second, it is comprehensive, ensuring that policies and actions respond to the diverse and interacting risks affecting migrants, displaced individuals and host communities. Third, it is context-specific, considering the root causes and specific manifestations of diverse and interacting insecurities. Fourth, it is prevention-oriented, taking proactive responses to current and future risks in order to enhance the benefits of migration and displacement, while preventing new crises from erupting.

Established in 1999, the application of human security at the United Nations provides some invaluable lessons on the interlinked challenges of migration, whether due to economic drivers, violence, environmental disasters, or persistent and abject poverty. Human security programmes illustrate the complexity and the need to address migration in a people-centred, comprehensive and integrated fashion. By combining institutional policies and processes with community-based empowerment responses and actions, human security programmes have drawn attention to the risks and insecurities faced by vulnerable groups and communities and have promoted responses that aim to address gaps in the management of migration so as to benefit both migrants and their host communities.

The quest to migrate has been and will continue to be a constant in human history. Therefore, responding to this phenomenon in a comprehensive and humane manner is vital, if we are to maximize its benefits and ensure that those who are most vulnerable and marginalized are not left behind.

Mehrnaz Mostafavi, Chief, United Nations Human Security Unit

PART I

Exercises in Blurring

Whose Security? Introductory Remarks on People on the Move and the Reclaiming of Security

Gerd Oberleitner and Stefan Salomon

1 Boundaries and the Production of Space

On 5 January 2015, the Lebanese government introduced visa requirements for Syrian nationals. The introduction of visa requirements effectively resulted in restricting access of Syrians seeking international protection in Lebanon. Already in the preceding months, Palestinians from Syria were denied entry at the border.[1] The high number of Syrian refugees arriving to Lebanon,[2] the volatile political arrangements along ethnic and religious lines, highly fragile state institutions, the absence of any significant international assistance to Lebanon and the socio-economic effects on the Lebanese population,[3] effectively resulted in the Lebanese government announcing that they could not host more refugees.[4] Although Lebanon is bound by the prohibition of *refoulement* (i.e. not to push any refugee back or to prohibit entry at its border), the generally vocal UN High Commissioner for Refugees (UNHCR) did not protest, let

---

1 IRIN, 'A Timeline of Syria's Closing Borders' (8 January 2015) <http://newirin.irinnews.org/syrian-refugees-restrictions-timeline>.

2 Although official UNHCR data indicate 1,03 Mio. Syrians officially registered as refugees in Lebanon (as of June 2016 – see UNHCR, 'Syrian Regional Refugee Response: Inter-Agency Information Sharing Portal' <http://data.unhcr.org/syrianrefugees/country.php?id=122>, the overall number of Syrian refugees in Lebanon is estimated at 1,5 Mio. – see Government of Lebanon and the UN, 'Lebanon Crisis: Response Plan 2015-16' (Year Two, 2016) 1, 3.

3 According to data of the World Bank approximately 170.000 Lebanese were pushed into poverty by the high number of Syrian refugees arriving to the country – see IRIN, 'A Timeline' (n 1).

4 The Lebanese Minister of Interior announced on a media conference on the introduction of the restrictive measures that Lebanon has "no capacity anymore to host more displaced." BBC, 'Syria Conflict: Lebanon Refugee Curb Prompts UN Concern' (*BBC News*, 5 January 2015) <http://www.bbc.com/news/world-middle-east-30685174>.

Salomon, Heschl, *et al.* (eds.), *Blurring Boundaries: Human Security and Forced Migration*
 ISBN 978-90-04-32686-6. pp. 3-21.

alone other governments.[5] The silence of the international community seems to acknowledge that the security of those who flee (Syrians) and those who provide protection (Lebanese) are equally at stake. It also illustrates that in such a situation, the right not to be *refouled,* a right that does not permit derogation under any circumstances,[6] becomes meaningless.

After a line of tragic boat incidents where hundreds of migrants drowned in the Mediterranean Sea, the Italian government launched on 18 October 2013 the lifesaving operation *Mare Nostrum*, extending rescue operations well beyond Italy's defined Search and Rescue (SAR) area. Although the Italian government certainly was not legally obliged to provide enhanced rescue operations beyond its SAR zone, Italian leaders seem to have been driven by a moral imperative to save the lives of migrants in distress at sea.[7] In November 2014, *Mare Nostrum* was replaced by the more narrow EU operation *Triton,* which almost immediately resulted in a spike of deaths at sea and eventually culminated in the black week in April 2015 where more than 1.200 migrants drowned in the Mediterranean Sea.[8] The EU and its Member States responded by launching the maritime operation *Sophia* to disrupt human smuggling networks on the EU plane[9] and secured international support by lobbying the UN Security Council to adopt resolution 2240, that permits states to inspect and seize vessels suspected of engaging in human smuggling.[10]

---

5 UNHCR merely demanded the Lebanese government to outline how the restrictions would work and to ensure that the most vulnerable would still get access, see ibid.

6 Elihu Lauterpacht and Daniel Bethlehem list in their comprehensive study some evidence that the norm of non-refoulement might constitute a peremptory norm of international law – see Elihu Lauterpacht and Daniel Bethlehem, 'The Scope and Content of the Principle of Non-Refoulement: Opinion' in Erika Feller and others (eds.), *Refugee Protection in International Law* (Cambridge University Press 2003) 141.

7 After a series of tragic boat accidents off the island of Lampedusa, the public pressure for taking action in Italy increased; the government declared a day of mourning and subsequently launched operation *Mare Nostrum.* On a detailed discussion see Riley M Townsend, 'The European Migrant Crisis' (AMF Publishing 2015) 93-96.

8 Death by Rescue, 'Main Narrative' <https://deathbyrescue.org/report/narrative/>.

9 Council of the EU, 'Council Decision (CFSP) 2015/778 on a European Union Military Operation in the Southern Central Mediterranean (EUNAVFOR MED)' (19 May 2015) OJ L 122/31.

10 UNSC, 'Resolution 2240' (9 October 2015) UN Doc S/RES/2240.

Federica Mogherini, the European Union High Representative for Foreign Affairs and Security Policy, stated "that the European Union is finally ready to take its own responsibilities: saving lives, welcoming refugees, addressing the root causes of the phenomenon, dismantling criminal organisations."[11] These situations illustrate a complex interplay and shifts between legal obligations, moral imperatives and policy strategies based on different security perspectives. Yet, welcoming refugees and saving lives, as Mogherini announced, never materialized into enhancing legal and thus safe access for those seeking protection. In this context, the absence of legal migration routes, curbing human smuggling (as part of strengthening prohibition and deterrence regimes) produces a situation where migrants need to be saved from distress at sea in the first place.

These two randomly chosen examples above merely illustrate a larger global context of a complex interplay between the increasing adoption of prohibition and deterrence regimes of countries in the Global North and the effects on migrants, refugees and other countries. That 2015 represented the year with the highest number of people, more than 65 million, forcibly displaced since the end of the Second World War merely aggravates and reinforces this interplay.[12] Already before the events commonly referred to as 'migration crisis', Lebanon hosted more than 500.000 Palestinian refugees with a total population of four million and the numbers of migrants drowning in the Mediterranean Sea has been steadily on the rise since the mid-1990s. These situations are merely symptomatic for steady trends: more than 86% of refugees remain in the Global South while the discourse continues to be predominantly on the 'refugee crisis' in the Global North; the increasing sophistication of deterrence and prohibition policies of states in the Global North; or the blurring of lines of jurisdiction exercised by states that aim to curb migration are but a few examples.

These trends essentially concern the same phenomenon: the blurring of boundaries. Like the flows of people they aim to stop, boundaries themselves are restructured into flows, disaggregated into multiple components that are contracted and expanded wherever and whenever needed for a specific purpose.[13] Boundaries, like the people who cross

---

11 Federica Mogherini, 'High Representative/Vice-President Federica Mogherini's Remarks at the UN Security Council, New York' (11 May 2015) UN Doc 150511_03_en.

12 UNHCR, 'Global Trends: Forced Displacement in 2015' (UNHCR 2016) 2.

13 On the problematic of disaggregating sovereignty in the context of transnational migration controls, see Itamar Mann, 'Dialectics of Transnationalism: Unauthor-

them, are being managed.[14] Disaggregation, contraction and expansion result in boundaries becoming elusive. Elusiveness, however, does not translate into not being there, but as being everywhere, the quality of ubiquity. If boundaries are elusive and ubiquitous at the same time, the question then is how to grasp and approach them analytically.

The late Sir Ian Brownlie remarked in his seminal work *African Boundaries* that the primary function of boundaries consists in allocation.[15] Brownlie understood allocation primarily as the allocation of territory to a state, other political units or non-self-governing peoples. It seems to be a view that persists in international law, as a quick look at the dockets of the International Court of Justice (ICJ) confirms: Still, the vast majority of cases before the ICJ are boundary disputes, allocating territory or rights of usage to one or the other party. Also, territory in this sense is an entirely legal creature, as it confers a mass of land (or sea) to a state, but the right to exercise jurisdiction over the assigned part. Yet, the function of elusive and ubiquitous boundaries is not to delimit territory, and thus jurisdiction, but, to the contrary, to regulate and control the movement of people beyond one's territory and jurisdiction. Therefore, the function of boundaries in international law requires fundamental reconceptualization. This book offers such a reconceptualization. It argues that the function of boundaries lies in the production of space.

For Henri Lefebvre, who was amongst the most acclaimed philosophers and sociologists of the 20th century, space was foremost a product. Lefebvre argued that every society produces its own space, hence, things and people do not merely appear in a space; rather space *appears* through societal creative practices that are, in fact, practices of appropriation.[16] Thus understood, space simultaneously is the product and process of societal production. If things and people do not merely appear in a certain space, as Lefebvre argues, but rather appear in a specific mode related to that space, as the latter appears itself through the practices of appropriation, then, we see these practices of appropriation most visibly in the law.

---

ized Migration and Human Rights, 1993-2013' (2013) 54(2) Harvard International Law Journal 315.

14 "The Union shall develop a common immigration policy aimed at ensuring, at all stages, the efficient management of migration flows [...]" – Consolidated Version of the Treaty on the Functioning of the European Union [2012] OJ C 326/47, Art 79.

15 Ian Brownlie, *African Boundaries: A Legal and Diplomatic Encyclopedia* (C Hurst & University of California Press 1979) 3.

16 Henri Lefebvre, *The Production of Space* (Blackwell 1991) 38-46.

Thus, this book argues that boundaries are primarily set forth in the law and, therefore, the *locus* of the production of space is law. If the locus of the production of space is law, space is not a singular, but a multitude of different spaces, each space circumscribed by boundaries set forth in the law: the prohibition on the use of force and its exceptions, the delimitation of the SAR area and concomitant legal obligations, spaces of jurisdiction and human rights obligations. Different spaces might overlap or they might be kept apart, depending on the specific instance.

Although space has a spatial dimension – people are arrested, turned back, sentenced and detained *somewhere* – it is less about exercising power over certain spatial features than effectively appropriating space by rearranging, if one adheres to a bundle of rights theory,[17] the substance of the subjective legal positions of persons. Consequently, space does not merely appear through things and persons, but, at the same time, the boundaries that circumscribe space set forth the possibilities of things and persons to appear in a space, i.e. the conditions of appearance.

When, for instance, the Australian High Court holds the offshore detention scheme as in conformity with the constitution, absent any direct detention by the government,[18] spaces are thereby construed not merely as a reduction of the sticks in the bundle of legal personhood, but where personhood, understood in the legal-philosophical aspects as sharing the same humanity, is muted as a matter of migratory policy.[19] Similarly, Greek laws on detention centres and the removal of 'irregular migrants' under the authority of the EU-Turkey agreement,[20] the amendments in

---

17 Hans Kelsen, *Pure Theory of Law* (University of California Press 1967, reprinted by The Law Book Exchange 2005) 173.

18 *Plaintiff M68-2015 v Minister for Immigration and Border Protection* (3 February 2016) High Court of Australia 1, para. 29-37.

19 See in particular the extracts from the official Wilson Security incidents report that meticulously documents the grave psychological and psychosomatic effects of detention on the physical and mental health of both detainees and staff – Ben Doherty and David Marr, 'The Worst I've Seen – Trauma Expert Lifts Lid on 'Atrocity' of Australia's Detention Regime' (*The Guardian*, 19 June 2016) <https://www.theguardian.com/australia-news/2016/jun/20/the-worst-ive-seen-trauma-expert-lifts-lid-on-atrocity-of-australias-detention-regime>.

20 European Commission, 'Communication from the Commission to the European Parliament, the European Council and the Council: Next Operational Steps in the EU-Turkey Cooperation in the Field of Migration' (COM/2016 166 final, 16 March 2016); European Council, 'EU-Turkey Statement' (Press Releases and Statements, 18 March 2016) <http://www.consilium.europa.eu/en/press/press-

Austrian asylum law on fast-track procedures and prolonged detention at the border,[21] or the enhanced powers of the military by government decree[22] in Hungary and the amendment of the penal law that make it a crime to enter Hungary except at official border crossing points,[23] set forth boundaries in the law that produce and circumscribe spaces in which the substance of legal personhood is rearranged.

Conceiving boundaries analytically as the constitutive element of the production of space permits to trace the modes and modalities of that production, as well as its effects.[24] The contributions contained in this volume aim at tracing the profoundly existential and normative effects on the individual human being. Beyond a mere critique of these effects, the contributions also offer alternative paths and actions that ought to be taken.

Human security, in this regard, represents an existing discourse on the international plane that recognizes the multitude of threats that profoundly affect the well-being and existence of the individual human being. Linking the conceptualization of boundaries, understood as the production of space in law, with human security, as a discourse on the international plane to highlight the effects on the individual thus represents a fruitful and promising combination.

---

releases/2016/03/18-eu-turkey-statement/>; European Council, 'European Council Conclusions (Press Releases and Statements, 17-18 March 2016) <http://www.consilium.europa.eu/en/press/press-releases/2016/03/18-european-council-conclusions/>.

21 Austrian Federal Act Concerning the Granting of Asylum (Asylum Act 2005 – AsylG 2005)Section 5.

22 Hungarian 269/2015. (IX. 15) Government Decree Announcing a Crisis Situation Caused by Mass Immigration and Establishing the Rules Related to the Declaration, Maintenance and Termination of the Crisis Situation.

23 Act C of 2012 on the Hungarian Criminal Code 2012 (2012).

24 Beyond the function of rearranging the legal sticks in the bundle of rights, boundaries also produce social and political identities beyond the immediate effects on the rights of persons concerned. Richard Ford eloquently described that the functioning of territorial jurisdiction produces political and social identities by separating them not merely spatially, but legally (native from foreign, slave from free, citizen from alien, migrant from refugee), see Richard T Ford, 'Law's Territory (A History of Jurisdiction)' (1999) 97(4) Michigan Law Review 843, 844

2 The Dimensions of Human Security

Traditional notions of security conceive security primarily as state centred and focused on a state's territory and its institutions. This traditional notion of security is broadly reflected in international law. International law traditionally gave, when it came to the constitutive components of states – territory, population, public authority – priority to territory and authority.[25] At best, populations always played a secondary role. The concept of human security, introduced in the 1994 Human Development Report, sought to reformulate such a conception of security and instead positioned the individual as the core analytical unit. Accordingly, the individual human being, and not the state is the primary referent of security.

The 1994 Human Development Report, in essence, argued that what people seek in their everyday lives is not primarily national security (of the state, its borders and territory), but economic, food, health, environmental, personal, collective and political security.[26] This idea was not entirely new, but drew on earlier re-conceptualizations of the social dimensions of security and its global, common or comprehensive reach. The Palme Commission of 1982, the Brandt Commission (1980/1983) and the Brundtland Commission of 1988, for instance, had already argued that national security cannot be considered as the appropriate strategy to respond to multi-layered threats. When the UNDP report rooted the notion of human security in the development discourse, it added social dimensions to such a comprehensive meaning of security.

Accordingly, the individual needs to be understood in its agency and consequently needs to be empowered to respond to the multitude of threats. As the Commission on Human Security, (set up in 2001 and composed of 12 renown personalities, among them Sadako Ogata, the former United Nations High Commissioner for Refugees, and Nobel Economics Prize Laureate Amartya Sen as co-chairs) puts it in its 2003 Report *Human Security Now*, human security means

> to protect the vital core of all human lives in ways that enhance human freedoms and human fulfilment. Human security means protecting fundamental freedoms – freedoms that are the essence of

---

25 Georg Jellinek, *Allgemeine Staatslehre* (Verlag Dr Max Gehlen 1966).

26 UN Development Programme, 'Human Development Report 1994' <http://hdr.undp.org/sites/default/files/reports/255/hdr_1994_en_complete_nostats.pdf>.

> life. It means protecting people from critical (severe) and pervasive (widespread) threats and situations. It means using processes that build on people's strengths and aspirations. It means creating political, social, environmental, economic, military and cultural systems that together give people the building blocks of survival, livelihood and dignity.[27]

In 2012, the UN agreed on a common understanding of human security in UN General Assembly resolution 66/290 of 25 October 2012. Noting the interlinkages between development, human rights and peace and security as the three pillars of the United Nations, the General Assembly considered human security as "an approach to assist Member States in identifying and addressing widespread and cross-cutting challenges to the survival, livelihood and dignity of their people."[28] Yet, at the same time, the resolution was cautious not to shake the foundations of the state-centred security discourse too violently. For the General Assembly, human security adds to national security without replacing it and enables governments to retain their primary role and responsibility for ensuring the survival, livelihood and dignity of their citizens, with the international community only complementing and supporting governments in their responses to current and emerging threats. In particular, a clause to preserve state sovereignty was integrated in the text so that human security should only be implemented with full respect for the purposes and principles enshrined in the Charter of the United Nations, which includes full respect for the sovereignty of States, territorial integrity and non-interference in matters that are essentially within the domestic jurisdiction of States. In particular, human security is not meant to be a responsibility to protect in disguise.[29] Interestingly enough, resolution A/RES/66/290 explicitly mentions the "primary role and responsibility [of governments] for ensuring the survival, livelihood and dignity of *their citizens*" while remaining conspicuously silent on forced migration or displacement.[30]

---

27 Commission on Human Security, 'Human Security Now' (2003) 4.

28 UN General Assembly, 'Resolution Adopted by the General Assembly on 10 September 2012: Follow-Up to Paragraph 143 on Human Security of the 2005 World Summit Outcome' (25 October 2012) UN Doc A/Res/66/290, para. 3.

29 See Edward Newman, 'The United Nations and Human Security: Between Solidarism and Pluralism' in Mary Martin und Taylor Owen, *Routledge Handbook of Human Security* (London and New York Routledge 2014) 225.

30 UN General Assembly, A/Res/66/290 (n 28) para. 3(g) (emphasis added).

At no place the resolution mentions forced migration or displacement, although, at the time the resolution was adopted, scores of people were displaced by the violent conflicts that erupted in the course of the events of the Arab Spring. Resolution A/RES/66/290 thus represents a further step away from the endorsement of human security as laid out in the 1994 Human Development Report.

3 Human Security and People on the Move

From a state-centred perspective of national security, mass migration or forced migration across borders can be perceived as endangering state security, both with regard to the physical forms of state security – borders and territory – as well as the underlying foundation of state security – the ability to autonomously control territory and regulate movements across borders and thus preserve state sovereignty as the precondition for the existence within the Westphalian model of Statehood. Human security may allow for a more effective understanding of migration and its effects.[31] There is hardly any situation of greater human insecurity than forced migration and displacement. Increasingly, processes of migration are as dangerous as the conditions people escape from, particularly where state power is simultaneously expanded and contracted.

The Commission on Human Security had already explicitly related the concept not only to violent conflicts, but among others also to people on the move. The Commission argued that applying a human security perspective to people on the move included the necessity to comprehensively analyse not only the movement of persons, but also their decisions to move.[32] Already in 1997, UNHCR highlighted the key role of human security in understanding the complexity of patterns of forced displacement. Understanding forced migration as complex mixture of various insecurities to people's lives, including economic decline, unbalanced development, systematic violence and warfare, shows that the conceptual "distinction between voluntary and involuntary migration is not always

31 See similarly Francesco Vietti and Todd Scribner, 'Human Insecurity: Understanding International Migration from a Human Security Perspective' (2013) 1(1) Journal of Migration and Human Security 17, 18.

32 Commission on Human Security, 'Human Security Now' (n 27) 45.

an easy one to sustain."[33] 'Economic migration', generally considered as 'voluntary' migration, involves in most instances the involuntary condition of poverty or economic decline, while every migratory movement involves an element of choice that represents the complex mixture of insecurities experienced by people. This also reveals that refugeehood and migranthood, or involuntary and voluntary migration, are fluid and historically contingent categories, shifting over time.[34] In the context of a general crackdown on immigration, the humanitarian focus on refugees as distinctive categories of migrants, deserving particular protection, contributes to exacerbate policies that consider migrants as suspicious, and latently bogus, category. Adopting a human security approach shows that such a conceptual distinction does not adequately reflect the reality of human movement. Given that a human security perspective considers security ultimately as shared security, this can indeed be understood as attempting to understand and respond to people on the move "rather than simply closing the door behind us in order to keep the less fortunate people outside".[35]

Furthermore, the Commission on Human Security also emphasized the need for international cooperation to respond to situations of insecurity for groups and individuals in migration and highlighted the positive example of the freedom of movement granted within the European Union in this regard.[36] How hollow this praise sounds a decade later, with freedom of movement having become one of the most divisive issues within the European Union. The Commission also proposed the development of an international migration framework with appropriate institutions, which allows for an orderly and safe movement of persons, increasing migratory opportunities while ensuring a burden-sharing between states.[37] For the Commission, the bottom line was that consultative and cooperative efforts cannot be achieved under a national security paradigm.[38]

33 UNHCR, 'The State of the World's Refugees: A Humanitarian Agenda' (UNHCR 1997) 14.

34 Katy Long, 'When Refugees Stopped Being Migrants: Movement, Labor and Humanitarian Protection' (2013) 1(1) Migration Studies 4, 5.

35 Vietti and Scribner, 'Human Insecurity' (n 31) 23.

36 Commission on Human Security, 'Human Security Now' (n 27) 47.

37 Ibid.

38 See Vietti and Scribner, 'Human Insecurity' (n 31) 27.

The basic assumption of human security – that the individual human being resides at the core of security and is the ultimate referent – rests on two key terms: threats and empowerment. As to the former, human security advances a conceptual shift. Accordingly, threats need to be understood broadly so as to encompass a variety of threats to the live, livelihood or dignity of humans. It thus encompasses a conceptual move from abstract and general references to threats, such as '*ordre public*', 'national security' or 'threat to the functioning of public institutions' towards a more comprehensive conceptualization of threat. Comprehensiveness in this regard may be understood along two lines.

First, human security does not categorically prioritize the interests of citizens over interests of non-citizens. Although such categorical prioritization is not specific to the law and the boundaries established therein, law nevertheless functions uniquely in that the interests of outsiders only count if they can be framed in legal language. Human security offers simultaneously a discourse beyond the law, while remaining attached to it through its broad acceptance by the international community. This might be called the transcending function of human security. By rigorously focusing on the effects on individual human beings, it transcends a categorical prioritization of citizens over non-citizens in a strong sense.[39] This is related to the second line: human security offers a rich discursive potential for a *critical* politics on universalism, which of course, requires that this discourse includes a critical stance towards its own limitations and conditions.[40] Empowerment, however, might also be instrumentalised for playing different groups of refugees out against each other.[41] Advancing gender equality or vulnerability in contexts of resettlement or distribution of resources in refugee camps, for instance, might result not in advancing autonomy and restricting governance, but eventually work as a means of effecting governance. The introduction of visa requirements for Syrian refugees by the Lebanese government, mentioned

---

39 Similar other discourses exist of course. They remain however largely confined to academia and some few activists. For the probably most eloquent argument see Arash Abizadeh, 'Démocratie, Nation et Ethnie: le Problème des Frontières, Raison Publique' (2013).

40 Étienne Balibar has pointed both to the inherent violence as integral condition of a politics and discourse of universalism – see Étienne Balibar, 'Sur L'Universalisme: Un Débat avec Alain Badiou' (*European Institute for Progressive Cultural Policies*, Transversal Texts, 2007) <http://eipcp.net/transversal/0607/balibar/fr>.

41 As pointed out by the contribution of Dana Schmalz in this volume.

earlier, illustrates these limitations and probably impossibility of its own conditions, namely to guarantee the human security simultaneously of Syrian refugees and Lebanese hosts. Understanding human security as a critical discourse also entails a critical stance towards its own limitations and tensions.

Switching perspectives in the analytical inquiry from migration, as phenomenon to be managed, to people on the move, sheds light onto the multitude of threats migrants and refugees experience. That also reveals the agency claimed by migrants and refugees, in fact, reclaims their ability to act. Claiming one's agency in a world where human mobility is distributed in highly unequal terms, packing things up and leaving might thus not merely be the oldest form to escape poverty, but indeed be a form of political protest. Refugees who claim freedom of movement in sit-in protests at the French-Italian border or who resist deportation are indeed a case in point.[42]

Looking at the Dublin regulation, probably the most contentious issue in EU Member States over the last decade, reveals some interesting insights. The Dublin Regulation represents a hierarchical system of determining the EU Member State responsible for the examination of an application of international protection. Such a system of allocation is crucial for the overall functioning of the Area of Freedom, Security and Justice (AFSJ). The criteria establishing the responsible EU Member State for examining an asylum application do not take into account – neither under the current Dublin-III Regulation, nor under the proposal amending the Dublin Regulation – preferences of asylum seekers, such as language skills, extended family members or social contacts in a specific country, which would mean having at least a minimal choice.[43] During

42 Al Jazeera, 'Italy Drags Migrants Away from French-Italian Border' (17 June 2015) <http://www.aljazeera.com/news/2015/06/italy-drags-migrants-french-italian-border-150616151510276.html>.

43 European Parliament and EU Council, 'Regulation (EU) 604/2013 of the European Parliament and of the Council of 26 June 2013 Establishing the Criteria and Mechanisms for Determining the Member State Responsible for Examining an Application for International Protection Lodged in one of the Member States by a Third-Country National or a Stateless Person (Recast)' [2013] OJ L 180/31, Arts 7-16; European Commission, 'Proposal for Regulation Establishing the Criteria and Mechanisms for Determining the Member State Responsible for Examining an Application for International Protection Lodged in one of the Member States by a Third-Country National or a Stateless Person (Recast)' (COM/2016 270 final, 4 May 2016).

the consultation process on the amendment of the existing Dublin Regulation some EU Member States pointed out that, "preferences [of asylum seekers] could not be fully ignored as this would almost inevitably result in secondary movements". Other EU Member States insisted that "applicants are seeking international protection [...] and that, therefore, they should not be provided with excessive room for choosing the final country of asylum, since the rationale of Dublin is not that of an (economic) migration scheme."[44] This interpretation of Member States suggests a sharp line distinguishing between physical safety provided by international protection and all remaining considerations that refugees might have in regard to building their future lives. Such a distinction is not merely ill conceived, but flies in the face of the complexity of migratory processes, migrants' choices and remains firmly rooted in traditional understanding of security. If the European Union is understood as a transformative political space, the notion of 'security' in the Area of Freedom, Security and Justice "could also include a human security dimension, in particular security of residence for refugees and migrants".[45] The Dublin Regulation certainly would look and function differently, if a human security perspective were to be taken into account.

If human security is to be employed meaningfully in the global discourse on security beyond a mere repetition of commonplaces, as illustrated in UN General Assembly resolution 66/290, for instance, and still remains grounded in its two key components – the comprehensive understanding of threat and empowerment of the individual – the inclusion of the preferences of non-citizens certainly needs to be addressed. This seems only possible if human security includes a critical and emancipatory stance towards legal doctrine and political concepts, as well as towards its own limitations and conditions.

4 International Law and the Idea of Human Security

Although the core of human security represents the focus on the individual and its general acceptance by states as a discourse, the development of human security over the last two decades includes diffused and differ-

44 European Commission (COM/2016 270 final) (n 43) 13.

45 Cathryn Costello, *The Human Rights of Migrants and Refugees in European Law* (Oxford University Press 2016) 21.

ent understandings and conceptualizations.[46] Human security is less an analytical tool, even though it has found its way into the practice of international organisations, continues to be promoted by a number of states and is used as an advocacy strategy by some NGOs. While there is no authoritative definition or interpretation of the meaning and scope of human security, human security nevertheless allows approaching situations of fragility, violence or insecurity from a perspective, which challenges the wisdom of state-centred discourse and state-centred responses. Human security in this sense deepens security in a vertical way beyond arguments of national security and broadens the perception of security to encompass situations, actors and agents differently and interdependently.[47]

Therefore, instead of viewing human security as an analytical tool or coherent concept, we propose to focus on the discursive potential for a *critical* politics of universalism. Human security thus functions as an idea. Idea is thereby understood in its etymological meaning in ancient Greek: *eidénai,* 'to know' or 'to understand'. Idea thus understood entails two dimensions: an epistemological dimension and an ontological-constitutive dimension.[48] We propose to place human security in the epistemological dimension. Similar to the technique of framing, human security employed as an idea assists in questioning processes of knowledge formation and thus unveiling and exposing underlying premises and assumptions.[49]

Conceptualising human security as idea brings it close to critical approaches in international relations and international law. While the similarities between the comprehensive notion of threat as part of human security and critical strands of international relations have frequently

---

46 See Shahrbanou Tadjbakhsh and Anuradha Chenoy, *Human Security: Concepts and Implications* (New York Routledge 2007) 9-38. Other proponents understood it narrowly, i.e. as a response to threats against the physical integrity of persons and communities or focused merely on its economic aspects. The Harvard Program for Human Security defines human security as the "expected number of years spent outside a state of generalized poverty".

47 Gerd Oberleitner, 'Human Security' in David P Forsythe (ed.), *Encyclopedia of Human Rights* (Oxford University Press 2009) 488.

48 See Paul Guyer and Rolf-Peter Horstmann, 'Idealism' in Edward N Zalta (ed.), *The Stanford Encyclopedia of Philosophy* (Fall 2015 Edition) <http://plato.stanford.edu/archives/fall2015/entries/idealism/>.

49 Karen O'Brien and others, 'The Framing of Climate Change: Why it Matters' in Karen O'Brien and others (eds.) *Climate Change, Ethics and Human °Security* (Cambridge University Press 2010) 6.

been noted, its relation to international law, let alone refugee or migration law, has received less attention.[50] Human security is related to two fields of international law in particular: international legal theory and human rights.

Recent scholarship in international legal theory emphasises the growing role of the individual in international law.[51] Although human rights represent the traditional field of international law that is concerned with the individual, Anne Peters, Co-Director of the Max Planck Institute, argues that, beyond the sphere of human rights, the individual constitutes the primary reference unit, or the 'natural person', of international law.[52] These tendencies in international legal theory chime well with the rigorous focus of human security on the individual human being.

The relation between human rights and human security has often been described as mutually reinforcing and complementary.[53] Their historical connection is often being traced back to the broader vision of Franklin D Roosevelts "Four Human Freedoms", the freedom from fear,

50 The comprehensive volume edited by Alice Edwards et al. discusses extensively the relation between human security and different theories of international relations, noting in particular the close relation between human security and critical security studies – see Alice Edwards and Carla Ferstman (eds.), *Human Security and Non-Citizens: Law, Policy and International Affairs* (Cambridge University Press 2010). Even the leading handbooks on human security do not contain a chapter on migration – see Martin and Owen (eds.), *Routledge Handbook of Human Security* (n 29). Although it is the leading handbook in the field, it does not contain a chapter specifically dedicated to migration – Michael R Redclift and Marco Grasso (eds.), *Handbook on Climate Change and Human Security* (Edward Elgar 2013) – and the recent publication dedicated to human security and international law merely contains one chapter on migration – Cedric Ryngaert and Math Noortmann (eds.), *Human Security and International Law: The Challenge of Non-State Actors* (Intersentia 2013).

51 Amongst a vast amount of literature see Kate Parlett, *The Individual in the International Legal System* (Cambridge University Press 2013); Daniel Bethlehem, 'The End of Geography: The Changing Nature of the International System and the Challenge to International Law' (2014) 25(1) European Journal of International Law 9; Anne Peters, *Jenseits der Menschenrechte: Die Rechtsstellung des Individuums im Völkerrecht* (Mohr Siebeck 2014).

52 Peters, *Jenseits der Menschenrechte* (n 51) 382.

53 Ademola Abass, 'An Introduction to Protecting Human Security in Africa' in Ademola Abass (ed.) *Protecting Human Security in Africa* (Oxford University Press 2010) 6.

freedom from want, freedom of speech and freedom of religion.[54] Thus, establishing a common value basis, at least human security's basic normative tenet, the intrinsic value of human dignity, is reflected as normative discourse in human rights. The ideas of human security can be found not only penetrating, but also laying the foundation for legal norms, such as the Ottawa-Convention against landmines, the Optional Protocol to the Convention on the Rights of the Child on children in armed conflict, or the protocol to the UN-Convention against transnational organised crime. Human security might thus serve as guidance both for adopting laws and for judicial interpretation.[55] Human rights can define the content of human security and describe its objectives and many of the threats to which human security is meant to respond. Given that the ultimate focus and beneficiary of both – human rights and human security – is the individual human being which is protected and empowered, sovereignty is positioned anew as a responsibility to respond appropriately to situations of insecurity; a development which *Kofi Annan* described as early as 1999 as the acknowledgment of "individual sovereignty."[56]

Yet, human security is broader than the law. Amartya Sen famously stated that human security is not to be incarcerated in the juridical frame.[57] The broader scope of human security thus serves to indicate the limits of the law. This is particularly salient when it comes to immigration and refugee law, a field of law, in which traditional notions of security prevail and crude cultural beliefs and imaginations often abound. Human security can thus be seen as a discursive strategy both to point out the limits of the law, including human rights law, and as a reclaiming of the security of (and partly by) people on the move.

---

54 Franklin D Roosevelt, 'Four Human Freedoms' (1984) 6(3) Human Rights Quarterly 384 (Excerpted from Address by President Roosevelt, 87th Congress Rec 44, 46-47, 1941).

55 See the *ordonnance* of the Conseil d'Etat in which the court seems to establish a positive duty to protect towards migrants who live in unpalatable conditions in an unofficial camp in Calais, Conseil d'État, 'Ordonnance 23 Novembre 2015, Ministre de l'Intérieur Commune de Calais' (No 394540, 394568) para. 9.

56 Kofi Annan, 'Two Concepts of Sovereignty' (The Economist, 18 September 1999).

57 Amartya Sen, 'Elements of a Theory of Human Rights' (2004) 32(4) Philosophy and Public Affairs 315, 319.

5 Overview of the Structure of the Book

Obviously, the contributions in this book have been written in the context of the 'migration crisis'. They have, however, also been written against, in the sense of opposing, the narrative of the 'migration crisis' by looking beyond its temporal and spatial dimension. Temporally, in terms of looking at broader historical contexts and into future migratory movements, in particular to environmentally induced migration. Spatially, in terms of looking beyond the geographical boundaries of the dominant narrative of the migratory crisis, i.e. EU Member States, by constantly reminding that that the overwhelming majority of displaced persons remain in the Global South. Although this book is subtitled *Human Security and Forced Migration*, it uses the term 'forced migration' only reluctantly and critically, as most migratory processes cannot be neatly differentiated along these categories. Although most of the contributions include a discussion of human security, not all include a comprehensive account of human security. Hence, the contributions ought to be read bearing in mind the conception of human security as an idea whose primary function lies in questioning processes of knowledge formation and exposing underlying premises and assumptions. Bearing these words in mind, the book is structured into five parts in total.

In the following chapter, *Dana Schmalz* discusses current dynamics in refugee protection from the theoretical angle of law's role in the production of superfluity. Her chapter embeds the questions of access to protection and responsibility sharing between states in a broader historical context and points to the ambivalence of current proposals for global solutions of responsibility sharing, as, without advancing the issue of mobility, these proposals are trading schemes of the non-arrival of refugees, law's production of superfluity.

The contributions in Part II engage with current legal regimes and practices on refugee protection, pointing to the spaces of exclusion and hardship produced also by these regimes and practices on protection. The common tune of the contributions is to call, to borrow the words of Seyla Benhabib, for "new political vistas", ant to explore legal possibilities and doctrines by which states that have violated human rights can be held liable.[58]

58 Seyla Benhabib, 'Critique of Humanitarian Reason' (*Eurozine*, 2014) <http://www.eurozine.com/articles/2014-07-18-benhabib-en.html> accessed 8 August 2016.

Maximilian Lakitsch picks up a similar theme by looking at the concept of state authority in the context of the dire situation of refugees in Lebanon. The situation in Lebanon is well known: of about 6 million residents, just about 4 million are citizens and thus have access to state services, the labour and the housing market. Instead of subscribing to an Agambian interpretation of authority, which views this exclusion and exposure to violence not merely as policy driven, but as the reflection of an ontological grounding of authority in violence, Maximilian argues that state authority has to be reconceptualised based on the individuals' evaluation of the authority's actions.

In the subsequent chapter, *Stefan Salomon* picks up a similar issue. Stefan looks at the relation between the use of force and refugee law in the context of the Syrian conflict, focusing on the shifting legal narrative from humanitarian intervention to self-defence. While refugees have been part of the humanitarian narrative, they remain largely absent as a matter of concern in the self-defence narrative. Even in the humanitarian intervention narrative, refugees were only to a limited extent 'objects of humanitarian intervention'. That, Stefan argues, reflects systemic aspects on the separation of the sphere of the law of force and refugee law.

Vassilis Tzevelekos starts with an analysis of UN Security Council resolution 2240 (2015) that transfers authority to states to inspect and seize vessels on the high sea, which are suspected of engaging in human smuggling and trafficking. Engaging with transnational phenomena, such as migrant smuggling or human trafficking, requires the involvement of a plurality of states and international organisations. The engagement of multiple duty bearers, Vassilis argues, results in a situation where they exercise parallel and overlapping jurisdiction. Therefore, if one of these duty bearers violates legal obligations (e.g. the duty to protect), the duty bearers may be held concurrently liable for the failure. Vassilis points out that a human security perspective permits to contextualise transnational phenomena and to shape specific policy responses that aim at protecting individuals.

Bríd Ní Ghráinne shifts the focus from the refugee situation in Europe to the broader situation of maritime interdiction regimes in South East Asia, reminding the reader that the large part of refugees remains in the Global South. Bríd focuses in particular on the events unfolding in the Andaman Sea in May 2015, pointing to a condition where those who cannot claim the rights attached to their citizenship claim any other rights. In the "human ping pong" between Thai, Malaysian and Indonesian authorities, they are reduced to their bare life. Bríd shows that although refugee law might not provide a remedy, the overarching framework of human rights law might provide some potential for action. The victims of human rights violations are however unlikely to claim their rights, which shows the unequal power situation between refugees and a state, in which the former depend on the goodwill of NGOs or foreign governments to take up their case.

The two contributions in Part IV both discuss environmental degradation and (forced) migration, approaching it from different perspectives.

Daniel Petz asks what the normative framework for planned relocations of populations ought to be. Focusing on an analysis of the *Guidance on Protecting People from Disasters and Environmental Change Through Planned Relocation*, the first guidance document on planned relocation, Daniel argues that a human rights based approach is capable of contextualising rights and thus appropriately addressing the needs of affected persons. A human rights based approach, Daniel insists, should however be supplemented by considerations on distributive justice in order to overcome shortcomings of a human rights based approach.

Susanna Villani looks at the possible impacts of environmentally induced migration on both individual human security and host states. Although the EU's legal framework, at least at the current stage, does not explicitly provide protection for environmental migrants, using human security in the external actions of the EU, Susanna argues, could establish the EU as a global forerunner in the protection of environmental migrants.

The final Part V returns in a way to the questions raised at the outset on victimhood and agency by discussing the legal situation of victims of human trafficking under a human security perspective.

Marco Borraccetti analyses the EU legislative framework on trafficking in human beings arguing that a lacuna exists in the protection of victims, depending on their nationality. He points out that this differentiation in providing protection is particularly salient concerning the right to stay and the punishment of victims' exploiters. The prevalence of traditional understandings of national security, Marco points out, is key in upholding such a differentiation in protection based on national origins. Applying a human security perspective would increase the protection of victims of human trafficking.

Global Responsibility Sharing and the Production of Superfluity in the Context of Refugee Protection

Dana Schmalz

1 Introduction

The agreement between the European Union and the Republic of Turkey from 18 March 2016 regarding the exchange of refugees has been criticized in political as well as legal terms from the very beginning.[1] It might go down in history as a questionable political decision with destructive consequences. Yet most likely, it will not go down as a singular event, but as part of a larger tendency we are facing with regard to forced migration and the distribution of freedom of movement. In this chapter, I will discuss this constellation and tendency drawing on the notion of law's "production of superfluity", which Susan Marks has proposed as conceptual lens for connecting phenomena in various areas of social life. Marks suggests that in addition to asking how law can contribute to safeguard the rights of persons, we must also assess how "law and legal institution may be helping to justify, normalize, naturalize and hence enable forms of misery against which protection is needed".[2]

In the context of refugee protection, this lens appears valuable as it might help to explain how policy choices not only impact on the immediate situation of persons rejected or admitted, but yield wider effects and shape the global situation. The context of the EU-Turkey agreement can be illustrative for such possible wider effects: Shortly after the agreement's adoption, Kenya, which for decades already belongs to the largest refugee receiving states, declared that it would close the Dadaab refugee

---

1 For legal assessments cf. Steve Peers, 'The Final EU/Turkey Refugee Deal: a Legal Assessment' (*EU Law Analysis*, 18 March 2016) <eulawanalysis.blogspot.de/2016/03/the-final-euturkey-refugee-deal-legal.html>; Rainer Hofmann and Adela Schmidt, 'Die Erklärung EU-Türkei vom 18.3.2016 aus Rechtlicher Perspektive' (2016) Neue Zeitschrift für Verwaltungsrecht-Extra 35(11), 1.

2 Susan Marks, 'Law and the Production of Superfluity' (2011) Transnational Legal Theory 2(1), 1, 21.

Salomon, Heschl, *et al.* (eds.), *Blurring Boundaries: Human Security and Forced Migration*
 ISBN 978-90-04-32686-6. pp. 23-47.

camps,[3] which had hosted at times more than 400.000 Somalian refugees.[4] A direct reference to the agreement with Turkey was not made, and the interrelation is only speculative. Yet the EU's willingness to pay for not receiving a substantive number of refugees and for not being directly confronted with a gross dilemma regarding its fundamental values might have worked as a message to a broader audience. In light of the agreement, assuming the task of hosting refugees without a similar return service would suddenly seem much less evident.

These occurrences and possible interrelations provide but one recent example of how legal measures shape the conditions of refugee protection on a global scale. They are situated in a growing discourse about the inadequacy of responsibility sharing in refugee protection today: Of more than 65 million displaced persons world-wide, 86 percent are hosted in states of the Global South.[5] It has long been pointed out, how the successive development of non-entrée regimes by states of the Global North contributed to a downward spiral in the conditions of access and the quality of protection.[6] This regards foremost the numerous protracted refugee situations, in which persons cannot return to their states of origins for decades but at the same time are denied local integration and access to numerous basic rights at their place of residence.[7]

In the following, I will first examine the interrelation between successive border securization regimes and the question of responsibility sharing in more detail (2). The development over the last decades attributed a growing role to the UN High Commissioner for Refugees (UNHCR) and further humanitarian organizations in material assistance,

---

3 Cf. Murithi Mutiga and Emma Graham-Harrison, 'Kenya says it will Shut World's Biggest Refugee Camp at Dadaab' (*The Guardian*, 11 May 2016) <www.theguardian.com/world/2016/may/11/kenya-close-worlds-biggest-refugee-camp-dadaab>.

4 Cf. Jack Redden (ed.), 'Dadaab – World's Biggest Refugee Camp 20 Years Old' (*UNHCR*, 21 February 2012) <www.unhcr.org/news/makingdifference/2012/2/4f439dbb9/dadaab-worlds-biggest-refugee-camp-20-years-old.html.>.

5 Cf. for figures: UNHCR, 'Global Trends: Forced Displacement in 2015' (UNHCR 2016) 2.

6 B. S. Chimni, 'The Geopolitics of Refugee Studies: A View from the South' (1998) Journal of Refugee Studies 11(4), 350, 352; James Milner, *Refugees, the State and the Politics of Asylum in Africa* (2009) 41.

7 Alexander Aleinikoff and Stephen Poellot, 'The Responsibility to Solve: The International Community and Protracted Refugee Situations' (2014) Virginia Journal of International Law 54(2), 198; cf. also for current numbers UNHCR, 'Global Trends' (n 5) 20.

creating situations of "humanitarian government". It is the triangular relationship between refugee hosting states in the Global South, UNHCR and humanitarian organizations, and donor states of the Global North, which appears key for understanding the problematic dynamics in the international refugee protection regime today. This combination of border securizations on the one hand and a "humanitarian reason"[8] in efforts to improve protection on the other marks the current situation and can be assessed with reference to a "production of superfluity".

For that endeavor, I will examine in an ensuing section the notion of superfluity as introduced by Susan Marks, and discuss its value as analytical concept (3). In particular, I will consider the debate regarding mechanisms of improved responsibility sharing through that conceptual lens. We find a growing debate in refugee law scholarship on responsibility sharing, which is important as it points out the highly inadequate situation today. At the same time, the debate engenders proposals for "global solutions", which involve a problematic logic of centralization. The choices of financial contributions and resettlement as "currencies" of taking a share in global responsibility for refugees risk legitimizing efforts to secure borders and restrict mobility on the other end, and thus ultimately contributing to a construction of refugees as a burden to be distributed. I will conclude by arguing that while we must not oppose endeavors for global solutions as such, a focus on mobility in addition to responsibility sharing appears central. Mobility as a perspective on the relationship between states and individuals rather than between states allows bringing into the picture the concrete challenges and decisions of persons. Conditions of mobility and the possibility to make choices about destinations thus appear as the minimal recognition of political agency that legal rules are able to provide for. In addition to a global perspective, we must for that purpose regard the particular situations at the border, in which conditions of access and mobility are negotiated (4).

---

8 Didier Fassini, *Humanitarian reason. A Moral History of the Present* (University of California Press, 2011); Seyla Benhabib, 'Critique of Humanitarian Reason' (*Eurozine*, 18 July 2014) <www.eurozine.com/articles/2014-07-18-benhabib-en.html>.

2 Access to Protection and the Question of Responsibility Sharing in International Refugee Law

In order to think about the ways in which law effects and can regulate the responsibility sharing for refugees, we must first of all consider the interrelation between states' border regulations and the corresponding question of access to protection on the one hand, and the distribution of responsibility for refugees between states on the other. This interrelation is apparent today and has shaped the evolution of the framework of international protection over the last 65 years. I will briefly outline the defining tensions in legal regulations regarding access to protection (a), before describing the evolution of the international framework of protection, with the correlation between increasing border securization and the distribution of responsibility for refugees (b). In that relation, I will point out the increasing role of humanitarian agencies in that fabric (c), before concluding the section with an overview on current tendencies and questions (d).

2.1 *The Paradoxical Conditions of Access to Protection*

The situation of refugees always relates to a dual challenge: the fact of fleeing one place, and of not having fully arrived in another. The notion of refugees thus encapsulates a certain state of in-between, of persons who cannot return to where they consider themselves or are considered to be at home, but who also have not made or have been able to make a new place their home. It is not only the loss of, or flight from, a home but "the impossibility of finding a new one",[9] which marks the refugee's situation, and which stands at the basis of the particular condition of rightlessness.[10] Hannah Arendt's analysis from 1951 pertinently captures this struggling for "a place on earth".[11] The experiences of refugees in the first half of the century had exposed this dilemma of how to guarantee not only rights to persons already admitted, but to guarantee the very access to rights.[12]

---

9 Hannah Arendt, *The Origins of Totalitarianism* (Schocken Books 1951) 293.

10 Cf. Ayten Gündoğdu, *Rightlessness in an Age of Rights: Hannah Arendt and the Contemporary Struggles of Migrants* (Oxford University Press 2015).

11 Arendt, The Orogins of Totalitarianism (n 9) 293..

12 Cf. in that regard Arendt's expression of the "right to have rights", Arendt, *The Origins of Totalitarianism* (n 9) 296.

When thinking about legal rules of refugee protection, we can distinguish the question of access to a territory and protection on the one hand, and the rights of persons once admitted – either preliminarily while awaiting decisions on their asylum claims, or as recognized refugees. While detailed rules exist as to the latter, the rights of persons once on the territory, we find very limited legal guidance regarding the access to territory and protection itself. These lacunae are partly systemic, and partly voluntary: In the processes of drafting new laws of refugee protection and universal rights conventions after 1945, states discretionarily decided to leave out the question of access to asylum.[13] The non-binding 1948 Universal Declaration of Human Rights (UDHR)[14] declares a "right to seek and to enjoy" asylum, but explicitly avoided a more far-reaching formulation.[15] The 1951 Geneva Refugee Convention equally remains silent on the question of access, with corresponding formulations having been carefully avoided by states in the process of drafting.[16] In 1967, the UN General Assembly adopted a Declaration on Territorial Asylum that addresses the questions;[17] a planned Convention on the issue, however, failed.

International legal provisions that would explicitly oblige states to let persons enter their territory in order to claim asylum thus hardly exist. Moreover, the effectiveness of universal rights legislation for border situations is very limited: The criterion for state obligations to be applicable is the criterion of jurisdiction.[18] Only towards persons, who fall within its jurisdiction, a state has obligations under human rights treaties. Yet whether a person falls under a state's jurisdiction is generally assessed on the basis of territorial presence.[19] Only under exceptional circumstances is extraterritorial jurisdiction established, with further preconditions as

---

13 Pauline Endres de Oliveira, 'Legaler Zugang zu Internationalem Schutz – Zur Gretchenfrage im Flüchtlingsrecht' (2016) Kritische Justiz 49(2), 167.

14 Universal Declaration of Human Rights [1948] 217 A (III).

15 Endres de Oliveira, 'Legaler Zugang zu Internationalem Schutz' (n 13) 3.

16 Cf. Paul Weis, *The Refugee Convention, 1951: The Travaux Préparatoires Analysed with a Commentary by Dr. Paul Weis* (Cambridge International Document Series, Cambridge University Press 1995) Art 26, Art 28.

17 Declaration on Territorial Asylum [1967] A/RES/2312(XXII).

18 Cf. European Convention for the Protection of Human Rights and Fundamental Freedoms (ECHR) [1950] Art 1; American Convention on Human Rights [1969] Art 1(1).

19 Seminally for extra-territorial application of the ECHR: *Cyprus v Turkey* App no 25781/94 (ECtHR, 10 May 2001).

to the effective control of a state over a person. This territorial approach of human rights obligations together with the dominant interpretation of what establishes "effective control" makes human rights legislation relatively silent with regard to border situations.[20]

At the same time, the boundaries of state obligations towards persons, both under refugee law and human rights law, are not a clear-cut issue but subject to debate and shifting interpretations.[21] As the case *Hirsi Jamaa et al vs. Italy* highlighted, particular practices and policies of border regulation and deterrence may well be found to be in violation of international law.[22] Nonetheless, the legal scope, in which states can engage in measures of deterrence and border securization, remains remarkably large.[23] In that vein, it belongs to the paradoxical features of the current situation that many states uphold differentiated regimes of refugee rights while at the same time engaging in costly and elaborate efforts to hinder persons from entering the territory where they can claim these rights.

2.2 *The Successive Establishment of Non-Entrée Regimes in Global Perspective*

The bases of the current legal framework of refugee protection were created after the end of World War II. In 1946, the International Refugee Organization (IRO) was founded as a temporary agency with the mandate to coordinate resettlement in post-war Europe. In 1950 it was replaced by the UN High Commissioner for Refugees (UNHCR), which assumed the role of a central international body to coordinate protection and to su-

---

20 Cf., however, for an alternative theory of human rights obligations in such circumstances Hamar Nann, 'Humanity at Sea' in *Maritime Navigation and the Foundations of International Law* (Cambridge University Press, 2016), 103.

21 Cf. for a discussion with regard to the interception of refugees at sea Guy S Goodwin-Gill, 'The Right to Seek Asylum: Interception at Sea and the Principle of Non-Refoulement' (2011) International Journal of Refugee Law 23(3), 443.

22 *Hirsi Jamaa and others v Italy* App no 27765/09 (ECtHR, 23 February 2012). The case concerned 24 claimants from Somalia and Eritrea, who in 2009 had been within a group of about 200 persons on three vessels navigating from Tripoli towards Lampedusa. They were intercepted by Italian authorities and transferred back to Libya without identification of any possible claims for asylum. The European Court of Human Rights found these acts to have violated Art 3 ECHR and Art 4 of Additional Protocol IV to the ECHR.

23 James Hathaway/Thomas Gammeltoft Hansen, 'Non-Refoulement in a World of Cooperative Deferrence', 53 Columbia Journal of Transnational Law (2015) 2, 235.

pervise the application of international refugee law.[24] Furthermore, the United Nations fostered the drafting of a new international agreement regarding refugees, leading to the adoption of the 1951 Convention on the Status of Refugees, the Geneva Refugee Convention (GRC).

While the experiences that led to these instruments were at the basis European – as was initially also the GRC's scope of application,[25] the regions in which persons were fleeing and in need of protection increasingly shifted to the Global South in the following decades.

Along with this evolution, the scope of activities carried out by UNHCR, which quickly broadened after its establishment: Originally foreseen as a coordinating agency, UNHCR soon became an important provider of material assistance.[26] In the years of 1950s and 1960s, its focus turned towards regions in Africa and Asia, beginning with refugees from China and Algeria in 1957.[27] Under the formula of "good offices", UNHCR began to provide material assistance, and for that purpose to independently raise funds. In the following years, UNHCR intensified its focus on refugees from the Global South, setting up new assistance programs and developing into an organization with global outreach.[28] World politics at the time were dominated by the Cold War. During the 1960s and 1970s, Western states were inclined to accept persons from states of Soviet territory or influence, while refugees from the Global South were widely hosted in neighboring countries. In total, this led to a relatively liberal system of protection.[29]

In the 1980s, however, the intensification of the Cold War contributed to violent proxy conflicts in Indochina, Afghanistan, Central America, North-eastern and Southern Africa. Together with ethnic tensions and oppositions arising from decolonialization this led to numerous protract-

---

24 Cf. the UN General Assembly, 'Statute of the UNHCR' (14 December 1950) A/RES/428(V).

25 The temporal limitation to events before 1 January 1951 and the possibility to declare a geographical limitation to persons coming from Europe were lifted by the 1967 Protocol to the GRC – UN General Assembly, 'Protocol Relating to the Status of Refugees' (31 January 1967).

26 Gil Loescher, 'The UNHCR and World Politics: State Interests vs. Institutional Autonomy' (2001) International Migration Review 35(1), 33, 35.

27 Ibid. 37; Astri Suhrke and Kathleen Newland, 'UNHCR: Uphill into the Future' (2001) International Migration Review 35(1), 284, 293.

28 Loescher, 'The UNHCR and World Politics' (n 26) 39.

29 Suhrke and Newland, 'UNHCR' (n 27) 285.

ed refugee situations.[30] UNHCR's work consisted to an ever-larger extent in material assistance, operating refugee camps that often persisted for many years. The far-reaching powers of administrative decision-making turning UNHCR in a partly surrogate for state agencies and the militarized nature of spaces for protection gave rise to widespread criticisms regarding UNHCR's work on the ground.[31]

In the time after 1990, the regime of international protection came under unprecedented pressure. The problems can be described as a consequence of the geopolitical situation, but also as emanating from a crisis of basic premises of the regime. Refugee protection was built on the clear separation between refugees as being involuntarily displaced and migrants as voluntarily leaving a state in search for economic advantages elsewhere. This separation could be operated in the 1960s and 1970s due to relatively open immigration schemes in industrialized states that gladly received foreign workers on the one hand, and manageable numbers of forcibly displaced on the other.[32] However, once channels for immigration became restricted to highly trained workers while at the same time the violent and long-lasting conflicts caused high numbers of persons to flee, the separation became difficult to uphold.[33]

After the end of the Cold War, the number of refugees grew significantly. Secessions and dissolutions of states, for example in Yugoslavia, took place within or at the borders of Europe. The resulting sense of "losing control" led many European states to create more restrictive asylum laws.[34] Although the number of refugees went down in the following decades, states continued to establish comprehensive regimes of control, which included strict visa regulations, severe sanctions against carriers, readmission agreements, safe country lists, and the policy to return a person to the country of first asylum.[35] These "non-entrée regimes"[36] continuously shifted the responsibility for refugees to states in neighboring regions of conflicts.

30 Loescher, 'The UNHCR and World Politics' (n 26) 40.

31 Guglielmo Verdirame and Barbara Harrell-Bond, *Rights in Exile: Janus-Faced Humanitarianism* (Berghahn Books 2005) 113, 151; Chimni, 'The Geopolitics of Refugee Studies' (n 6) 350.

32 Suhrke and Newland, 'UNHCR' (n 27) 287.

33 Ibid. Cf. also Emma Haddad, *The Refugee in International Society* (Cambridge University Press 2008), 152.

34 Ibid., 290.

35 Ibid., 291.

36 Chimni, 'The Geopolitics of Refugee Studies' (n 6) 352.

The shifting of responsibility firstly works through the direct effects of border regulations: By restricting access and returning persons to states of previous sojourn, the current regime of protection boils down to a rule of "responsibility by proximity".[37] Whether the shifting of responsibility thereby taking place is in line with human rights obligations in many cases never becomes subject to legal scrutiny. The effect of physical distance, which measures of deterrence yield, regularly precludes already the applicability of human rights provisions.[38] But even if applicable, practical conditions regularly hinder persons to claim their rights under such instruments.[39] Moreover, the policies of border securization and deterrence also work as communications, and will often reduce the motivation of states that are left with the responsibility for refugees, thus leading to a downward spiral in the overall quality of reception.[40]

2.3 *Humanitarian Reason in Refugee Protection*

Central to the dynamics in the regime of international protection is furthermore the role attributed to humanitarian organizations in the current constellation. This role emerges from and contributes to sustain the distribution of responsibility between states, but also impacts on the overall perception of refugees. Speaking about "humanitarian reason"[41] in refugee protection, camps are an important phenomenon to begin with. At the same time, the phenomenon is more complex both in the sense that refugee camps cannot be viewed as uniform phenomenon, and in that a critique of humanitarian reason must look

37 Cf. for the expression by Peter Sutherland: UN News Center, 'Interview: "Refugees are the Responsibility of the World… Proximity doesn't Define Responsibility." – Peter Sutherland' (2 October 2015) <www.un.org/apps/news/story.asp?NewsID=52126#.V5YPuFc7TTo>.

38 Cf. above at n 21 et seq.

39 The case *Hirsi* (n 20) was illustrative also of the practical improbability of persons affected by measures of deterrence being able claim their rights before a human rights court: The case could only come before the ECtHR because the Italian Refugee Council had traced the later applicants in Libyan camps, investigated their treatment and provided the counsels for court proceedings. The 24 persons represented before the court stand against thousands who faced similar push-back practices. For an analysis see also Sonja Buckel, *"Welcome to Europe": Die Grenzen des Europäischen Migrationsrechts* (1st edn, Transcript 2013) 289.

40 Milner, Refugees (n 6) 41.

41 See Fassin, Humanitarian reason (n 8); Benhabib, 'Critique of Humanitarian Reason' (n 8).

beyond protection in camps. In a broad ethnographic study, Michel Agier has offered impressions on the diversity of camps ranging from mainly self-organized settlements, over transit centers, to camps created and operated by UNHCR and humanitarian agencies.[42] Refugee camps thus vary in their size and composition, in their circumstances of creation and duration of existence, in their organization, and of course geographical position. At the same time, it is widely agreed that living conditions in camps involve to varying degrees a limitation of rights and freedom.[43] There have been numerous criticisms of refugee camps, which highlight how encampment harms persons' autonomy.[44] The Agambenian critique of camps as "spaces of exception" has thereby been outmost influential,[45] but was also questioned as too one-dimensional.[46]

I have described above the growing involvement of UNHCR in material assistance: To the extent that states in neighboring regions of conflicts were unable to provide for effective protection alone, UNHCR together with numerous partner organizations stepped in. Regularly, though by no means exclusively, this assistance took and continues to take place in refugee camps.[47] The involvement, initially construed as emergency relief, in practice often persisted for many years if not decades. In such protracted refugee situations, the assistance by UNHCR and other, both governmental and non-governmental, organizations regularly results in encompassing service infrastructures in parallel to those of the local population.[48] These situations have been described as UNHCR adopting

42 Michel Agier, *Managing the Undesirables: Refugee Camps and Humanitarian Government* (Polity Press 2011) 39.

43 Ibid., 65. Cf. also UNHCR, 'Policy on Alternatives to Camps' (UNHCR 2009) 4.

44 Jennifer Hyndman, 'Refugee Self-Management and the Question of Governance' (1997) Refuge 16(2), 16; Liisa H Malkki, *Purity and Exile: Violence, Memory, and National Cosmology among Hutu Refugees in Tanzania* (The University of Chicago Press 1995); Verdirame and Harrell-Bond, *Rights in Exile* (n 31).

45 Giorgio Agamben, *Means without End: Notes on Politics* (University of Minnesota Press 2000) 39.

46 Judith Butler and Gayatri Chakravorty Spivak, Who Sings the Nation-State? Language, Politics, Belonging (Seagull Books 2007) 39.

47 UNHCR, 'Operational Protection in Camps and Settlements: A Reference Guide of Good Practices in the Protection of Refugees and Other Persons of Concern' (UNHCR 2006).

48 Verdirame and Harrell-Bond, *Rights in Exile* (n 31) 241.

the role of a "surrogate state",[49] both in the perception of refugees themselves,[50] and in the amount of authority exercised.[51]

But while certain functions of administrative decision-making and the provision of services can be substituted, the substance of a genuine political community in which persons can obtain political membership and strive for autonomous lives cannot. The far-reaching antinomies of humanitarian government are illustrated by UNHCR endeavors for inclusion: Recognizing the problems that encampment and dependence on humanitarian assistance pose for refugees, UNHCR from the 2000s on aimed to set up more inclusionary governance mechanisms: The intention to enhance refugee participation in all operations was firstly advanced by the UNHCR Executive Committee in 2001,[52] and framed in the following as "community-based approach".[53] A specific handbook followed in 2008.[54]

Examinations of the practical implementation and effects, however, highlight the problems in these inclusionary policies in refugee camps: The election of refugee representatives and other structures of participation would often not confer actual power to influence decisions taken about the matters of the camp.[55] Refugee representatives in those studies were found to serve as bridges for passing orders, supporting governance rather than controlling it.[56] On a more systemic level, Simon Turner has criticized the concept of "community" in the use by UNHCR policies as

49 Amy Slaughter and Jeff Crisp, 'A Surrogate State? The Role of UNHCR in Protracted Refugee Situations' (New Issues in Refugee Research, Research Paper No. 168, UNHCR 2009).

50 Katharina Inhetveen, *Die Politische Ordnung des Flüchtlingslagers* (Transcript 2010) 128.

51 Maja Smrkolj, 'International Institutions and Individualized Decision-Making: An Example of UNHCR's Refugee Status Determination' in Armin von Bogdandy and others (eds.), *The Exercise of Public Authority by International Institutions* (Springer 2010) 165.

52 Executive Committee of the High Commissioner's Programme, 'Reinforcing a Community Development Approach' (20th Meeting of the Standing Committee, EC/51/SC/CRP.6, 15 February 2001).

53 UNHCR, 'Operational Protection in Camps and Settlements' (n 47) 16.

54 UNHCR, 'A Community-Based Approach in UNHCR Operations' (UNHCR 2008).

55 Inhetveen, *Die Politische Ordnung des Flüchtlingslagers* (n 50) 181.

56 Ibid., 171.

actually opposed to politics:[57] Community in his view works as a notion used to ensure a smooth running of distributive and other administrative procedures, thereby de-legitimizing opposition as egoistic and contrary to the interest of "the community". In a similar vein, Jennifer Hyndman has emphasized the dangers of misconceiving refugees in a camp as uniform subjects.[58] Such image of the refugees as a uniform group reduces the persons to interests ascribed to them from an abstract point of view, or identified in general ways. A similar critique has been advanced with regard to the term "empowerment",[59] pointing to the risk that certain groups of refugees are played off against others. For instance, the principle of gender equality then risks being instrumentalized for governing purposes.[60] Moreover, "empowerment" can result in fostering refugee participation as a feeling rather than agency.[61] In that sense, inclusionary policies run the risk, while claiming the exact opposite objective, to take part in the victimization refugees.[62]

In a discourse of victimization, measures circumscribing free agency, such as prohibitions, obligations, and controls, are framed as necessary for protection. Such limitation of free agency vice versa is likely to actually create a far-reaching dependency on humanitarian assistance in all areas of life, which in turn supports a picture of refugees as passive victims. Most importantly, the discourse also underlines how the described flaws in endeavors for better inclusion of refugees relate back to the overall fabric of international protection: Once put in the hand of humanitarian agencies, thorough protection will foremost depend on the continuance

57 Simon Turner, 'Biopolitics and Bare Life in a Refugee Camp. Some Conceptual Reflections' in Katharina Inhetveen (ed.), *Flucht als Politik: Berichte von Fünf Kontinenten* (2006) 53.

58 Jennifer Hyndman, *Managing Displacement: Refugees and the Politics of Humanitarianism* (Rüdiger Koppe Verlag 2000) 138.

59 Simon Turner, 'Angry Young Men in Camps: Gender, Age and Class Relations Among Burundian Refugees in Tanzania' (New Issues in Refugee Research, Research Paper No. 9) 3.

60 Elisabeth Olivius, 'Displacing Equality? Women's Participation and Humanitarian Aid Effectiveness in Refugee Camps' (2014) Refugee Survey Quarterly 33, 93. Cf. in that context also the critical remarks about promotion and display of gender equality and women roles in the Sahrawi refugee camps, Elena Fiddian-Qasmiyeh, The Ideal Refugees: Gender, Islam, and the Sahrawi Politics of Survival (Syracuse University Press 2014) 47.

61 Turner, 'Angry Young Men in Camps' (n 59) 54.

62 Cf. also Agier, *Managing the Undesirables* (n 42) 65.

of funding.[63] Yet the dependence on funding favors the framing of a situation as emergency and incentivizes the depiction of refugees as victims.[64] Moreover, in order to claim funding, humanitarian agencies have to keep refugees as their "persons of concern" separated from the general population to be clearly visible.[65]

The structural problems of "humanitarian government"[66] or more generally "humanitarian reason"[67] in refugee protection thus directly relate back to the power structures between states of the Global North and of the Global South and the corresponding politics of refugee protection.[68] Based on studies about urban refugees in Jordan and other Middle Eastern countries, Patricia Ward in that sense has argued that the role of UNHCR for the protracted refugee situations should not be overestimated: While the policies of UNHCR merit critical reflection, also a reconsideration of the relationship between UNHCR, host states and donor states is necessary.[69]

2.4 *Current Tendencies in the Correlation of Border Regulation and Responsibility Sharing*

I suggested in the beginning that the agreement between the EU and Turkey from March 2015 is expressive for a broader tendency in refugee protection that we are witnessing at the moment. I thereby do not mean to refer to measures of deterrence or the transferral of responsibility to states at the European periphery alone. As I have tried to show in this section, such successive development of non-entrée regimes has been taking place at least since the beginning of the 1990s, and finds its basis in the relative silence of the international refugee protection regime on the issues of access and responsibility sharing. The numerous measures of deterrence contributed to an ever-increasing inequality in

63 Patricia Ward, 'Refugee Cities: Reflections on the Development and Impact of UNHCR Urban Refugee Policy in the Middle East' (2014) Refugee Survey Quarterly 33(1), 77.

64 Slaughter and Crisp, 'A Surrogate State?' (n 49) 6.

65 Michael Kagan, '"We Live in a Country of UNHCR": The UN Surrogate State and Refugee Policy in the Middle East' (UNHCR New Issues in Refugee Research, Research Paper No. 201, UNHCR 2011) 6.

66 Agier, Managing the Undesirables (n 42) 65.

67 Benhabib, 'Critique of Humanitarian Reason' (n 8).

68 Heather L Johnson, *Borders, Asylum and Global Non-Citizenship* (Cambridge University Press 2014) 47.

69 Ward, 'Refugee Cities' (n 62) 93.

the international distribution of responsibility for refugees, harming the overall quality of protection and putting the meaningfulness of the international regime into question.

Based on this description, the EU-Turkey agreement does not appear that exceptional but rather as a continuation of the preceding evolution. At the same time, the agreement encapsulates in a particularly clear manner the logic of tradability of refugees, or, rather, of the non-arrival of refugees. This logic found expression when shortly after its conclusion the president of Turkey, discontented about the agreement's implementation, threatened to "flood Europe with migrants".[70] The idea that one could threaten a continent with migrants did not seem to surprise anybody as such, rather it appeared in line with the general reasoning of the deal. I have pointed to the message that this reasoning might have conveyed on refugee protecting states that were not immediately affected but well aware of the gross inequality in international burden-sharing.[71]

Finally, it is important to note how the logic of tradability also played out with regard to funding: material bases for providing assistance to refugees are scarce in many places, and UNHCR and humanitarian agencies had long called on states to provide more means in relation to the Syrian refugee crisis. It was, however, only the arrival of a higher number of Syrian refugees in Europe – and thus the realization that persons were willing to take this journey despite the many obstacles and perils, which prompted an increase in support of refugee assistance in Jordan and the Lebanon, "to stem the exodus".[72] Contributing to make living conditions bearable in those neighboring countries of Syria thus was considered a worthwhile investment in order to have persons not moving onwards to Europe. Financial support of humanitarian work in that sense regularly goes hand in hand with "strategies of containment", states urging UN organizations to assist displaced persons in their states of origin or nearby.[73]

---

70 Cf. Reuters, 'Turkey's Erdogan Threatened to Flood Europe with Migrants: Greek Website' (8 February 2016) <http://www.reuters.com/article/us-europe-migrants-eu-turkey-idUSKCN0VH1R0>.

71 See n 3 et seq.

72 Cf. Deutsche Welle, 'German, Austrian Political Leaders Call on EU for Billions in Refugee Aid' (19 September 2015) <www.dw.com/en/german-austrian-political-leaders-call-on-eu-for-billions-in-refugee-aid/a-18724959>.

73 Hyndman, *Managing Displacement* (n 58) 2.

This is of course one specific reading of the reasoning behind those policies, and I neither claim this to constitute the only motives, nor do I mean to imply that individual actors are cynic in their attitudes towards refugee protection. Rather it is my proposition that we should take note of this structural logic for analytical purposes, as it can illuminate our reflections about how legal measures can improve but also worsen the current situation. Susan Marks' notion of "law's production of superfluity" is helpful in that regard. Marks suggests that legal rules can contribute to frame social interrelations in such a way as to "produce superfluity", meaning the perception of persons as unneeded and dispensable, their mere existence being a problem, or threat. This resonates with many of the phenomena we see. In the current European context, the lens of superfluity is particularly pertinent since the construction of persons as superfluous is largely counterfactual: The persons whose presence is construed as dispensable and whose arrival as threatening are in many ways needed if we believe demographic and economic analyses.[74] This counterfactuality does not diminish but rather underline the relevance of the concept. At the same time, the notion indicates how the plight of refugees does not stand for itself but can be situated in broader social phenomena.

3 Superfluity as a Conceptual Lens: The Problems of "Global Solutions" for Refugee Protection

In this section, I shall examine the concept of superfluity as proposed by Susan Marks in more detail (a), and consider on that basis propositions for "global solutions" for refugees (b). While these propositions tackle the important aspect of responsibility sharing, both the *global* and the *solutions* part come with problems. If we consider the production of superfluity as a central feature of the challenge, schemes for responses will have to recognize the necessity to oppose rather than increase this drift (c).

---

74 Cf. e.g. Patrick Kingsley, 'Refugees will Repay EU Spending Almost Twice Over in Five Years – Report' (*The Guardian*, 18 May 2016) <www.theguardian.com/world/2016/may/18/refugees-will-repay-eu-spending-almost-twice-over-in-five-years-report>; Christian Bodewig, 'Is the Refugee Crisis an Opportunity for an Aging Europe?' (*Brookings*, 21 September 2015) <www.brookings.edu/blogs/future-development/posts/2015/09/21-refugee-demographics-europe-bodewig>.

3.1 *Susan Marks: The Notion of Superfluity in Legal Analysis*

Susan Marks writes in the tradition of critical legal theory, pointing to the role of law not only in regulating but also in generating and shaping relations of power in social life.[75] In her text from 2011 Marks explores "how international law may contribute to the production of superfluity".[76] Introducing the analytical lens of law's production of superfluity, she begins by pointing out the diversity of meanings present in the notion:[77] That something is superfluous on a first level can mean that it exists in "quantitative excess", that there is too much of it, an oversupply. On a second level, it refers to a "practical redundancy", meaning that there is no need for it. On a third level, finally, it relates to the idea of "noxious waste", which is not simply unnecessary but harmful. These different layers of meaning resonate in the later use of the concept.

A first reference point for Marks in developing the concept of superfluity is Hannah Arendt's "Origin of Totalitarianism".[78] The most well-known part of the book is certainly the chapter on the "perplexities of the rights of men", in which Arendt analyses the dilemma of law to guarantee rights independently of political membership.[79] Arendt famously describes how rights that were imagined as universal proved ineffective exactly the moment they would have been needed the most. For refugees and stateless persons, who lacked effective membership in any political community, those universal rights were of no use when no state would accept them, when they were denied the very "place on earth".[80] While these reflections are central to critical refugee law scholarship today, they also more generally touch upon conditions of marginality and precarity. In that sense, Arendt's analysis is essential to her thinking about the human condition, to which the possibility to "appear to others", thus the possibility of a political existence is central.[81] Accordingly, the fact that persons "do not matter", that their opinions are not significant and their actions

---

75 Marks, 'Law and the Production of Superfluity' (n 2).

76 Ibid., 2.

77 For the following differentiations cf. ibid., 3.

78 Arendt, *The Origins of Totalitarianism* (n 9).

79 Ibid., 290.

80 Ibid., 293.

81 Hannah Arendt, *The Human Condition* (1st edn, 1958) 50. For the centrality of "Origins of Totalitarianism" in Arendt's thought cf. also Christian Volk, *Arendtian Constitutionalism: Law, Politics and the Order of Freedom* (Hart 2015) 10.

not effective,[82] forms a preliminary to the possibility of their elimination.[83]

Read as a thinker of superfluity, Arendt offers a conceptual link between the lack of political membership and de-individualization of persons, and the perception as dispensable. This is illustrated in her reflection about the fates of refugees and stateless as compared to persons considered criminals: "The best criterion", Arendt writes, "by which to decide whether someone has been forced outside the pale of the law is to ask if he would benefit by committing a crime."[84] Yet, as Susan Marks points out, Arendt's reflections about superfluity reach far beyond the chapter on the perplexities of human rights and her considerations about the figure of the refugee. Foremost, Arendt suggests that a correlation exists between superfluous money and superfluous wealth on the one hand, and superfluous people on the other.[85] In that vein, Marks traces Arendt's thinking about the relationship between capitalism and imperialism, and on how the changing perception of wealth and the idea of unlimited growth and accumulation "spilled over into the political domain".[86]

Firstly, Arendt describes how expansion appeared as the only option for superfluous capital, which otherwise would have been menacingly parasitical.[87] At the same time, every stage of industrial growth left behind persons, who had become "superfluous", eliminated from producing society.[88] Both aspects, superfluous capital and superfluous people, then relate to imperialism, the dynamics of which Arendt describes with reference to South Africa as paradigmatic example. In South Africa during the gold rush, thus concerned in an ironic way with a useless object of mere wealth, as Arendt underlines, the superfluous money could finance the digging, which was carried out by "superfluous men".[89]

Arendt thus suggests that a characteristic correlation exists between superfluity of capital and the construction of persons as superfluous, between the continuous necessity of growth and the production of

82 Cf. Arendt, *The Origins of Totalitarianism* (n 9) 293.

83 With reference to Arendt: Étienne Balibar, *Equaliberty: Political Essays* (Duke University Press 2014) 170; Nanda Oudejans, *Asylum: a Philosophical Inquiry into the International Protection of Refugees* (Boxpress 2011) 79.

84 Arendt, *The Origins of Totalitarianism* (n 9) 286.

85 Ibid., e.g. 150, 189.

86 Marks, 'Law and the Production of Superfluity' (n 74) 10.

87 Arendt, *The Origins of Totalitarianism* (n 9) 150.

88 Ibid.

89 Ibid., 188.

superfluity on the side of goods as well as on the side of people. In that regard, Susan Marks links her assessment of Arendt with a reading of Zygmunt Bauman as a contemporary thinker of superfluity. From Zygmunt Bauman, Marks takes in particular the idea of waste as co-product of all production, and the corresponding notion of "wasted humans", a perception of humans as disposable.[90] Marks traces Bauman's reflections on how progress by necessity entails a devaluation of previously prevailing modes of existence,[91] and how the shift from a society centered on production to a society centered on consumption plays out in that regard.[92] Bauman's thought is particularly insightful for the case of refugees and migration in that he links the presence of superfluity as a social phenomenon to fears about immigration: The forced migrant, who depends on a state's discretion to even admit him to its territory, embodies, in Bauman's analysis, the "presentiment of [one's] own disposability".[93]

In a similar vein, Étienne Balibar describes different axes along which social exclusion occurs, on the one hand the one of nationality, and on the other hand the one of class.[94] While the very rich can establish themselves, "materially and symbolically, beyond the distinction between the national and the foreign",[95] the very poor are construed as "internal foreigners, threatening or superfluous."[96] While Balibar's focus here is on the superfluity produced along the lines of class, this construction of superfluity is illuminating to understand fears and social oppositions in relation with questions of immigration.

While these social analyses are central for understanding internal political processes with regard to refugees, we can also use the considerations about superfluity to think about international law instruments. Susan Marks in that respect refers to the debate about camps as spaces of exception, or spaces of elaborate *legal* rule.[97] Both sides are important in her opinion: the reflections about regimes of exceptionalism, for in-

90 Marks, 'Law and the Production of Superfluity' (n 2) 11, with reference to Zygmunt Bauman, *Wasted Lives: Modernity and Its Outcasts* (Polity 2004) 5.

91 Marks, 'Law and the Production of Superfluity' (n 2) 11.

92 Ibid., 12.

93 Bauman, *Wasted Lives* (n 90) 56.

94 Balibar, *Equaliberty* (n 83) 253.

95 Ibid., 254.

96 Ibid.

97 Marks, 'Law and the Production of Superfluity' (n 2) 18.

stances analyses of the legal framing of Guantánamo Bay,[98] and the calls to situate these critiques in a broader context, looking also at largely neglected disasters such as HIV in sub-Saharan Africa.[99] On that basis, she suggests that "superfluity is a problem not just for law, but also of law",[100] and that our reflections should include not only how law can remedy the perception of persons as superfluous, but also how it might contribute to this perception.[101]

3.2 *Global Solutions for Refugees*

This suggestion is central when thinking about the global framework of refugee protection as it stands today, and about the proposals for reform. For that purpose, I will now turn to the considerations about responsibility sharing in refugee protection and the discussion about possible steps to overcome current flaws.

One of the most outspoken scholars on the question of global responsibility sharing in refugee protection for a long time is James Hathaway. Advocating a "Global Solution to a Global Refugee Crisis", Hathaway underlines that a fair system must take into account the circumstances of all states rather than follow the interests of a few powerful ones.[102] He views the 1951 Convention to contain sufficient guidance for a functioning international system of protection: Firstly, he reads it to constitute an agreement between states in favor of a model of refugee empowerment rather than charity.[103] Moreover, he points to the principle of international cooperation laid down in the convention's preamble.[104] It is thus, in Hathaway's view, not the inadequacy of rules but an insufficient implementation of those rules by states, which puts the current system under pressure and makes living conditions for refugees so utmost precarious in many places.

---

98 Ibid., with reference to Fleur Johns, 'Guantánamo Bay and the Annihilation of the Exception' (2005) European Journal of International Law 16(4), 613.

99 Marks, 'Law and the Production of Superfluity' (n 2) 19, with reference to Ralph Wilde, 'Casting Light on the "Legal Black Hole": Some Political Issues at Stake' (2006) European Human Rights Law Review 5, 552.

100 Marks, 'Law and the Production of Superfluity' (n 2) 21.

101 Ibid., 20, 21.

102 James Hathaway, 'A Global Solution to a Global Refugee Crisis' (2016) European Papers 1(1), 93.

103 Ibid., 96.

104 Ibid.

On that basis, Hathaway proposes a five-point plan for a global solution. This plan builds on the idea of a "common but differentiated responsibility" of states for refugees,[105] which would be implemented a "managed model, with […] pre-determined burden (financial) sharing and responsibility (human) sharing quotas".[106] By agreeing on financial contributions and quota for resettlement, states would in that vision create a system that allows dealing with newly emerging refugee situations. While the focus of Hathaway's plan lies on an international administration of refugee protection, he also points to the idea of refugees "voting with their feet",[107] thus as reacting to the respective situations and taking part in the distribution of responsibility by making migration decisions.

A different proposal addressing the need for a better regime of responsibility sharing has been advanced by Alexander Aleinikoff and Sarah Cliffe.[108] They argue that new mechanisms need to be set up in order to overcome the current deadlock of the system. For that purpose, they sketch the creation of a multi-stakeholder platform, in which states, international institutions, non-governmental and private actors come together to work towards solutions.

Aleinikoff and Cliffe also point to the steps that international institutions are beginning to take for improving the global structures of protection: A "Solution Alliance" has been created between several UN agencies and the World Bank, which strives to work towards models of assistance that focus on refugee self-reliance and support hosting communities.[109] In June 2016, the UN General Assembly advanced a draft proposal for a Global Compact on Responsibility Sharing for Refugees, which stressed the "centrality of the principle of responsibility sharing"

105 Ibid., 98.

106 Ibid., 97.

107 Ibid., 98.

108 Alexander Aleinikoff/Sarah Cliffe, 'A Global Action Platform and Fund for Forced Migrants: A Proposal' (Netzwerk Flüchtlingsforschung, 25 July 2016) <http://fluechtlingsforschung.net/a-global-action-platform-and-fund-for-forced-migrants-a-proposal>.

109 Executive Committee of the High Commissioner's Programme, 'Update on Solutions' (60th Meeting of the Standing Committee, EC/65/SC/CRP.15, 6 June 2014); cf. also Solutions Alliance <www.solutionsalliance.org>.

and identified concrete steps to work towards a better international cooperation.[110]

3.3 *Considering Proposals for Global Solutions through the Lens of Superfluity*

Looking at these proposals with a focus on the question how the projected measures might contribute to or contravene the production of superfluity, the assessment is mixed. Two questions appear central in my opinion: Firstly, the question how an emphasis on responsibility sharing relates to the issue of mobility. And secondly, the question to which extent centralized approaches can take into account the concrete situations at the border.

I have discussed how states' regulation of borders and the global question of responsibility sharing relate. Not only does the securization of borders in one place shift responsibility for refugees to another state, but also do strategies of containment have shaped today's international structure of protection more generally, including the growing role of humanitarian actors and the corresponding expansion of humanitarian reason in reactions to displacement. These dynamics contribute to the construction of refugees as "superfluous" in at least two ways: Firstly, the more access to territory is restricted, the more the *need* for such access becomes in itself problematic. On a first level, it is the emergence of territorial borders and limitations to free movement, which gives rise to the very concept of the refugee.[111] But also on the level of today's regulation of displacement, the more access is precluded, the more persons will appear *in need* of access. Those persons more and more forced on the same routes, on which it still appears possible to enter a territory, in turn are perceived as uncontrollable masses the admittance of which would threaten the public order, or for which the resources for redistribution can never suffice.[112] Border

---

110 UN, 'Draft for a Global Compact On Responsibility Sharing for Refugees' (30 June 2016) para. 6 <http://www.un.org/pga/70/wp-content/uploads/sites/10/2015/08/Refugees-and-Migrants-30-June-2016.pdf>; the adoption of the Global Compact at the UN Summit failed, instead the New York Delaration was addopted, cf. <http://refugeesmigrants.un.org/declaration>.

111 Patricia Tuitt, *False Images: Law's Construction of the Refugee* (Pluto Press 1996) 110; Dana Schmalz, 'Der Flüchtlingsbegriff zwischen kosmopolitischer Brisanz und nationalstaatlicher Ordnung' (2015) Kritische Justiz 48(4), 390, 399.

112 For articulations of fears about losing control in legal terms cf. Otto Depenheuer, 'Flüchtlingskrise als Ernstfall des Menschenrechtlichen Universalismus' in Otto Depenheuer and Christoph Grabenwarter (eds.), *Der Staat in der Flüchtlingskrise:*

regulations and measures of border securization in that sense take part in a production of superfluity, which subsequently becomes an important factor in the debate about the need for border regulation and social stability itself.

On a different level, the humanitarian reasoning in reacting to forced migration also contributes to a production of superfluity, in that it creates circumstances of dependence, in which persons are foremost recipients of aid. Under those circumstances in which refugees are forced to *wait* for a "durable solution", they are largely excluded from activities that reach beyond the daily concerns. This relates both to an outside-perception of refugees as objects for whom a solution has yet to be found, and to a self-perception of "boredom, impotence, and superfluity".[113] Legal regulations here work both to preclude persons from a full political existence, and from access to a genuine public sphere. I have described in that regard how humanitarian actors actively seek to remedy these effects by introducing policies for inclusion and empowerment, but how these policies also tend to ultimately deepen rather than overcome structures of domination. Foremost, the dependence on funding is likely to reinforce a discourse of victimization.

Looking at the proposals for global solutions, the first important point is thus the stand they take on the question of access and border regulation. While the issues of responsibility sharing and borders directly relate, not every endeavor improving responsibility sharing will also tackle the conditions of access. The draft for a UN Global Compact on Responsibility Sharing for Refugees in that regard subsumed under the necessary measures for improving responsibility sharing for instance the commitment to prevent the "need to flee, or the need to move onwards".[114] Such proposed commitment to prevent onwards migration is likely, however, to reinforce rather than question the dominant "strategies of containment".[115] In that sense, setting up strategies on responsibility

Zwischen gutem Willen und geltendem Recht (Schöningh 2016) 18, 20; Josef Isensee, 'Menschenwürde: Rettungsinsel in der Flüchtlingsflut?' in ibid., 231.

113 Gündoğdu, *Rightlessness in an Age of Rights* (n 10) 143, with reference to Aamer Sultan and Kevin O'Sullivan, 'Psychological Disturbances in Asylum-Seekers Held in Long Term Detention: A Participant-Observer Account' (2001) The Medical Journal of Australia 175(11-12), 593.

114 UN, 'Draft for a Global Compact On Responsibility Sharing for Refugees' (n 111) para. 9.

115 Hyndman, *Managing Displacement* (n 58) 2.

sharing must carefully avoid legitimizing at the same time the increasing securization of borders and restrictions on mobility. Thinking in terms of the "production of superfluity", those measures otherwise risk contributing to the problem they aim to resolve.

James Hathaway's proposal appears split in his perspective on the mobility of refugees, as he generally relies on centralized mechanisms of distribution, but also underlines the role of refugees deciding on directions.[116] Equally, Alexander Aleinikoff and Sarah Cliffe point to "state policies of deterrence" as central part of the problem,[117] while the proposed platform necessarily also subscribes to a logic of centralization in order to improve coordination of funding and resettlement. This thrust towards more centralized administration of responses to refugee situations must not exclude simultaneous endeavors to strive for better conditions. On the one hand, the implementation of responsibility sharing can to different degrees include refugees' choices about destinations. Besides that, the question of access and the role of political agency also in the decisions about migrating are not outside the scope of legal regulation, both in its positive and its negative reach.

4 Responsibility Sharing and Political Membership: Mobility as a Key Concept

Thinking about the framework of refugee protection through the lens of law's production of superfluity, I have pointed to the ambivalences in proposals for global solutions. They are important in that they issue a vehement call to address the flaws in the current system and oppose regional misperceptions about the own role in the picture. At the same time, both the *global* and the *solutions* part in the propositions come at a risk: The *global* comes at the risk of shifting attention from concrete border situations to a more abstract commitment to design responses. It might be the concreteness of the border situation, however, which allows framing the question of refugees not as a humanitarian but as a political one. The *solutions* in turn risks subscribing to the logic that refugees form a temporary problem that one day will be resolved. From the complex intertwinement that the notion of the refugee has with the legitimacy

116 Cf. Hathaway, 'A Global Solution to a Global Refugee Crisis' (n 102).

117 Cf. Aleinikoff/Cliffe, 'A Global Action Platform and Fund for Forced Migrants' (n 108).

framework of nation states and political membership more generally, the horizon of solution can ultimately only stand for a respective dealing with concrete situations.

Yet it would certainly be wrong to on that basis entirely reject the endeavors for global instruments. To draw such finding would subscribe to a strict opposition between principles and pragmatism, which as such cannot be upheld.[118] A critical perspective on possible legal measures on the international level instead must recognize that those measures not only react to factual circumstances but themselves contribute to and frame these very circumstances. With regard to responsibility sharing this means underlining that there is no static mass to be distributed, or no definite number of persons for whom the responsibility is to be shared. Rather, the notion of the refugee and its delimitations both from voluntary migrants and from citizens are themselves not stable but determined through law. In that regard, thinking about superfluity in refugee protection also points to the broader implications of the figure of the refugee in our time.[119]

This brings us back to the initial considerations how the question of access is central to the cause of refugees. We are speaking, to quote Arendt again, about "a problem not of space but of political organization".[120] To address this question, we must thus include the condition of political membership in our thinking about refugees, and concretely in the reflections about possible global solutions. There are numerous sites, in which these conditions of political membership are problematic and relevant to law.[121] In the context of the present considerations about responsibility sharing, recognizing the role of political membership points foremost to the role of mobility.

While responsibility sharing forms the key concept for thinking about inter-state relations regarding protection, it does not address the relationship between states and refugees themselves. Yet the agency of

---

118 For a contemporary account of Hegelian thought and the need to relate normative reasoning with social analysis cf. Axel Honneth, *Freedom's Right: The Social Foundations of Democratic Life* (Columbia University Press 2014) 5.

119 Itamar Mann, 'Refugees' (2011) Mafte'akh 2e, 81; Patricia Tuitt, 'Rethinking the Refugee Concept' in Frances Nicholson and Patrick Twomey (eds.), *Refugee Rights and Realities: Evolving International Concepts and Regimes* (Cambridge University Press 1999) 106.

120 Arendt, *The Origins of Totalitarianism* (n 9) 294.

121 Cf. e.g. Johnson, *Borders, Asylum and Global Non-Citizenship* (n 68) 164.

refugees forms an essential factor in the reality of the legal framework and the conditions of its implementation. By making decisions about where to go, by objecting to unbearable conditions of shelter in one place by moving to another, refugees take part in describing and shaping the global picture of protection. Conceiving it as an essential challenge of refugee law to avoid the production of superfluity, we might thus take mobility as a central principle to guide our reflections. Mobility on the one hand relates to the question of responsibility sharing, in that persons by making migration choices react to inadequate distribution of responsibility between states and its respective effects. But mobility also relates to the perception of refugees as autonomous actors rather than fungible numbers.

For the reflections about legal measures this means on the one hand that centralized efforts must work towards including mobility into the picture. This might be at the minimum by foreseeing a central role of refugees in decisions on destinations. It further might be by fostering international agreements on mobility rights for refugees, as it finds a certain precursor in the institution of the Nansen Passports.[122] But the argumentation I have advanced foremost underlines that we cannot disregard the role of particular border situations. In addition to a global perspective that strives for solutions, it is the analysis of how conditions of mobility are negotiated in these places and how law structures conditions of access, which will remain essential understanding the problem.

---

122 For considerations in that direction cf. Matthew J Gibney, 'Refugees and Justice Between States' (2015) European Journal of Political Theory 14, 448.

PART II

The Politics of Refugee Law

The Exceptional Case of Refugees in Lebanon: An Argument for Rethinking the Concept of State Authority

Maximilian Lakitsch

1 Introduction

When the war in Syria started in 2012 and people had to leave their homes and lives behind, many of them found refuge in Lebanon. They were welcomed despite Lebanon's permanent political fragility that keeps it on the verge of violent conflict. After more than a million Syrians were registered as refugees in Lebanon by the beginning of 2014, the government drastically slowed down the immigration process. By summer 2016, officials estimate 1,5 million Syrians to be residing in Lebanon. Adding the Syrians to the approximately 500.000 refugees of Palestinian descent who have been in the country since 1948 and 1967 respectively, this renders Lebanon an exceptional case. Of about 6 million residents in Lebanon, 4 million are citizens who enjoy government services and unconstrained access to economy and the labor market, while 2 million depend on the goodwill of the state, UN agencies and NGOs.

The vulnerability and the arbitrariness those 2 millions of refugees are exposed to represents a serious humanitarian problem. However, it does not only restrain the individual and deprives it from its basic human needs, it constitutes a fertile ground for violent conflicts between various Lebanese, Syrian and Palestinian factions. After briefly sketching the fragile political conditions in Lebanon and describing the situation of the Palestinian and Syrian refugees, the paper will describe the precarious state of the refugees as a manifestation of the traditional concept of authority. Finally, an alternative paradigm of authority will be introduced that is based on the well-being of the individual. Being framed as *human security* and adopted by the international community, the applicability of this concept to the case of refugees in Lebanon demonstrates that the corresponding discussion about this concept is far more than an exclusive academic discussion beyond reality.

Salomon, Heschl, *et al.* (eds.), *Blurring Boundaries: Human Security and Forced Migration*
 ISBN 978-90-04-32686-6. pp. 51-72.

2 Lebanon's Permanent Refugee Population

2.1 *Brief History of Lebanon – Its Sectarian Background*

The state of Lebanon is an artificial product that is the result of French colonial strategies. Following the distribution of zones of influence in the Middle East between France and Britain as stated in the Sykes-Picot Agreement of 1917, the French relied substantially on the Maronite Church in enacting its authority over Greater Syria. The Maronite Church had already stated an interest in an independent state comprising of Mount Lebanon, which is predominantly Christian, as well as of coastal towns from Byblos over Beirut to Tyre and Sidon in the South and Baalbek and the Bekaa valley in the East. A survey among the population of what was to become Lebanon overwhelmingly was in favor of being included into a Greater Syria as an autonomous region that would be ruled by the Hashemite prince Faisal. Whereas most Maronites objected, other Christian churches sided with most Muslims who opted for the integration into Syria. Nevertheless, France followed its strategy of *divide et imperia* and carved five states out of Greater Syria following the Arab revolt: Greater Lebanon, Aleppo, Damascus, the Alawi state and Jabal al-Duruz. Greater Lebanon became Lebanon and the rest was turned into Syria lateron.[1]

In 1926, France granted Greater Lebanon a constitution that renamed it into the "Republic of Lebanon". The government and administrative posts were equally distributed among the various sects. In 1943, Lebanon became independent. Its constitution distributes the leading government posts among the three largest sects: the president has to be Maronite, a Sunni the Prime Minister, and a Shiite shall be the speaker of the parliament. The state authority was concentrated within the hands of the president. At the same time the imbalance of the distribution of governmental seats overwhelmingly favored the Maronites. That was legitimized with a census in 1932, when the Maronite dominance was still uncontested. However, fertility rates within the Muslim population were already two to four times higher than within Maronite families. As a consequence, Christian dominance in terms of multitude vanished over the following years. That became obvious in the 1960s and led to a redistribution of power towards more equality.[2]

---

1 Fawwaz Traboulsi, *A Modern History of Lebanon* (Pluto Press 2007) 75-87.

2 Ibid., 88-123.

2.2 *Palestinian Refugees in Lebanon*

Following the creation of the state of Israel and the first Arab-Israeli war in 1948, about 120.000 Palestinians fled to Lebanon. Whereas the Lebanese authorities at first tried to resettle them to Syria which rejected those requests, the refugees were finally granted residence in refugee camps around citrus plantations and coastal industrial sites due to the economy's demand of workforce.[3] The Israeli occupation of the West Bank in 1967 and the deadly expulsion of the PLO from Jordan increased the Palestinian presence in Lebanon to a number of 350.000 people.[4]

The PLO relocated its base to Lebanon and Beirut. That actually constituted many Palestinians' identity as such in the first place. In 1969, the Cairo Agreement between the Lebanese government and the PLO leadership granted Palestinians autonomy within the camps. With the PLO leadership forced out of the country in 1982 after the Israeli invasion of Lebanon, the social and economic institutions vanished and the Palestinian economy collapsed. After all, with the relocation of the PLO the recipient of capital from the Gulf countries for the support of the Palestinian cause was out of Lebanon. The Oslo accords in the 1990s worsened the situation as they redirected more money away from the Palestinians living in Lebanon. To this day, the Lebanese authorities have not tried to extend their authority to the camps again.[5]

According to UNRWA, the number of refugees of Palestinian origin amounted to about 433.000 people by June 2011. Almost two thirds of them live in refugee camps throughout the country, the rest in gatherings around those camps or in other parts of the country. Further statistical data emphasizes the poor living conditions of the Palestinian refugees in Lebanon. Two thirds of those registered subsist on less than six USD per day, six percent even on just about two USD. The chances for empowerment are modest when the education record is taken into account: more than 60% of the youth do not finish ninth school grade and only half of those between 16 and 18 years are still enrolled in schools. Most students attend UNRWA schools whose average education standards mostly make it difficult for its alumni to meet the criteria of Lebanese universities and thus break out of the poverty of the camps.

---

3 Ibid., 113-114.

4 Robert Fisk, *Pity the Nation: Lebanon at War* (3rd edn, Oxford University Press 2001) 73-74.

5 Jad Chaaban and others, 'Socio-Economic Survey of Palestinian Refugees in Lebanon' (Final Draft, American University of Beirut 2010) 3-5.

Palestinian refugees in Lebanon lack most basic human rights. Above all, they have no right to own property and are restricted from most working areas – the employment sector excludes non-Lebanese citizens from many jobs. In addition to that, they have only minimum access to the legal system. In some camps, Palestinians without an ID card from UNRWA are not even allowed to leave.[6]

The Palestinian refugee camps, in the beginning a gathering of tents with basic infrastructure, became cramped concrete ghettos with basic infrastructure. As the Lebanese state considers the camps as enclaves outside its authority, it is UNRWA that has to provide housing, water, and electricity. However, those services do not transcend the official borders of the camps and are thus unavailable for the crowded surroundings of the camps which are also not being taken care of by the Lebanese government.[7] Thus, Palestinians in the camps and their surrounding are not only socially excluded, but also spatially.

As the urbanization of Beirut took off in the 1960s and 1970s, its suburbs became cramped with poor and working-class people – many of them Shiites – from Burj Hammoud East of Beirut to the airport south of Beirut. As those neighborhoods swelled, they grew into a single metropolitan area that also incorporated the Palestinian camps of Tall al-Zatar from the East to Mar Iliyas, Sabra, Shatila and Burj al-Barajneh in the West. Thus, this agglomeration, which made up almost half of Beirut's population with approximately 1 million, constitute the so-called poverty belt. As a consequence, the Palestinian camps also became a place for poor Lebanese and other refugees like the ones from Iraq – simply because living was affordable in the concrete barracks of the camps.[8]

War in Syria of course also brought many Palestinians to Lebanon. In its annual report for 2015, UNRWA counts 41.000 Palestinian refugees from Syria. It particularly emphasizes this group as UNRWA considers it to be among the most vulnerable: About 93% depend on regular and humanitarian assistance concerning food, shelter, health care and education.[9] Many Palestinians from Syria rented rooms and houses in already existing camps. That did not only lead to dangerous extensions of

6 UN Relief and Works Agency for Palestine Refugees, 'Palestinian Refugees: A Special Case' (UNRWA Lebanon 2011).

7 Chaaban and others, 'Socio-Economic Survey' (n 5) ix-x.

8 Traboulsi, *A Modern History of Lebanon* (n 1) 161-162.

9 UNRWA, 'Annual Operational Report 2015: for the Reporting Period, 1 January-31 December 2015' (UNRWA 2016).

additional floors in already fragile buildings, but has already more than tripled the rents inside the camps and their surroundings.[10]

Apart from the newly arrived refugees from Syria, most Palestinians are in almost the same situation in which they arrived or in which they were born into. As the status of the Palestinian refugees in Lebanon has hardly changed in the last 60 years, a study by the American University of Beirut for UNRWA speaks of "protracted refugees". They keep being excluded legally, economically and socially from people with Lebanese citizenship. Due to support from UNRWA and various national and above all international NGOs, the Palestinians are being provided with the basic services to survive. Nevertheless, their situation is far from desirable. Furthermore, given Lebanon's demography and the deep cleavages between its sects, the prospects for improving the situation for the Palestinians are modest at best.

2.3 *Reasoning behind the Exclusion*

The Palestinian presence had decisive effects on Lebanon. In 1968, the PLO launched raids in Israel from Southern Lebanon. As the ill-equipped Lebanese army could do nothing but let the PLO militia fight their war, the Lebanese government legitimized this presence through the Cairo accords. Anger within the Lebanese population grew as many suffered from the Israeli retaliation strikes that often hit areas far beneath the Palestinian areas of the south which were already being called "Fatahland". Consequently, the frictions between the Palestinians and the Maronites grew. Subsequently, tensions between Maronites and Lebanese Muslims rose as the latter were considered potential allies of the Palestinians due to their religion. Many Muslims indeed had some sympathy for the Palestinian cause. Frictions, however, also grew between the Palestinians and the Shiites who often were among the victims of the Israeli counter-attacks, as many of them lived in the poorer South due to economic reasons. The incident that opened Pandora's box was the killing of 27 Palestinians traveling in a bus by the Phalange, a Maronite militia. This event triggered a war by various factions that would last until 1990: religious (Maronite, Sunni, Shia, Druze), ideological (nationalist, socialist) and Palestinian

10 Haytham Mouzahem, 'Palestinian-Syrian Refugees Face Hardship in Lebanon' (*al-Monitor*, 7 November 2014) <http://www.al-monitor.com/pulse/originals/2014/11/palestinian-refugees-from-syria-to-lebanon-hardships.html> accessed 22 July 2016.

factions with shifting alliances and oppositions, including changing foreign allies (externally supporting, intervening or occupying).[11]

Given the Palestinian role in triggering the war and their significant military relevance until 1982, the sympathy within the Lebanese population among non-Sunni is modest. Above all, two and a half decades of civil war between its religious and ethnic groups led to the fragmentation of the Lebanese society along their group affiliations. Sectarian quota had already been a political issue before the war. Afterwards, however, it became a matter with the potential to decide about war and peace. Consequently, would the Palestinians who are dominantly Sunni be naturalized and made Lebanese, the Sunni dominance – given the slightly more than four million Lebanese citizens – would be difficult to deny and would probably result in claims for reflecting the distribution of political power. That, however, is highly precarious for the fragile sectarian balance. On the contrary, Christian Palestinians had no difficulty in being naturalized already in the 1950s.[12]

Nevertheless, despite all the advantages, many Palestinians have reservations to raise their voice and claim Lebanese citizenship. For them, such a step could be misinterpreted as giving up their right to return to their homelands. Thus, many Palestinian leaders in the Lebanese camps – at least officially – reject naturalization in favor of the right to return.[13]

2.4 *Syrian Refugees*

As the violent conflict in Syria became a full-blown war with regional involvement, many Syrians had to take refuge in neighboring countries. While most of them found shelter in Turkey, the second largest number of Syrians fled to Lebanon. Given the relatively small Lebanese population of four million inhabitants, already the official account of 1,07 million Syrian refugees in late 2015 is disproportionate. The government estimates actual data to be 500.000 above the official figures.[14] Nevertheless, the country has held its borders open and taken in refugees for a long

11 Fisk, *Pity the Nation* (n 4) 69-80.

12 Sari Hanafi, 'Palestinians in Lebanon: Status, Governance and Security' in Elizabeth Picard and Alexander Ramsbotham (eds.), *Reconciliation, Reform and Resilience: Positive Peace for Lebanon* (Accord Issue 24, Conciliation Resources 2012) 67-68.

13 Ibid., 68.

14 Government of Lebanon and UN, 'Lebanon Crisis Response Plan 2015-16: Year Two' (2015) 6.

time. Since settling in camps has been forbidden by the government in order to properly foster integration, many settled within the communities at first. However, available places soon were overcrowded, savings of the refugees were spent and many people moved to the camps or settled in gatherings with poor conditions.[15]

About 52% of Syrian refugees are considered extremely poor which means that they have to survive on less than 2,4 USD a day. Two thirds are in need of legal documents and residence permits. Thus, most of the Syrian refugees live in precarious conditions scattered throughout the country, mostly in informal gatherings. They also belong to Lebanon's most vulnerable.[16]

Considering Lebanon's sectarian social and political condition, an improvement of the Syrian refugees' situation is unlikely. The employment sector excludes non-Lebanese citizens from many jobs and a naturalization of the mostly Sunni Syrians also threatens the fragile sectarian power balance – although the labor market for Syrians is not as restricted as it is for Palestinians. That in turn leads to tensions between Syrians and Lebanese, as the Syrians are ready to work for a much lower wage.[17] Moreover, fear that the conflict will spill over from Syria to Lebanon is always present and is strongly associated with the refugees. At the end of June 2016 for example, eight suicide bombings on a single day shook a dominantly Christian town in Eastern Lebanon in the Bekaa valley. All of the assassins came from refugee camps. That of course contributes to racist sentiments and statements from population and politicians.[18]

2.5 *The Status of Lebanon's Refugees*

Already in late 2015, the Lebanese minister of social affairs, Rashid Derbas, explained:

15 Jeremy Loveless, 'Crisis in Lebanon: Camps for Syrian Refugees?' (2013) Forced Migration Review 43, 66.

16 Government of Lebanon and UN, 'Lebanon Crisis Response Plan 2015-16, 6-10.

17 Mohammad Nemr, 'Lebanese Minister: We Will Not Force Syrians to Leave' (*al-Monitor*, 28 October 2014) <http://www.al-monitor.com/pulse/politics/2014/10/lebanon-syrian-refugee-policy.html> accessed 22 July 2016.

18 Jean Aziz, 'Lebanon Reels under Weight of Syrian Refugee Crisis' (*al-Monitor*, 8 July 2016) <http://www.al-monitor.com/pulse/originals/2016/07/al-qaa-bombings-syrian-refugees-lebanon-reactions.html> accessed 22 July 2016.

> We explained to UN and Western officials who visited Beirut that a demographic, social, economic, environmental, security and military explosion is in the offing. Despite all the measures taken to try to alleviate the wave of displacement to Lebanon and prevent any further increase in the number of displaced, the fact remains that there are 1,117,000 Syrians officially registered in Lebanon. Add to these the foreign workers in Lebanon and the Palestinian refugees inside and outside the camps.[19]

There are about 6 million people in Lebanon. Only 4 million of them are in possession of a Lebanese passport and have adequate access to the national job market and social services. The remaining two million consist of Syrian and Palestinian refugees – some Palestinians have been in Lebanon for three generations. Lebanon has provided a safe haven for those who sought refuge and took care of their basic humanitarian needs. Any service beyond sensitively touches upon Lebanon's fragile peace that is built on a complex and thin foundation.

Hence, 2 million out of 6 million living in Lebanon are caught in the limbo between citizenship and toleration. They are being taken care of – but not more. The situation that was laid ground in 1948 with the first refugees from Palestine was significantly aggravated by the arrival of Syrian refugees. The refugees from Palestine and Syria, they all live in a situation of permanent vulnerability. They are basically caught between life and death, and some of them for generations.

In order to describe such situations and articulate the corresponding feeling of indignation, the Norwegian social scientist Johan Galtung introduced the term "structural violence". Galtung defined it as being present "when human beings are being influenced so that their actual somatic and mental realizations are below their potential realizations".[20] Thus, we have a broad spectrum of violence: from repression or discrimination over physical violence to murder. All those manifestations of violence have been present in the refugee camps throughout Lebanon and the informal gatherings: be it discrimination by state regulations or violence by

19 Jean Aziz, 'Lebanon Continues to Struggle under Weight of Syrian Refugee Crisis' (*al-Monitor*, 12 November 2015) <http://www.al-monitor.com/pulse/originals/2015/11/lebanon-syrian-displacement-crisis-international-action.html> accessed 22 July 2016.

20 Johan Galtung, 'Violence, Peace, and Peace Research' (1969) Journal of Peace Research 6(3) 167.

army raids or attacks by certain militias – Lebanon's refugee camps and gatherings are zones of violence. However, although Lebanon is an outstanding example in its magnitude and multitude, there are comparable situations in other countries. Those are also situated in modern states.

3 Zones of Violence in Modern States

The term modern state refers to a specific type of political community, which is constituted through a single social order that is enacted on the whole of a certain territory and thereby overrides local and particularistic regimes. The social order in its legally codified manifestation serves as the common agreement managing the actions of the institutions of authority that enact it as well as of the subjects that comply with it.[21] A crucial element of any enacted social order is a certain foundation for its persistence – the reason for compliance. Max Weber describes authority as the foundation for compliance. It means "the probability that a command with a specific content will be obeyed by a given group of persons".[22] Yet, in order to achieve *voluntary* compliance, what needs to be added, according to Weber, is the *belief in legitimacy*. He puts it simple: political legitimacy is the belief of people, that a specific sort of political domination which is enacted upon them is legitimate. He lists three types of legitimate authority according to their sources of legitimacy: rational, tradition, and charismatic.[23] And the modern state is characterized by its rational legitimacy that constitutes a reality that is transpersonal and intersubjective.[24]

---

21 Georg Jellinek, *Allgemeine Staatslehre* (3rd edn, Kronberg 1976) 58, 325-326; Johannes Kunisch, *Absolutismus: Europäische Geschichte vom Westfälischen Frieden bis zur Krise des Ancien Régime* (2nd edn, UTB 1999) 53-60; Marc Bloch, *Die Feudalgesellschaft* (Propyläen 1982) 180-257.

22 Max Weber, *Economy and Society: An Outline of Interpretative Sociology* (vol 1, University of California Press 1978) 53.

23 Ibid., 212-215.

24 Intellectually the word *modern* is tied to a dispute in French arts: the *Querelle des Anciennes et des Modernes.* The *Anciennes* argued in favour of the old classic authorities, which a society had to imitate and follow as well as possible, whereas the *Modernes* pointed out the very own character and worth of their epoch – it can be understood by itself. Thus, the world can indeed be described in its own value by penetrating it with human rationality – Rainer Piepmeier, 'Modern, die Moderne'

Thus, one could say that a crucial characteristic of the modern state is a certain agreement between state authority[25] and its subjects, which provides predictability of the authority's actions towards its subjects and serves as the foundation of its legitimacy. However, if we apply Galtung's comprehensive definition of violence and apply it to the concept of legitimate authority, so-called zones of violence can be characterized through the non-predictability of authority and its agents against individuals, from temporarily withholding certain desired goods to severe physical violence – all can be characterized by a comprehensive understanding of the term violence. In modern states such zones become manifest for example as torture and death of deportees in Austria,[26] ill-treatment of asylum seekers in Germany,[27] police violence against Roma in France and Italy,[28] or dead refugees at EU's external borders in Greece and Italy.

Violence within modern states also becomes manifest in the uncertainty about the immediate future like in the refugee camps located on Greek islands and on Lampedusa in Italy. Children, women, and men are held in camps for months without any further notice about their prospects, without legal advice, with nothing more than enough food to survive under partly severe hygienic conditions.[29] This precarious policy

---

in Joachim Ritter and Karlfried Gründer (eds.), *Historisches Wörterbuch der Philosophie* (vol. 6, Schwabe Verlag 1984) 54-62.

25 The term *state authority* refers to the institutions of authority which are tasked with enacting and upholding authority of the central government on the whole of the state territory.

26 See as an example the case of Bakari J.: In 2006 a Gambian deportee from Austria, Bakari J., was nearly beaten to death by policeman on the way to the airport. Austria Press Agency, 'Vernehmungsprotokoll zu den Misshandlungsvorwürfen. Zur Dokumentation: das Protokoll der Vernehmung von Bakary J. im Büro für besondere Ermittlungen der BPD Wien am 10. April 2006 von 11.15 bis 14 Uhr' (*no-racism.net*, 15 April 2006) <http://no-racism.net/article/1635> accessed 22 July 2016.

27 Tobias Schwarz, 'Abschiebehaft in Berlin: Die Darstellung der Haftsituation durch die Inhaftierten' (*Initiative gegen Abschiebehaft*) <http://www.initiative-gegen-abschiebehaft.de/download/Abschiebehaft%20in%20Berlin.pdf> accessed 22 July 2016.

28 Human Rights Watch, 'Everyday Intolerance: Racist and Xenophobic Violence in Italy' (Report, March 2011) 51-52.

29 Human Rights Watch, 'The EU's Dirty Hands: Frontex Involvement in Ill-Treatment of Migrant Detainees in Greece' (Report, Sep 2011); Human Rights Watch, 'No Refuge: Migrants in Greece' (Report, Nov 2009); Human Rights Watch, 'Pushed Back, Pushed Around: Italy's Forced Return of Boat Migrants and Asylum Seekers, Libya's Mistreatment of Migrants and Asylum Seekers (Report, Sep 2009); Human Rights

of detaining migrants culminated already before the fall of Gaddafi and the pre-detainment of migrants in Libya in 2009 in Lampedusa, as unbearable conditions led to the escape of 4.000 refugees who shouted repeatedly "freedom, freedom, freedom".[30] Soon the situation in Malta and Greece became similar, yet worsened in Greece where refugees whose request for asylum was granted have been confronted with daily despotism by the police.[31]

The situation of refugees at the EU's external borders is comparable to Lebanon, only that in Lebanon refugees have no hope for a citizen-like status that would open the door to the entire labour market or to social services and could thereby satisfy at least their basic human needs. However, Lebanon is not a state that would immediately classify as a modern state. Its institutions and apparatus might at first glance appear modern, but considering the definition of a modern state provided above, Lebanon can only partly be described as such. Even if arbitrary actions of the state authority's institutions are significantly fewer than in other non-OECD countries, the social order that is enacted on the Lebanese territory is not being considered as equally binding by all Lebanese citizens. Often, allegiance to a religious leader is stronger than to a common central government in Beirut. Furthermore, the country's religious sects often have militias that enable them to enforce their will upon the central government.[32]

Watch, 'Turned Away: Summary Returns of Unaccompanied Migrant Children and Adult Asylum Seekers from Italy to Greece' (Report, Jan. 2013).

30 par ARCI, 'Lampedusa Chronology: The Situation Inside Detention Centres' (*no-racism.net*, 27 February 2009) <http://no-racism.net/article/2835/> accessed 17 June 2012.

31 Human Rights Watch, 'Boat Ride to Detention Adult and Child Migrants in Malta' (Report, July 2012); Human Rights Watch, 'Unwelcome Guests: Greek Police Abuses of Migrants in Athens' (Report, Jun 2013); Human Rights Watch, 'Greece: Refugee "Hotspots" Unsafe, Unsanitary' (Report, May 2016).

32 Following a government's request of Hezbollah to dismantle its communication system in May 2008, the Shiite militia took over West Beirut within not even a day in order to demonstrate that it does not consider itself a subject of the Lebanese government. Fortunately, Hezbollah handed over the occupied areas to the Lebanese army two days after, but declared that it will continue its protest against the request by civil means. Hussein Abdallah, 'Day 5: Lebanese Dare to Hope Worst is Over' (*The Daily Star Lebanon*, 12 May 2008) <https://web.archive.org/web/20080517053917/http://www.dailystar.com.lb/article.asp?edition_id=1&categ_id=2&article_id=91930> accessed 22 July 2016.

Still, the structural similarity of the situation of refugees in Lebanon to the European example indicates some relation to the concept of a modern state.

4 The Modern Concept of State Authority – The Inner and the Outer Sphere of Law

The scandalous aspect of zones of violence in modern states is that they are situated next to spaces of enacted law, in which the relation between the authority's agents and the state's citizens is characterised by its predictability, which provides the foundation for a belief in the authority's legitimacy. But what if these acts of violence are crucially linked to the foundations of our political community? Walter Benjamin writes: "The tradition of the oppressed teaches us that the 'state of emergency' in which we live is the rule. We must arrive at a concept of history that corresponds to this. [...] The astonishment that the things that we see, are still possible in the twentieth century is not philosophical. It is not at beginning of knowledge, unless the effect that the idea of history from which it is derived, is not to keep."[33]

In his *Critique of Violence* Walter Benjamin states that it is violence which originally creates any ethical framework as a primordial reference for right and justice. Thus, it is actually violence, which ensouls the orders of right and justice.[34] Similarly, Carl Schmitt argues that originally power is not based on abstract principles of right and justice but on pure power. What originally constitutes power is the decision on the state of exception. Schmitt argues that the core and foundation of power has to transcend law, as it also has to persist beyond the status of enacted law. The pure decision on the removal of the legal order constitutes power beyond any legal framework. It literally constitutes *absolute* (lat. *ab-solutus* for *separated*) power as it presupposes nothing but itself.[35] If we follow Max Weber's definition of power as any chance to enforce one's own will even against opposition, then power as primordial event of the consti-

33 Walter Benjamin, 'Geschichtsphilosophische Thesen' in Walter Benjamin, *Zur Kritik der Gewalt und andere Aufsätze* (Suhrkamp 1971) 84. Translation into English by Maximilian Lakitsch.

34 Benjamin, 'Zur Kritik der Gewalt' in ibid., 29-47.

35 Carl Schmitt, *Politische Theologie: Vier Kapitel zur Lehre von der Souveränität* (9th edn, Duncker & Humblot 2009) 13-21.

tution of power is violence: this manifestation of power overrides any coercion and sets up its own constraints.[36] That is why Walter Benjamin names the type of violence constituting primordial order mythical violence. It is power for the purpose of power. Like misfortune comes upon the hero in the Greek *mythos* faithfully, mythical violence comes over individuals by imposing an order that did not exist before. Consequently, any rationalisation of order is secondary as it has constituted itself upon an act of violence. There are no such things as breaches of ethical regulations and principles on this basic stratum: guilt and delinquency come fatefully upon the individuals like the catastrophe comes upon the hero in the *mythos*.[37]

Thus, it is violence that originally creates and enacts rational and intersubjective order. Giorgio Agamben describes this matter in a more precise way than Benjamin and Schmitt do. Law itself has no being: Law always applies to life. That includes a twofold thesis: on the one hand, to even exist at all beyond the written letter, law needs to be incorporated by the individuals it is enacted upon. That means that law needs life as a bearer or fundament to exist at all. Yet, law also needs life in order to be enacted and validated. Agamben states that the letter of law is ensouled not by the decision on the state of exception, like Schmitt argues, but through the sovereign[38] exception of people from the legal order. That is because law needs a space beyond itself as reference. This place beyond the space of law is being constituted by the exception of people from the legal order. However, this space is not just beyond the sphere of law, it is banned from law: it is bound to the sovereign through its decision to abandon it. That means that the sovereign exercises power upon the banned life by maintaining the status of abandonment. So law is not just absent: law is present through its status of exception. The paradigm of originally banned life is the *homo sacer*: it is disposed to the sovereign to

---

36 Weber, *Economy and Society* (n 21) 52.

37 Benjamin, 'Zur Kritik der Gewalt' (n 32) 58.

38 Agamben uses the terms sovereign and sovereignty when he refers to Weberian understanding of authority (as ability or as entity that carries it out). Thereby, Agamben uses the definition of sovereignty by Jean Bodin as absolute and undivided ability of the king to enforce his own will on his subjects even against their will. Jean Bodin, *Der Staat* (Reclam 2005) 19.

an absolute extend through its abandonment from the sphere of profane as well as divine law.[39]

By enacting the legal order through the exception of individuals from it, the sovereign constitutes two spheres: the inner sphere of enacted law as well as the outer sphere of excepted law. The sphere of enacted law depends on the abandonment of people from the sphere of enacted law, which constitutes the sphere of excepted law. In the sphere of enacted law, the sovereign is bound by the legal order: It acts with legal legitimation. In the sphere of excepted law, the sovereign is not constrained be any order or principle: It acts beyond any type of legitimation – the sovereign acts a-legitimate. Law is valid, yet not enacted and does not prescribe anything, it is purely potential, as Agamben puts it. Whereas in the inner sphere of enacted law any individual in guaranteed certain fundamental rights through and vis-à-vis the sovereign – the individual is citizen – in the outer sphere of excepted law nothing stands between the individual and the Sovereign's pure power – the individual is bare life. So the individual as bare life finds itself helpless at the pure power's mercy.[40]

Consequently, while state borders confine the territory of the state's authority, it is the boundaries of those spheres of excepted law that define the way authority relates to its subjects: as citizens or as *homines sacri*. Within a state's territory, citizens and abandoned *homines sacri* live side by side, yet not together: the people in detention camps live next to German, Austrian, Italian, Greek, but also Lebanese citizens and their basic rights. Thus, it is basically the modern conception of authority that incorporates the dimension of violence into a social order and creates zones of exception. The refugees in Lebanon are a manifestation of the modern paradigm of authority.

5 Refugee Camps and Gatherings as Zones of Exception

Sari Hanafi on the situation of Palestinian refugees in Lebanon:

> After sixty years and three generations, Palestinian refugees cannot be considered within the category of "foreigners" who, in Lebanon, are usually temporary migrants. Reduced to their status

39 Giorgio Agamben, *Home Sacer: Die Souveränität der Macht und das Nackte Leben* (Suhrkamp 2002) 15-39, 92-112.

40 Ibid., 60-66.

> as individuals in need of shelter and food, the governance of their bare-life has been transferred to the hands of the police and military on the one hand, and to apolitical relief organizations like UNRWA, on the other. The Lebanese state has sustained a status quo (of sorts) by juggling the inclusion/exclusion duality, subverting the legal with the political and vice-versa. In other words, the Lebanese authorities are excluding Palestinians from the rights and benefits they ought to enjoy as residents of Lebanon while simultaneously including them as a security threat, as 'something' to be contained and thus subjected to strict control and surveillance.[41]

Palestinian refugees in Lebanon remain subjects to state authority while they do not have the rights of the subjects that mostly live beyond the walls of the camps: Lebanese citizens. Thus, it is the Lebanese state authority that makes the Palestinian camps and gatherings zones of exception. Consequently, along the modern conception of authority, the Lebanese central government exercises significant authority for the Palestinians by excluding them from social services, the labour market and other crucial services, thereby creating those spaces of exception. As authority in the camps is scattered and contested, individual despotism and violence is omnipresent.

Since the PLO was forced out of the country in 1982, no authority has managed to establish itself and exercise legitimate authority. As Inner-Palestinian governance within the camps is highly contested between factions like Fatah, Hamas, Islamic Jihad, UNRWA, and several NGOs, carrying out effective policies within the camps is barely possible. As a consequence, the individual depends on the goodwill of one of the authorities. The case of the Palestinians in the camps is a lively example of the daily life of the *homo sacer*. As a matter of fact, the camp dwellers are desperately caught between their authorities' inability to organise daily affairs, the unwillingness of the Lebanese state to grant all of its residents an adequate status and an imposed and reinforced dream of returning to the land of Palestine.[42]

---

41 Sari Hanafi, 'Governing Palestinian Refugee Camps in the Arab East: Governmentalities in Search of Legitimacy' (Working Paper Series, no 1, The Issam Fares Institute for Public Policy and International Affairs) 29.

42 Sari Hanafi, 'Palestinian Refugee Camps in Lebanon as a Space of Exception' (*REVUE Asylon(s)*, no 5, September 2008) <http://www.reseau-terra.eu/article798.html> accessed 22 July 2016.

While the identity of the camp dwellers has proven to be almost unrelated to the host country Lebanon, it also seems to be only loosely connected with a Palestinian identity. Rather, the camps seem to nurture a distinct urban identity disconnected from the world beyond their borders. The camp of *Ein al-Helweh* can serve as a paradigm for this shift. Being once known for its important role in resistance to the Israeli occupation, it seemingly can be barely linked to the Israeli-Palestinian conflict and a Palestinian identity anymore. Instead, ongoing radicalisation processes are directed towards Salafist activism that is linked Saudi-Arabia and sometimes Iran but not to Israel-Palestine anymore.[43]

Beyond their disconnectedness to the place of origin and the place of residence, Michael Agier describes them as being unrelated to time: They are "outside of the places and outside of the time of a common, ordinary, predictable world".[44]

The Syrian refugees were openly welcomed in the first weeks and months of the Syrian war. But the enormous influx of people was too much of a social and economic burden for the small country of Lebanon. Neither have UNHCR and the international community provided enough means to adequately cope with the basic human needs of the Syrians.[45] Consequently, most Syrian refugees became dwellers in the state authority's zone of exception: the Syrian refugee as a bare life faces the immediate power of the sovereign. A young Syrian woman who fled to Lebanon describes her situation: "We get threats in the street every day. Sometimes we wait until it gets dark [to go out]. We are addicted to rain because the streets are empty."[46] Probably a paradigmatic manifestation of bare life is the act of self-immolation.[47] In April 2014, a Syrian mother

---

43 Ibid.

44 Michael Agier, 'Between War and City: Towards an Urban Anthropology of Refugee Camps' (2002) Ethnography 3(3), 317, 323.

45 In 2014 the overall contributions for humanitarian means in Lebanon added up to 874 million USD, whereas the estimated financial requirements to properly deal with the situation nation-wide were 1,69 billion USD. Government of Lebanon and UN, 'Lebanon Crisis Response Plan 2015-16, 6.

46 Amnesty International, 'Hardship, Hope and Resettlement: Refugees from Syria tell their Stories' (February 2015) 4.

47 In 2016, two incidents of self-immolation were reported from an Australian offshore refugee camp. One of them, a young Iranian detainee, is depicted in a video before the self-immolation yelling desperately "This is how tired we are. [...] This action will prove how exhausted we are. I cannot take it any more". Ben Doherty, 'Self-immolation: desperate protests against Australia's detention regime'

set herself on fire out of desperation following the UN-announced cuts of food and monetary support. The Syrian refugee had nothing else than her bare life to protest against the deprivation of her basic human needs.[48]

6 Rethinking Authority beyond Exclusion

The crucial flaws of the mechanisms of constituting authority lie in its origins of violence that create a social order by excluding individuals from it. Both the individuals within the social order and the excluded ones are subjects of its power. However, the subjects included into the order are tied to the authority via a certain set of regulations that defines their relationship and makes the actions of the authority predictable: the citizens of a state are subjects on the foundation of national law and they have certain rights that protect them from a state authority's despotism. The subjects excluded from the social order are immediately related to authority. They absolutely depend on its mercy and permanently face uncertainty: the mercy of the Lebanese government, the mercy of UNRWA or UNHCR, the mercy of other factions.

It is especially the figure of the refugee which highlights crucial flaws of the common concept of sovereignty: Protection of basic human rights and the guarantee of basic human needs are tied to the concept of citizenship. Walter Benjamin and Carl Schmitt go a step further and claim that the basic layer of law that allows for justice, basic protection and being considered a citizen is already built on a foundation of violence. Giorgio Agamben frames this violence as exception from the sphere of law that is essential for the constitution of sovereignty. Thus, those spaces of exception are an existential necessity for any state governed along the common concept of sovereignty. Applying that to the example of refugees

(*The Guardian*, 3 May 2016) <https://www.theguardian.com/australia-news/2016/may/03/asylum-seekers-set-themselves-alight-nauru> accessed 27 Jul 2016. Yet, there are numerous acts of self-immolation, self-harm and suicide in Australian camps, which have been reported within the last years. Ben Doherty and David Marr, 'The worst I've seen – trauma expert lifts lid on 'atrocity' of Australia's detention regime' (*The Guardian*, 19 Jun 2016) <https://www.theguardian.com/australia-news/2016/jun/20/the-worst-ive-seen-trauma-expert-lifts-lid-on-atrocity-of-australias-detention-regime> accessed 27 Jul 2016.

48 Reuters, 'Syrian Self-Immolation Case Reflects Tragedy' (*al-Jazeera*, 3 April 2014) <http://www.aljazeera.com/news/middleeast/2014/04/syria-self-immolation-case-reflects-tragedy-20144216034370957.html> accessed 22 July 2016.

means that by transcending state borders one will always enter zones of exception if the state authority's protection of the country of origin does not extend to the country of destination.

The case of Lebanon emphasizes the absurdity of the connection between political authority and basic human rights in exceptional clarity. In fact, with one third of the residents being structurally exposed to permanent vulnerability, political stability and state authority are seriously endangered: tensions are already raising among the refugees, between the refugees and the citizens as well as among the Lebanese factions – with violent eruptions from time to time. Once the tensions have transformed into a violent conflict carried out between various factions on its territory, the central government will not be able to exercise its authority anymore.

In her definition of power, Hannah Arendt includes Max Weber's understanding of legitimacy of authority: power is the "human ability not just to act but to act in concert".[49] She argues that violence as an instrument to multiply strength to enforce one's will upon others is in opposition to power. Arendt asserts that a government that relies exclusively on the use of force and has no power base cannot persist. "Power is indeed of the essence of all government, but violence is not."[50] Whereas violence is superior to power, the cost of using violence is a loss of power.[51]

Thus, authority in order to be enacted presupposes the individuals' voluntary compliance. This compliance is necessary to impose a social order that is able to manage their daily interactions and prevent violent interaction. Furthermore, it is the institutions of authority which enact and uphold the social order by exercising authority in accordance with the foundation of legitimacy; this in return upholds the subjects' convictions that it is in their interest that the order is effective.

Thus, effective authority depends on its evaluation by the people it considers its subjects. Baruch de Spinoza already noticed: "[A]bsolute sovereignty, if any such thing exists, is really the sovereignty held by a whole people."[52] Only the power of the many can control the power of the many:

---

49 Hannah Arendt, *On Violence* (Harvest 1970) 44.

50 Ibid., 51.

51 Ibid., 43-56; Benjamin, 'Geschichtsphilosophische Thesen' (n 31).

52 Benedict Spinoza, 'Tractatus Theologico-Politicus' in Benedict Spinoza and A G Wernham (eds.), *The Political Works* (Clarendon Press 1958) 371.

> This corporate right, which is defined by the power of a people, is generally called sovereignty, and is entirely vested in those who by common consent manage their affairs of state [...]. If such functions belong to a general assembly of the people, then the state is called a democracy.[53]

Thus, "democracy" – as Spinoza calls it – is the ontological foundation of power: the mass constitutes authority, which is thus bound by the mass. Spinoza also draws the line to Hobbes when he states that, in a democracy:

> [...] No one transfers his natural right to another so completely that he is never consulted again, but each transfers it to a majority of the whole community of which he is a member. In this way all remain equal, as they were before in the condition of nature.[54]

As a result, the individuals never actually surrender their autonomy to the authority as Hobbes argued. The authority's power – meaning its ability to enact a certain social order – will depend on the subjects' evaluation of its usefulness. Furthermore, obedience to the authority is an obligation as long as the authority actually exercises ultimate authority and is thereby able to enact and uphold social order. If the authority's power to actually govern its subjects fades, the authority no longer has a right to act as such, as it is incapable of exercising.

In the tradition of Abraham Maslow, John Burton[55] and Edward Azar[56] an individual's actions and interactions are defined as being guided by the pursue for basic human needs and wants. Basic human needs are characterized by their non-negotiability as well as the destructive consequences in case of their deprivation. Thus, as Burton declares, "[t]he satisfaction of human needs and desires is [...] of systemic interest."[57]

---

53 Ibid., 277-279.

54 Ibid., 137.

55 John W Burton, 'Human Needs Versus Societal Needs' in Roger A Coate and Jerel A Rosati (eds.), *The Power of Human Needs in World Society* (Lynne Rienner 1988).

56 Edward A Azar, *The Management of Protracted Social Conflict: Theory and Cases* (Dartmouth 1990).

57 Burton, 'Human Needs Versus Societal Needs' (n 51) 43.

Consequently, the actual foundation of enacted authority and a social order is every individual that is considered a subject to authority and whose basic human needs are being provided for.

Human security, as defined by UNDP in 1994, also connects individual well-being with social order, thereby making it a prerogative for state authority: "Without peace, there may be no development. But without development, peace is threatened."[58] It argues that human security consists of safety from hunger, disease and repression, and second, of security of being deprived of this safety. As an interrelated element, human development is mentioned as a process of increasing one's choices and options. Human security encompasses the ability to take those choices freely. Thus, both human security and human development are linked: failure in the one might endanger the other. Failure in human development leads to deprivation of basic human needs like nutrition, sanity but also political as well as economic access and that might lead to inner-societal violence.[59]

Human security means that people are provided the basis to autonomously lead their lives the way they desire. In doing that, they take care of their own development and the development of their community and the state.[60] Thus, it constitutes national security on the foundation of individual human security that is basically understood like Galtung's comprehensive definition of peace as freedom of any kind of repression.

Basically, by rethinking security and shifting the perspective from the central state authority to the individual aims at shifting the paradigm of understanding sovereignty as ontologically linked to the fulfilment of the individual's basic human needs. Thereby it has a lot of revolutionary potential that it was not able to unfold so far. Annick Wibben sees UNDP's critical understanding of human security from 1994 undermined by the Commission on Human Security's report of 2003.[61] There, the conditionality of national security is not based on human security anymore, but

---

58 UN Development Programme, 'Human Development Report 1994' (Oxford University Press 1994) iii.

59 Ibid., 23.

60 Ibid., 24.

61 This questionable development was then also affirmed by the UN through the adoption of UN General Assembly resolution 66/290 of 25 October 2012.

seen as mutually related. Along such reshifts, human security is often being misused to emphasize conventional interpretations of security.[62]

7 Lebanon's Fragile Foundation of State Authority

With its more than 6 million residents and just about 4 million citizens that have full access to state services and the economy, Lebanon poses a strong argument in favor of reshifting the paradigm of state authority towards the individual well being. Many camps have already become cities of their own beyond any relation to their surroundings but their geographical position. Various gatherings comprising of many Syrian refugees are on the way of becoming such zones of exception. According to Walter Benjamin, Carl Schmitt and Giorgio Agamben's analyses of authority, exposing the refugees to vulnerability and violence is not an obviously policy-driven action, but is structurally related to the conception of authority that is ontologically based on violence.

Following Hannah Arendt's interpretation of Max Weber and Baruch Spinoza's understanding of power, the individuals' evaluation of the authority's actions is what actually constitutes authority. The concept of human security is the international community's paradigm to frame this idea and to turn the traditional relation of authority and basic human rights around: not authority is the ontological foundation that grants the right for the provision of basic human needs, but the provision of basic human needs is the foundation that constitutes authority as such in the first place.

Many Syrians will probably return to their home country one day. However, right now they are still in Lebanon and their humanitarian situation is worsening. The Palestinians do not have a country to return to. Their situation has been serious for all their lifetime. Those almost 2 million refugees are not part of the ontological foundation of the Lebanese state authority. Taking seriously the individual-centered concept of human security would not only satisfy the basic human needs of the refugees, but would also contribute to not endangering state authority in light of rising tensions between Lebanese citizens, Syrian refugees and Palestinians. Being often an academic topic, the case of Lebanon poses a strong argu-

62 Annick T R Wibben, 'Human Security: Toward an Opening' (2008) Security Dialogue 39(4), 455, 455-458.

ment of the benefits of an individual-based concept of authority, which is also framed as human security.

The Missing Link between Law on Force and Refugee Law: Some Preliminary Remarks in Context

Stefan Salomon

1 Setting the Scene

Most refugees escape from wars. The overwhelming majority of refugees arriving to EU Member States, escaped wars that have or had an international dimension – Syria, Iraq, Afghanistan, Somalia, Kosovo[1] – which, arguably involves questions on the use of force. Moreover, military intervention by a state against the territory of another state may result in an increase of persons fleeing from that violence. UNHCR data, for instance, suggests a strong correlation between the U.S. led intervention in Afghanistan in 2001 and an increase of Afghan refugees.[2] Although a lively public debate takes place in the U.S. and Germany, in particular, on moral responsibilities of granting asylum to Afghan refugees and, more narrowly, to those who worked for the allied forces in Afghanistan,[3] a discussion of the legal aspects of the relation between use of force and refu-

1 Eurostat, 'Countries of Origin of (Non-EU) Asylum Seekers in the EU-28 Member States, 2014 and 2015' <http://ec.europa.eu/eurostat/statistics-explained/index.php/File:Countries_of_origin_of_(non-EU)_asylum_seekers_in_the_EU-28_Member_States,_2014_and_2015_(thousands_of_first_time_applicants)_YB16.png> accessed 29 July 2016.

2 UNHCR, 'Afghan Refugee Statistic February 2005' <http://www.unhcr.org/en-us/421316072.pdf> accessed 29 July 2016.

3 On the U.S. context see in particular the article series in the New York Times, 'Is America Responsible for Afghan Refugees' (6 April 2016) <http://www.nytimes.com/roomfordebate/2016/04/06/is-america-responsible-for-afghan-refugees>. On the Afghan personnel that worked for the ISAF forces in Afghanistan and who would be at threat after the withdrawal of troops from Afghanistan, see inter alia Azam Ahmed, 'Afghans Who Helped the U.S. Fear That Time for Visas Has Run Out' (*New York Times*, 24 March 2014) <http://www.nytimes.com/2014/03/25/world/asia/afghans-visas-us.html>; Frankfurter Allgemeine Zeitung, 'Die Übersetzer' (24 September 2012) <http://www.faz.net/aktuell/feuilleton/debatten/dolmetschen-in-afghanistan-die-uebersetzer-11899993.html?printPagedArticle=true#pageIndex_2>; Anne Allmeling, 'Bedroht und im Stich Gelassen' (*Deutschlandfunk*, 25 August 2014) <http://www.deutschlandfunk.de/bundeswehrhelfer-in-afghanistan-

Salomon, Heschl, *et al.* (eds.), *Blurring Boundaries: Human Security and Forced Migration*
 ISBN 978-90-04-32686-6. pp. 73-98.

gee law is virtually absent. Whereas the relation between international humanitarian law (*ius in bello*) and refugee law has been the field of rich doctrinal production,[4] its mutual insights incorporated into both refugee law and international humanitarian law,[5] no such elaboration has been undertaken in regard to the relation between the use of force and refugee law. Although the Geneva Refugee Convention (GRC) emerged as "never-again" from the experience of a war that produced millions of refugees, it mentions 'war' only four times: in article 1F(a) excluding persons who have committed war crimes from refugee status;[6] derogation clause in times of war;[7] and the now defunct continuity of residence provision pertaining to refugees from the Second World War.[8] Similarly, the EU Qualification Directive mentions 'war' only twice: As exclusion from refugee status and subsidiary protection if there are serious reasons that the person has committed a war crime.[9] Equally, other regional protec-

---

bedroht-und-im-stich.724.de.html?dram:article_id=295577> all accessed 29 July 2016.

4 E.g. Mélanie Jacques, *Armed Conflict and Displacement: The Protection of Refugees and Displaced Persons under International Humanitarian Law* (Cambridge University Press 2015). Elspeth Guild, for instance, analyses how the legitimacy of an individual's claim to international protection depends on how the international community views the conflict, i.e. whether a situation of violence is defined as armed conflict – see Elspeth Guild, *Security and Migration in the 21st Century* (Polity Press 2009) 69. Similarly, Catherine Dauvergne observes that the dividing line between successful and unsuccessful claims involving objections to military service depends, inter alia, on the characteristics of the conflict in question, on the actors who are involved and on the compliance with international humanitarian law – Catherine Dauvergne, 'Toward a New Framework for Understanding Political Opinion (2016) 37 Michigan Journal of International Law 243, 266-268.

5 Geneva Convention (IV) Relative to the Protection of Civilian Persons in Time of War Geneva [1949] 75 UNTS 287, Art 44.

6 Convention Relating to the Status of Refugees [1951] 189 UNTS 13, 137.

7 Ibid., Art 9.

8 Ibid., Arts 10(1) and (2).

9 Directive 2011/95/EU of the European Parliament and of the Council of 13 December 2011 on Standards for the Qualification of Third-Country Nationals or Stateless Persons as Beneficiaries of International Protection, for a Uniform Status for Refugees or for Persons Eligible for Subsidiary Protection, and for the Content of the Protection Granted [2011] OJ L 337/9 (Qualification Directive), Art 12(2)(a) and 17(1)(a).

tion instruments do not mention war beyond the exclusion clause.[10] In short, 'war' is largely absent in refugee law.[11]

In the first section, I point out that the absence of 'war' in refugee law reflects a broader absence of 'war' in international legal language. As "resort to armed force", the International Criminal Tribunals (ICTY) definition of armed conflict,[12] is, however, still permitted as a matter of self-defence or on the basis of a Security Council mandate, I subsequently analyse the shifting narrative – from humanitarian intervention to self-defence – on the use of force in the Syrian conflict. As the use of force by states has been, more often than not, attached to legal justification, despite any obligation to do so,[13] these narratives illustrate as a spectacle of state power and a seismograph that records how a state wants to be seen (publicly displayed morals). In the second section, I relate the humanitarian narrative to refugee law, arguing that the construction of the refugee as object of humanitarian intervention in the law of force reduces her to a passive object of benevolent intervention. In section three, I formulate some speculative remarks on the effects of the changing narrative of the use of force in the Syrian conflict, arguing that the legal narrative of a conflict relates to the people fleeing from that conflict.

---

10 Convention Governing the Specific Aspects of Refugee Problems in Africa [1969] 1001 UNTS 45; Convention on Asylum [1928] (Havana Convention).

11 Refugee law is understood, for the purpose of this chapter, as the ensemble of the norms of international refugee law and regional asylum law, a legal complex that is referred to in EU law as the 'law of international protection' – Qualification Directive 2011/95/EU (n 9). Hence, the term 'refugee' in this chapter is not used within the confines of the doctrinal understanding of Article 1A(2) of the Geneva Refugee Convention, but in a broader understanding encompassing also the status of subsidiary protection. Doing so is based, on the one hand, on the jurisprudence of the Court of Justice of the European Union that increasingly extends protection standards for refugees to other statuses of protection by referring to "a uniform status to all beneficiaries of international protection" (see inter alia, joined Cases C-443/14 and C-444/14 *Kreis Warendorf v Ibrahim Alo and Amira Osso v Region Hannover*, ECLI:EU:C:2016:127, para. 32). On the other, on a theoretical argument that focuses on the effects on the human rights caused by displacement, rather than the causes of displacement – e.g. Matthew Gibney, 'Refugees and Justice Between States' (2015) 14 European Journal of Political Theory 448, 452-456.

12 *Prosecutor v Dusko Tadić* [1995] ICTY, Decision on the Defence Motion for Interlocutory Appeal on Jurisdiction, IT-94-1-A, para. 70.

13 Dino Kritsiotis, 'Theorizing International Law on Force and Intervention' in Anne Orford and Florian Hoffmann, *The Oxford Handbook of the Theory of International Law* (Oxford University Press 2016) 655-683, 656.

To be sure, I consider both modern war and refugeehood as legal creatures. Modern warfare takes place largely as a struggle in the law.[14] Equally, modern refugeehood is largely produced by and in the law.[15] Hence, I describe in this chapter the legal rules pertaining to the justification of 'war' (the force of law) and refugee law as two separate legal spheres. The separation of these two legal spheres facilitates the continued view of the refugee as an object of humanitarian intervention or security concerns, while reducing her capability of acting as a political subject. Certainly, this is not the only 'mechanism' facilitating this paradox, but, given the relation between 'war' and refugeehood, certainly has a crucial function in upholding that paradox.[16]

2 On the Use of Force

2.1 *The Absence of War in International Law*

The absence of the term 'war' is not peculiar to refugee law. 'War' was supposed to have vanished from the vocabulary of international legal language since the outlawing of aggression in the Covenant of the League of Nations.[17] The UN-Charter includes 'war' as a "never again" reference

14 Nathaniel Berman speaks of law's central role in the "construction of war as a separate sphere of human activity" – Nathaniel Berman, 'Privileging Combat? Contemporary Conflict and the Legal Construction of War' (2004) 43 Columbia Journal of Transnational Law 4. And probably most prominently on this issue, David Kennedy, 'Lawfare and Warfare' in James Crawford and Martti Koskenniemi, *The Cambridge Companion to International Law* (Cambridge University Press 2012) 158-184.

15 Roger Zetter, 'More Labels, Fewer Refugees: Remaking the Refugee Label in an Era of Globalization (2007) 20(2) Journal of Refugee Studies 172.

16 Matthew Gibney sees the fundamental issue in the irreconcilable tension between democratic politics, which requires "some degree of closure and degree of closure and a privileging of the claims of insiders over outsiders" – Matthew Gibney, 'Asylum: Principled Hypocrisy' in Bridget Anderson and Michael Keith (eds.), *Migration: The Compas Anthology* (Compas 2014) 163-164. The irreconcilability of that tension presupposes the validity of a specific understanding of the boundaries of the demos, an understanding that is contested, for instance, by Arash Abizadeh who argues for a, in principle, unbounded demos thus requiring the justification of closed borders. See: Arash Abizadeh, 'Democratic Theory and Border Coercion: No Right to Unilaterally Control Your Own Borders' (2008) 36 Political Theory 37 – or by Giorgio Agamben, arguing for rethinking fundamental political categories; see: Giorgio Agamben, 'We Refugees' (1995) 49 Symposium 114-119.

17 Covenant of the League of Nations [1919] Art 10.

to past experiences. First, 'war' is set out as purpose in the preamble "to save succeeding generations from the scourge of war, which twice in our lifetime has brought untold sorrow to mankind", and second as reference to the Second World War.[18] The UN-Charter defines 'war' only in the negative, its very purpose being to banish war from the realm of international relations whose anarchy ought to be replaced by the rationality of international law. The International Law Commission (ILC), in its first session, considered whether war should be included as a topic of enquiry in its program of work. The ILC decided that war had ceased to be a relevant topic of enquiry for the codification of law:

> It was suggested that, war having been outlawed, the regulation of its conduct had ceased to be relevant. On the other hand, the opinion was expressed that, although the term "laws of war" ought to be discarded, a study of the rules governing the use of armed force – legitimate or illegitimate – might be useful.[19]

'War' as a legal term, as the International Law Association (ILA) points out, has been replaced in international legal language by the definition of 'armed conflict', a term international lawyers are much more comfortable using.[20] The replacement of the term 'war' by the term 'armed conflict' in the Geneva Conventions, for instance, should make it harder for states to argue that their acts merely represent police actions or self-defence.[21] Yet, the negative definition of war – and hence its absence – by and in the law, reminds in some way of Hans Joas observation of modern social theory. Although much of modern social theory emerged as a result of personal experiences of war (just think of Jürgen Habermas or Talcott Parsons), social theory itself largely abstained from war as an object of inquiry.[22]

---

18 Charter of the United Nations [1945] 1 UNTS XVI, Arts 77 and 107 (UN Charta).

19 UN, *Yearbook of the International Law Commission 1949: Summary Records and Documents of the First Session Including the Report of the Commission to the General Assembly* (UN New York 1956) 281.

20 Mary O'Connell, *What is War?* (Brill 2012) 9.

21 Jean Pictet, *Commentary on the Geneva Conventions of 12 August 1949, Vol I* (International Committee of the Red Cross, 1952) 32.

22 Hans Joas and Wolfgang Knöbl, *Kriegsverdrängung: Ein Problem in der Geschichte der Sozialtheorie* (Suhrkamp 2008) 10-11. Joas and Knöbl argue that the absence of war as an object of inquiry in modern social theory is a legacy from enlightenment philosophy and political theory that characterize 'war' as social anomaly and transient aberrance.

The figure of the refugee was for the international lawyer equally a legal anomaly. Writing on the international protection of refugees, three years after the entry into force of the Geneva Refugee Convention (GRC), Paul Weiss, the then legal advisor of the UN High Commissioner on Refugees (UNHCR), wrote that "[f]or the lawyer, the status of a person who is deprived of national protection is "anomalous"… He has been called flotsam, *res nullius*".[23] Well up to the 1950s virtually all major studies on refugees included in their titles the "Refugee Problem",[24] an expression that sounds strangely familiar in the current political context. This phrasing reflected the predominant mood and conviction at the drafting conference of the GRC that the "refugee problem" would be resolved in a few decades. I will return to this point in a bit. For now, it is enough to note that refugees were considered as a transient phenomenon that would be resolved.

Article 2(4) UN-Charter includes a comprehensive prohibition on the use of force "against the territorial integrity or political independence of any State, or in any other manner inconsistent with the purposes of the United Nations".[25] Two well-known exceptions to the use of force are included in the UN-Charter: the exclusive authorisation of the Security Council to "take action by air, sea, or land forces as may be necessary to maintain or restore international peace and security";[26] and the unilateral use of force by states to exercise the "inherent right of individual or collective self-defence".[27] Thus, although 'war' is absent in international legal language, agreement exists only on the point that the UN-Charter contains a general prohibition on aggressive wars. The most basic disagreement on the use of force came to the fore in the NATO intervention Kosovo in 1999 with many writers and at least two states arguing that the last part of article 2(4) UN-Charter ("in any manner inconsistent with the purposes of the United Nations") could not be construed as to prohibit the use of force to end crimes against humanity

23 Paul Weiss, 'The International Protection of Refugees' (1954) 48(2) American Journal of International Law 193, 193.

24 See in particular the influential study of John H Simpson – John H. Simpson, 'The Refugee Problem' (1938) 17 International Affairs 607. Also J L Rubinstein, 'The Refugee Problem' (1936) 15(5) International Affairs 716; G J Van Heuven Goedhart, 'The Problem of Refugees' (1953) 82 RdC.

25 UN Charter, 1 UNTS XVI (n 18) Art 2(4).

26 Ibid., Art 42.

27 Ibid., Art 51.

or genocide as a matter of last resort.[28] I describe this legal justification for intervening militarily as the humanitarian reason narrative.[29]

In the following section I focus on the Kosovo intervention, illustrating the broader issue of how refugees became objects of military intervention in the legal justifications provided on the intervention. To understand the current scope of the humanitarian intervention debate on Syria, the humanitarian reason narrative has to be understood. Although the Kosovo intervention was not the first time a humanitarian reason narrative was employed in regard to refugees Kosovo still represents the most powerful narrative on humanitarian intervention.[30]

2.2 *Refugees as Objects of Humanitarian Intervention*

Michael Reisman, in his 1990 article "International Law after the Cold War", argued that the disappearance of "[s]ymmetrical doctrines of

28 Christine Gray, *International Law and the Use of Force* (Oxford University Press 2008) 33-51.

29 I will only deal with the doctrine of humanitarian intervention and not the subsequent theory of the Responsibility to Protect, as both share the same humanitarian reason narrative – e.g. Brian Barbour and Brian Gorlick, 'Embracing the Responsibility to Protect: A Repertoire for Measures Including Asylum for Victims' (2008) 20 International Journal for Refugee Law 533.

30 The UK openly relied on a humanitarian intervention doctrine in the aftermath of the Iraq conflict in 1991 with the aim to provide protection to refugees and displaced persons by establishing 'safe havens', together with U.S. and French armed forces – Gray, *International Law* (n 28) 35-37; Howard Adelman, 'Humanitarian Intervention: The Case of the Kurds' (1992) 4 International Journal of Refugee Law 4, 5. The UN Security Council adopted resolution 688, in which it requested the UN Secretary General to "address urgently the critical needs of the refugees and displaced Iraqi population" (para. 5); in this regard, the Security Council "insists that Iraq allow immediate access by humanitarian organizations to all those in need of assistance in all parts of Iraq" (para. 3). The moral necessity-legal restraint dilemma of the Kosovo intervention was equally present in this intervention, as resolution 688 (1991) was not taken under chapter VII and the U.S. army can hardly be described as a 'humanitarian organization' that needs to be granted access (although the U.S. argued that resolution 678 (1990) was still operative, thus permitting the use of force, the same 'legal basis' the U.S. government relied on in its legal argumentation on using force against Iraq). As Peter Malanczuk aptly described tis moral necessity-legal restraint dilemma: "[f]rom a purely moral and humanitarian point of view there seems to be little difficulty in welcoming the allied military intervention in Iraq to protect the Kurdish refugees" – see Peter Malanczuk, 'The Kurdish Crisis and Allied Intervention in the Aftermath of the Second Gulf War' (1991) 2 European Journal of International Law 114, 123.

selective intervention", by the reduction of the role of military strategy at the international plane, would no longer skirt the prohibition on the unilateral use of force.[31] With the legitimacy of domestic authority now deriving from international human rights, the narrative of interventions, Reisman noted, would adapt accordingly. Yet, Reisman had no delusions that interventions would function in a "regular and non-selective manner each time that circumstances required it", as others have argued later on.[32] Because interventions, Reisman argued, "are perforce reflections of the world power process, the arena of their operation will continue to be the internal affairs of smaller and weaker states".[33]

As Reisman predicted, after 1990 the UN Security Council indeed turned its attention increasingly to crimes against humanity, massive violations of human rights, and genocide. In this context the Security Council started to consider large displacements of populations, in particular refugee flows, as threat to international peace and security.[34] The Security Council used different formulas by which it referred to refugees. It either referred directly to "massive flows of refugees towards and across international frontiers… which threaten international peace and security",[35] or it mentioned the obligation of a state to guarantee the "right of refugees and displaced persons to return in safety and security to their homes".[36] The Security Council included refugees in its resolutions taken under chapter VII of the UN-Charter which either expressly permitted the use of force by UN Member States,[37] in resolutions which were taken under chapter VII but did not include express permission on

31 Michael Reisman, 'International Law After the Cold War' (1990) 84 American Journal of International Law 859, 860-861.

32 George Abi-Saab, 'Wither the International Community?' (1998) 9 European Journal of International Law 248, 264.

33 Reisman, 'International Law' (n 31) 861.

34 For an overview see Guy Goodwin-Gil and Jane McAdam, *The Refugee in International Law* (Oxford University Press 2007) 5.

35 E.g. UNSC, 'Resolution 688' (5 April 1991) UN Doc S/RES/688; UNSC, 'Resolution 841' (16 June 1993) UN Doc S/RES/841.

36 E.g. UNSC, 'Resolution (15 September 1999) UN Doc S/RES/1264.

37 Notably Resolution 940 (1994) – UNSC, 'Resolution 940' (31 July 1994) UN Doc S/RES/940 – in which it authorised the use of force against the military regime in Haiti. In this resolution the UN Security Council highlighted the "desperate plight of Haitian refugees". Already in previous resolutions the Security Council referred to refugee flows from Haiti as threat to international peace and security – e.g. UNSC, 'Resolution 841' (n 35).

the use of force,[38] and in resolutions that were not taken under chapter VII, which did not prevent states from intervening and relying on those resolutions, amongst others, in their legal justifications.[39]

In the unilateral NATO military intervention in Kosovo, refugees were part of the humanitarian intervention narrative. The UN Security Council noted in resolution 1199 (1998) its concern with "the flow of refugees into northern Albania, Bosnia and Herzegovina and other European countries as a result of the use of force in Kosovo", and acting under chapter VII of the UN-Charter, it called upon the Yugoslavian government to facilitate the safe return of refugees and displaced persons to their homes in Kosovo.[40] At the NATO Summit in April 1999 U.S. Deputy Secretary of State Strobe Talbott referred to refugee flows, both as a matter of political instability and humanitarian concern, in his description of the changing role of NATO's strategy.[41] (It is hard not to note the striking parallels to the NATO assistance operation in the Aegean Sea, in the wording of NATO, "providing support to assist with the consequences of this humanitarian crisis" to the Greek government and the European Border and Coast Guard Agency, Frontex.)[42] Although only Britain and Belgium explicitly

38 UNSC, 'Resolution 1970' (26 February 2011) UN Doc S/RES/1970.

39 Adelman, 'Humanitarian Intervention' (n 30).

40 UNSC, 'Resolution 1199' (23 September 1998) UN Doc S/RES/1199.

41 "With the end of the Cold War, new, less spectacular, but more diversified threats have arisen. Disputes over ethnicity, religion or territory, can, as we've already seen, trigger armed conflict, which in turn can generate cross-border political instability, refugee flows and humanitarian crises that endanger European security", US Deputy Secretary of State, Strobe Talbott, quoted in Bruno Simma, 'NATO, the UN and the USE of Force: Legal Aspects' (1999) 10 European Journal of International Law 1, 14. The return of refugees appeared as one point of the five objectives in the Statement on Kosovo issued by the NATO Summit in Washington DC, 23-24 April 1999.

42 Providing support in the context of a humanitarian crisis permits NATO to redesign its institutional role and function and thus reinvent its purpose of an otherwise odd organization – see NATO, 'Assistance for the Refugee and Migrant Crisis in the Aegean Sea' <http://www.nato.int/cps/en/natohq/topics_128746.htm>. Ruben Andersson observed a similar institutional project of redesigning at the Guardia Civil in the 2000s that reinvented its institutional purpose from an odd Franco paramilitary organization to humanitarian life saving. See Ruben Andersson, *Illegality, Inc.: Clandestine Migration and the Business of Bordering Europe* (University of California Press 2014).

relied on a *right* to humanitarian intervention,[43] the intense public debates in Germany on the country's engagement in the NATO intervention in Kosovo were largely driven by the plight of Kosovar refugees.[44]

Surely, references to refugees vary both in state practice and the practice of the Security Council. Nevertheless, refugees are integral part of the humanitarian reason narrative. In fact, one could argue that humanitarian intervention explicitly aims, at its basis, at the protection of refugees, either by ending persecution or ethnic cleansing thus avoiding that a person becomes a refugee, or that a person stops being a refugee (the right to return referred to by the Security Council). The wording "*towards* and across international frontiers" used by the Security Council is an expression of the underlying *telos* of protection, as the wording 'towards' would not include refugees, because under the Geneva Refugee Convention the refugee is a person that is outside the borders of her country.[45] Refugees in this sense are objects of intervention in the language of the humanitarian reason narrative, as it is their lives that need to be saved and their persecution that needs to be brought to an end.

The Kosovo intervention in this sense illustrates equally the limits and the vision of international law. Generally, it is considered that the broadly shared opinion is that intervention was generally deemed illegal yet morally justified, or in the famous words of Bruno Simma, "there do occur hard cases in which terrible dilemmas must be faced and imperative political and moral considerations may appear to leave no choice but to act outside the law".[46]

Yet, these imperative political and moral considerations presuppose two main issues. First, it presupposes that the measures that are being taken are in fact the appropriate measures and means to end persecution and save lives. Taking the appropriate measures includes, however, not merely that one knows what the appropriate means are, but also that the processes in which it is established that *these* are the most appropriate means – and not

---

43 See in particular Tony Blair's speech in Chicago on 22 April 1999 on the 'Doctrine of the International Community' <http://www.number-10.gov.uk/public/info/ index.html> accessed 29 July 2016.

44 Sebastian Sahla, 'Between Fear and Compassion: How Refugee Concerns Shape Responses to Humanitarian Emergencies – The Case of Germany and Kosovo' (LSE Working Paper Series, No 13-140, 2013).

45 UNSC, 'Resolution 688' (n 35).

46 Bruno Simma, 'NATO, the UN and Use of Force: Legal Aspects' (1999) 10 European Journal of International Law 1, 22.

others – are spoken in the language of humanitarian intervention (and not the language of refugee law), which channels the course of actions into a certain direction. It is the language of military experts (advising on precision strikes), legal experts (advising on the legality of humanitarian intervention), PR experts (advising on public opinion), and sometimes even moral philosophers.[47] This is the domain of expert language.[48]

Second, the necessity to save lives, in particular if spatially distanced, requires representation in a specific language that renders them cognizable as objects of compassion and as rallying cries of public moral outrage. They have to be represented both morally (the language of the philosopher's child in the pond) and legally (the international lawyer's victims of crimes against humanity). Didier Fassin directs our attention to the underlying "politics of suffering", a moral affect that is the secular remnant of the enlightenments dual legacy that all life is sacred and that suffering has to be reduced.[49]

2.3 *The Turn to Self-Defence*

2.3.1 Turning Points

It is against this background of the production of objects of humanitarian intervention that the interventions of Western states in the Syrian conflict have to be viewed. I only deal with interventions by EU Member States and the U.S.[50] Looking at these interventions reveals a shift in the narrative

---

47 If one wants to believe that the French philosopher Bernard-Henri Levy played a crucial role in convincing French President Nicolas Sarkozy to intervene in Libya – Angelique Chrisafis, 'French Intellectuals Feud over Libya Campaign' (*The Guardian,* 26 April 2011) <https://www.theguardian.com/world/2011/apr/26/french-intellectuals-feud-libya-campaign> accessed 29 July 2016.

48 On a critique on the role of expert knowledge, see: David Kennedy, *A World of Struggle: How Power, Law, and Expertise Shape Global Political Economy* (Princeton University Press 2016).

49 Didier Fassin, *Humanitarian Reason: A Moral History of the Present* (University of California Press 2012) 248.

50 Russia relies on intervention by invitation grounds, supporting the regime of President Bashar Al-Assad. There seems to be, at least, a correlation between the intervention by invitation narrative and Russia's practices to indefinitely detain and forcibly deport Syrian asylum seekers to Syria – see in particular the facts of the case *L.M. and others v Russia* App nos. 40081/14, 40088/14, 40127/14 (ECtHR 2015), 15 October 2015. In the period of 1 January 2011 to 1 November 2014 a total of 1.714 Syrians applied for refugee status in Russia: None had been granted refugee status – ibid., para. 66.

on the use of force, a shift from a humanitarian narrative that prevailed in the early days of the Syrian conflict, but failed to be transformed into a self-defence narrative. In August 2013 the Syrian government allegedly used chemical weapons against its civilian population in Ghouta, a rebel held suburb of Damascus. A few days after this attack, the U.S. Senate Foreign Relations Committee agreed on a draft resolution that would authorise the use of limited force against Syria in order to respond to and deter the use of weapons of mass destructions in order to protect the civilian population in Syria.[51] Although the draft resolution was endorsed by the majority leaders of the U.S. Senate and the House, achieving broader political support in Congress subsequently failed.[52] Similarly, the British government advanced using force against the Syrian regime based on humanitarian intervention grounds,[53] but the UK House of Commons ruled out a government motion narrowly, which, in turn, ultimately defeated political support in the U.S. Congress on the use of force against the Assad regime.[54] Harold Koh, the former legal advisor at the U.S. State Department, pointedly remarked that, while "American and British executive officials were thinking 'Kosovo, Halabja, and Rwanda,' their publics were thinking 'Iraq.'"[55]

---

51 Preamble, Section 2, Syria Joint Resolution For Markup, Senate Foreign Relations Committee; Harold Koh suggests that the U.S. justification on using force was based on the R2P doctrine – see Harold H Koh, 'Syria and the Law of Humanitarian Intervention: Part I: Political Miscues and U.S. Law' (*Just Security*, 26 September 2013) <https://www.justsecurity.org/1158/koh-syria/>; Harold H Koh, 'Syria and the Law of Humanitarian Intervention: Part II: International Law and the Way Forward' (*Just Security*, 4 October 2013) <http://www.ejiltalk.org/syria-and-the-law-of-humanitarian-intervention-part-ii-international-law-and-the-way-forward/> accessed 29 July 2016.

52 New York Times, 'Where Lawmakers Stand on Military Action in Syria' (5 September 2013) <http://www.nytimes.com/interactive/2013/09/05/us/politics/syria-vote-tracker.html> accessed 29 July 2016.

53 UK Parliament, 'Conditions for Using Force in Humanitarian Intervention: Standard Note 6761' (*House of Commons Library*, 29 August 2013) <http://researchbriefings.parliament.uk/ResearchBriefing/Summary/SN06716> accessed 29 July 2016.

54 The UK House of Commons ruled out a government motion on the possible use of force in Syria by 272 votes to 285, thus defeating the motion by mere 13 votes – Nicholas Watt and others, 'Blow to Cameron's Authority as MPs rule out British Assault on Syria' (*The Guardian*, 30 August 2013) <http://www.theguardian.com/politics/2013/aug/30/cameron-mps-syria> accessed 29 July 2016.

55 Koh, 'Syria and the Law of Humanitarian Intervention: Part I' (n 50).

While military intervention against Syria on humanitarian grounds did not receive sufficient political support, military intervention, however, became politically feasible and legally justifiable on self-defence grounds.[56] Politics and law in a symbiotic relation, each directing the subsequent paces of the other, enabled by the exposure of large parts of the population to the violence of gruesome beheadings.[57]

2.3.2 The Self-Defence Narrative

On September 23, 2014, U.S. Representative to the UN Samantha Powers informed UN Secretary General Ban Ki-moon that the U.S. would exercise the right to self-defence against ISIS. Although the collective self-defence argument relies on the request of the Iraqi government and the threat ISIS posed to the Iraqi territory and its population, the U.S., and subsequently other governments, additionally rely on an individual self-defence argument based on the threats ISIS poses to their national security and territorial integrity. The U.S. letter to Ban Ki-moon specified that,

> ISIL and other terrorist groups in Syria are a threat not only to Iraq, but also to many other countries, including the United States and our partners in the region and beyond. States must be able to defend themselves, in accordance with the inherent right of individual and collective self-defense [...][58]

Indeed, other countries duly followed. In November 2014, the UK government informed the Security Council that it would exercise its right to self-defence against ISIS. Although the British government relied in this

---

56 Peter Moore, 'One Year Later, Americans Back Military Action in Syria' (*YouGov*, 29 August 2014) <https://yougov.co.uk/news/2014/08/29/one-year-later-americans-back-military-action-syri/>; Toby Helm, 'Cameron Edges Closer to Airstrikes as Support Grows on Both Sides of Commons' (*The Guardian*, 22 November 2015) <https://www.theguardian.com/world/2015/nov/22/david-cameron-closer-vote-syria-airstrikes-commons-support>; Will Dahlgreen, 'Support Grows for RAF Airstrikes, even into Syria' (*YouGov*, 17 September 2014) <https://yougov.co.uk/news/2014/09/17/now-majority-also-support-raf-air-strikes-syria/> all accessed 29 July 2016.

57 Will Self, 'We are Passive Consumers of the Pornography of Violence' (*The Guardian*, 23 December 2014) <http://www.theguardian.com/news/2014/dec/23/-sp-passive-consumers-pornography-violence> accessed 29 July 2016.

58 UNSC, 'Letter Dated 23 September 2014 from the Permanent Representative of the United States of America to the United Nations addressed to the Secretary-General' (23 September 2014) UN Doc S/2014/695.

letter that it is "taking measures in support of the collective self-defence of Iraq",[59] the British government specified ten months later that the UK "has undertaken military action in Syria against the so-called Islamic State in Iraq and the Levant (ISIL) in exercise of the inherent right to individual and collective self-defence… This [action] was a necessary and proportionate exercise of the *individual right to self-defence of the United Kingdom.*"[60] In September 2015, the French foreign minister declared that France would join the U.S. government in carrying out airstrikes on ISIS targets in Syria "under Article 51 of the United Nations Charter, in other words, in self-defence",[61] which was soon followed by a letter to the UN Security Council stating that "France has taken actions involving the participation of military aircraft in response to the attacks carried out by ISIL from the territory of the Syrian Arab Republic."[62]

Most of the governments that invoked self-defence were cautious to highlight that self-defence is used against ISIS and not the Syrian government or territory.[63] The political mood that enabled and channelled

---

59 UNSC, 'Identical Letters Dated 25 November 2014 from the Permanent Representative of the United Kingdom of Great Britain and Northern Ireland to the United Nations addressed to the Secretary-General and the President of the Security Council' (26 November 2014) UN Doc S/2014/851.

60 UNSC, 'Letter Dated 7 September 2015 from the Permanent Representative of the United Kingdom of Great Britain and Northern Ireland to the United Nations addressed to the President of the Security Council' (8 September 2015) UN Doc S/2015/688 (*emphasis added*).

61 Radio France International, 'France May Launch Strikes in Syria "in Self Defence"' (11 September 2015) <http://en.rfi.fr/americas/20150911-france-may-launch-strikes-syria-self-defence-fabius> accessed 29 July 2016.

62 UNSC, 'Identical Letters Dated 8 September 2015 from the Permanent Representative of France to the United Nations addressed to the Secretary-General and the President of the Security Council' (9 September 2015) UN Doc S/2015/745. Already on July 24, 2015, the Turkish government informed the Security that it will use force against ISIS on Syrian territory, exercising the individual right to self-defence, referring to recent attacks from ISIS against its citizens and territory and the imminence of further attacks – UNSC, 'Letter Dated 24 July 2015 from the Chargé d'Affaires a.i. of the Permanent Mission of Turkey to the United Nations addressed to the President of the Security Council' (24 July 2015) UN Doc S/2015/563.

63 E.g. UNSC, 'Letter Dated 9 September 2015 from the Permanent Representative of Australia to the United Nations addressed to the President of the Security Council' (9 September 2015) UN Doc S/2015/693, "These operations are not directed against Syria or the Syrian people […]"; UNSC, 'Letter Dated 7 June 2016 from the Permanent Representative of Belgium to the United Nations addressed to the President

the use of force within the expressed self-defence justification, as it seems, reflects this understanding that force is being used not against the Syrian government but against ISIS.[64] Yet, as the world's geographical surface is covered by territorial states, violence used against any non-states actor necessarily is always directed against the territory of a state (unless it is used on the high sea). The Syrian government indeed denounced at the Security Council the air strikes as "flagrant violation" of its sovereignty.[65] Hence, a legal argument on imputability and space has to be brought forward (see below).

Virtually none of the letters by which states informed the Security Council that they would exercise the right to self-defence referred to refugees in the reasons provided. Also the resolutions of the Security Council that were referred to as legal basis for exercising the right to self-defence, notably resolution 2249 (2015), merely include the standard phrase that "Member States must ensure that any measures taken to combat terrorism comply with all their obligations under international law, in particular international human rights, refugee and humanitarian law".[66] Note that this wording refers to a set of already existing legal obligations (international refugee law), whereas the humanitarian narrative includes the refugee as social appearance, as object of protection. The refugee disappears as object of concern in the self-defence narrative.

2.3.3 Self-Defence and Space

Leaving questions on whether self-defence can be, as a matter of law, exercised against non-state actors or on the materialization of the immediacy requirement of self-defence aside (as I am not concerned with the actual legality) – all questions that blossomed as a field of academic enquiry after 9/11 – I enquire into the spatial elements on which the self-defence arguments are based and their effects.

---

of the Security Council' (9 June 2016) UN Doc S/2016/523, "Those measures are directed against [ISIS] and not against the Syrian Arab Republic."; UNSC, 'Letter Dated 3 June 2016 from the Permanent Representative of Norway to the United Nations addressed to the President of the Security Council' (3 June 2016) UN Doc S/2016/513, "The measures are directed against ISIL, not against the Arab Republic of Syria."

64 Moore, 'One Year Later' (n 56).

65 Sputnik International, 'Damascus Accuses US-Led Coalition of Breaking Int'l Law, State Sovereignty' (1 October 2015) <http://sputniknews.com/middleeast/20151001/1027841733/syria-coalition-airstrikes-violation.html>.

66 UNSC, 'Resolution 2249' (20 November 2015) UN Doc S/RES/2249.

Using force against ISIS on the territory of Syria is based on the argument that the Syrian government is unwilling or unable to stop the acts committed by ISIS. Self-defence against ISIS on the territory of Syria is thus based on the fact that Syria does not "exercise effective control" over the territories occupied by ISIS, a formula that, in the Syrian context, was first employed by the UN Secretary-General as a reaction to the U.S. invocation of self-defence, long before governments employed that same reasoning.[67] The German government, for instance, stated that:

> ISIL has occupied a certain part of Syrian territory over which the Government of the Syrian Arab Republic does not at this time exercise effective control. States that have been subjected to armed attack by ISIL originating in this part of Syrian territory, are therefore justified under Article 51 of the Charter of the United Nations to take necessary measures of self-defence, even without the consent of the Government of the Syrian Arab Republic.[68]

The argument that a state lost effective control over part of its territory and is thus unable to stop the acts that originate from that territory is very close to the 'unwilling or unable' test.[69] The 'unwilling or unable' test is part of the necessity requirement. Assuming *arguendo* the acceptance of the 'unwilling or unable' test,[70] the reasoning goes as follows: it may be necessary for a state to use force against a non-state actor located on the territory of another state if the latter is unable or unwilling to take action against the non-state actor. Thus, the necessity to exercise force against

---

67 Ryan Goodman and Sarah Knuckey, 'Remarkable Statement by UN Secretary General on US Airstrikes in Syria' (*Just Security*, 23 September 2014) <https://www.justsecurity.org/15456/remarkable-statement-secretary-general-airstrikes-syria/> accessed 29 July 2016.

68 UNSC, 'Letter Dated 10 December 2015 from the Chargé d'Affaires a.i. of the Permanent Mission of Germany to the United Nations addressed to the President of the Security Council' (10 December 2015) UN Doc S/2015/946.

69 Marko Milanovic points out that the 'unwilling or unable' test and the loss of effective control are very close, but not necessarily the same – Marko Milanovic, 'Belgium's Article 51 Letter to the Security Council' (*EJIL: Talk!*, 17 June 2016) <http://www.ejiltalk.org/belgiums-article-51-letter-to-the-security-council/>.

70 Which is an issue of itself: Ashley Deeks argues that states have not followed the 'unwilling or unable' doctrine as a matter of legal obligation – Ashley Deeks, '"Unwilling or Unable": Toward a Normative Framework for Extraterritorial Self-Defense' (2012) 52 Virginia Journal of International Law 483.

ISIS (and on the territory of the state where it acts) rests on the inability of that state to exercise effective control over parts of its territory.

Weaving together the two arguments that (i) violence is not directed against the Syrian government and the Syrian people and (ii) the loss of effective control produces spaces that appear, because of having lost control, as spaces of inhumanity and violent recess on which one's weaponry is to be discharged. This belies the very materiality of the intervention and of violence. It belies the fact that it is the buildings of the Syrian government and Syrian citizens that are bombed, its infrastructure crippled, its property destroyed and its citizens killed.[71]

Moreover, the coordinates of these spaces of extreme violence disappear: violence is enacted extraterritorially in spaces that are circumscribed functionally, either by gross human rights violations (in the case of humanitarian intervention) or the absence of effective control (in the case of self-defence). When the Security Council adopted on 20 November Resolution 2249 (2015), upon the initiative of the French government, that "calls upon Member States to take all necessary measures…on the territory under the control of ISIL",[72] it is not merely the resolution itself that is a masterpiece of "constructive ambiguity",[73] permitting UN Member States equally to denounce the use of force

71 Emma Graham-Harrison and Spencer Ackerman, 'US Airstrikes Allegedly Kill at Least 73 Civilians in Northern Syria' (*The Guardian*, 20 July 2016) <https://www.theguardian.com/world/2016/jul/20/us-airstrike-allegedly-kills-56-civilians-in-northern-syria> accessed 8 August 2016.

72 Operative paragraph 5 of the resolution is as follows: "Calls upon Member States that have the capacity to do so to take all necessary measures, in compliance with international law, in particular with the United Nations Charter, as well as international human rights, refugee and humanitarian law, on the territory under the control of ISIL also known as Da'esh, in Syria and Iraq, to redouble and coordinate their efforts to prevent and suppress terrorist acts committed specifically by ISIL also known as Da'esh as well as ANF, and all other individuals, groups, undertakings, and entities associated with Al-Qaida, and other terrorist groups, as designated by the United Nations Security Council, and as may further be agreed by the International Syria Support Group (ISSG) and endorsed by the UN Security Council, pursuant to the statement of the International Syria Support Group (ISSG) of 14 November, and to eradicate the safe haven they have established over significant parts of Iraq and Syria".

73 Dapo Akande and Marko Milanovic, 'The Constructive Ambiguity of the Security Council's ISIS Resolution' (EJIL: Talk!, 21 November 2015) <http://www.ejiltalk.org/the-constructive-ambiguity-of-the-security-councils-isis-resolution/> accessed 29 July 2016.

against on Syrian territory as well as to justify it.[74] The ambiguity of the spatial coordinates thus constructed renders the ambiguity of these spaces of intervention ubiquitous. Ubiquity then becomes an essential quality of these spaces and violence enacted wherever these spaces appear.[75]

3 On Refugee Law

3.1 *Proximity and Distance*

I have pointed out above that refugees as objects of humanitarian intervention do not merely appear, rather they are produced and acquire meaning in the specific context of the language on humanitarian intervention as part of the force of law sphere. Protection acquires meaning in the sphere of the law of force. Law in this sense functions by channelling action into

74 The wording of "all necessary means" generally is the code for using force, particularly in the context where UN Member States already notified the UN Security Council of exercising their right to self-defence against ISIS on the territory of Syria. Yet, at the same time, the Security Council does not refer to chapter VII UN-Charter and highlights in the operative paragraph that the actions have to be taken "in compliance with international law", including the prohibition of the use of force. In the statements before the UNSC French representative pointed out "that collective action could now be based on Article 51 of the United Nations Charter" – UNSC, '7565th Meeting: Threats to International Peace and Security Caused by Terrorist Acts' (20 November 2015) UN Doc SC/12132 – rubberstamping, in effect already existing actions of states, while still permitting the Russian government to denounce future actions as violating article 2(4) UN-Charter.

75 A note of concern here: Self-defence requires in addition to necessity (no other means) immediacy (before or after armed attack), a criteria that also distinguishes it from reprisals that are prohibited under international law. Extending self-defence infinitely renders it thus indistinguishable from reprisals. US President Barack Obama, in his letter to the US Congress invoking self-defence against ISIS, referred to self-defence as a temporally indefinite response to constant threats: "It is not possible to know the duration of these deployments and operations. I will continue to direct such additional measures as necessary to protect and secure U.S. citizens and our interests against the threat posed by ISIL." – The White House, 'Letter from the President – War Powers Resolution Regarding Iraq: Text of a Letter from the President to the Speaker of the House of Representatives and the President pro tempore of the Senate (*Office of the Press Secretary*, 23 September 2014) <https://www.whitehouse.gov/the-press-office/2014/09/23/letter-president-war-powers-resolution-regarding-iraq>. This is, of course, something that has been pointed out before – Frederic Megret, 'War'? Legal Semantics and the Move to Violence' (2002) 13 European Journal of International Law 361.

one direction and not another, and, probably more importantly, provides legitimacy to one action while rendering alternative ways of defining the problem inconceivable.[76] Proximity and distance represents a key feature in channelling action into one direction while excluding available alternatives. Proximity and distance, as I understand it, contains two dimensions: a spatial dimension and a (de-)politicising dimension that relates to the 'politics of suffering' mentioned above.

First, humanitarian interventions are carried out beyond the territory of a state. Whether it is bombing from 10.000 feet in Kosovo or intervening in Libya or Iraq, interventions are extraterritorial projects, spatially distanced from the territory of the intervening state and the constituencies and parliaments that demand for them.[77] Redeeming protection, to the contrary, requires spatial proximity. One has to be at the border or in the territory of a state to lodge an asylum application.[78] Jurisdiction, and thus the application of human rights norms such as the principle of non-refoulement, is only exceptionally exercised beyond the territory of a state.[79] One has to be at the territory of a state or under the control of its organs to vindicate protection from that state.

The actions taken by the EU and its Member States in the context of the Syrian conflict illustrate that. Since the adoption of the European Agenda on Migration in May 2015, more than 65 legislative instruments were adopted on the EU level.[80] Yet, these amendments and actions that have been taken are probably most telling not in what they do but in what they abstain from doing. While the proposed amendments on le-

---

76 E.g. Kritsiotis, 'Theorizing International Law' (n 13).

77 Probably nowhere has this proximity distance pattern been more tragically obvious than in the left-to-die boat case where the dinghy with 63 migrants on board was left floating off the coast of Libya, despite the presence of numerous war ships and surveillance aircraft that engaged in the military operation Unified Protector in Libya. The facts and failures are meticulously detailed in Forensic Architecture, 'The Left-To-Die Boat: The Deadly Drift of a Migrants' Boat in the Central Mediterranean' <http://www.forensic-architecture.org/case/left-die-boat/#toggle-id-2> accessed 8 August 2016.

78 Directive 2013/32/EU of 26 June 2013 on Common Procedures for Granting and Withdrawing International Protection (Recast) OJ L 180/60, Art 3(1).

79 E.g. *Ilascu and others v Moldova and Russia* App no 487877/99 (ECtHR, 08 July 2004) para. 312.

80 For an overview see European Commission, 'European Agenda on Migration – Legislative Documents' <http://ec.europa.eu/dgs/home-affairs/what-we-do/policies/european-agenda-migration/proposal-implementation-package/index_en.htm>.

gal instruments that apply for asylum seekers largely aim at laying down clearer rules and partly enhancing the protection, the legislative documents abstain from creating an "asylum space", to borrow a term from Alexander Aleinikoff, i.e. possibilities for refugees to get to the place where asylum can be claimed.[81]

Refugee law does not provide for mobility rights of refugees. The lack of mobility rights increases existing inequalities between countries and results in dire consequences for those who attempt to seek protection. I will briefly illustrate that by discussing the two main avenues for mobility: resettlement and visa. On the global level no obligation exists to cooperate with other states by providing resettlement, nor to provide 'humanitarian visa' for those seeking protection. The European Commission stresses in its strategic documents that "more legal channels are needed to enable people in need of international protection to arrive in the EU in an orderly, managed, safe and dignified manner".[82]

The EU Commission has foreseen a total of 22.504 resettlement places over a period of two years (2015-2016); as of June 2016, only 7.272 persons have been resettled from third countries.[83] UNHCR estimates that in 2017 more than 1,19 Million resettlement places are urgently needed, while it

81 Alexander Aleinikoff, 'ICON*S Conference, Session 2: "Migration and Movement"' (*Verfassungsblog*, 17 June 2016) <http://verfassungsblog.de/icons-conference-session-2-migration-and-movement-with-philippe-sands-alexander-aleinikoff-and-ayelet-shachar/>.

82 European Commission, 'Towards a Reform of the Common European Asylum System and Enhancing Legal Avenues to Europe (COM/2016 197 final, 6 April 2016) 14. Enhancing legal avenues for persons seeking international protection is also a policy goal in the European Agenda on Migration, see European Commission, 'A European Agenda on Migration' (COM/2015 240 final, 13 May 2015).

83 European Commission, 'Recommendation on a European Resettlement Scheme' (C/2015 3560 final, 8 June 2015) para. 7; European Commission, 'Fourth Report on Relocation and Resettlement' (COM/2016 410 final, 15 June 2016) Annex 3; Under the relocation mechanism that aims at distributing refugees within the EU only 2.826 of a total of 98.256 persons, as of July 2016, were relocated from Greece and Italy to other EU member states. This non-functioning relocation from southern EU member states (Italy and Greece) illustrates to some degree the broader global situation, where still 85% of the refugees remain in the global south, see European Commission, 'Member States Support to Emergency Relocation Mechanisms' (12 August 2016) <http://ec.europa.eu/dgs/home-affairs/what-we-do/policies/european-agenda-migration/press-material/docs/state_of_play_-_relocation_en.pdf> all accessed 29 July 2016.

expects to submit 170.000 refugees for resettlement.[84] As currently less than 1% of refugees are resettled globally and more than 85% of refugees remain in countries of the Global South, the EU resettlement scheme will hardly contributes to alleviate this imbalance.

As there is no right to access protection, states are under no legal obligation to issue entry permits or visa for persons seeking international protection. Whereas up to 1990 each EU Member State had its own visa policy towards third countries, the 1990 Convention Implementing the Schengen Agreement required harmonisation of visa policies of EU Member States.[85] The visa policies adopted since then require nationals from virtually all major refugee-producing countries to obtain short-term visa in order to travel legally to EU Member States. While visa mobility over the past 40 years increased in general, it is primarily the mobility rights of nationals from wealthy OECD countries that increased. The mobility rights of nationals of African countries, in particular, decreased which results in a global "mobility divide".[86] In the context of the gruesome conflict in Syria, the number of visa issued for Syrian nationals by EU Member States embassies since the outbreak of the conflict almost dropped to zero.[87] Moreover, visa requirements for Syrians were introduced by Algeria, Egypt, Morocco, Libya and Tunisia, "most likely under pressure from the EU" in order to avoid that Syrians used the well-functioning 'route' from northern African countries to Italy.[88] These policies impacted the decisions of Syria's neighbouring countries: Lebanon, Jordan, and Turkey introduced visa requirements for Syrian nationals and partly closed their border to Syrian refugees.

As proposed amendments of visa legislation on the EU plane envisage the suspension of visa exemptions for third country nationals in situations of emergency, the absence of asylum space is likely to exacerbate the

---

84 UNHCR, 'Global Resettlement Needs 2017' (22nd Annual Tripartite Consultations on Resettlement, June 2016).

85 For an overview of the institutional developments see Steve Peers, *EU Justice and Home Affairs Law* (Oxford University Press 2011) 226-271.

86 Stefan Mau and others, 'The Global Mobility Divide: How Visa Policies Developed Over Time' (2015) 41(8) Journal of Ethnic and Migration Studies 1192, 1194.

87 European Commission, 'Complete Statistics on Short-Stay Visa Issued by the Schengen States' <http://ec.europa.eu/dgs/home-affairs/what-we-do/policies/borders-and-visas/visa-policy/index_en.htm#stats>.

88 Marten Den Heijer and others, 'Coercion, Prohibition, and Great Expectations: The Continuing Failure of the Common European Asylum System' (2016) 53 Common Market Law Review 607, 620-621.

systemic pattern of proximity and distance.[89] The fact that until 2002 six European countries accepted asylum applications in their embassies and another six permitted access to their territory for international protection in exceptional circumstances seems like a far cry from distant past in the current context.[90]

Second, spatial distance, as pointed out above, requires representation of the objects of humanitarian intervention as victims that are to be saved. The figures quoted above however indicate not merely an imbalance in the distribution of refugees between countries of the Global North and Global South, but also a stark inequality in mobility rights between these countries. If one looks through the lens of inequality at the humanitarian intervention narrative, the refugee as object of humanitarian intervention reflects these structures. The refugee is reduced to the passive recipient of benevolence, who has to wait to be saved by those who are called into action. The reduction of the refugee as passive object of suffering that merits intervention and rescuing (in the case of maritime operations) tends to mask the underlying political dimension: inequality is replaced by suffering and injustice is articulated as misfortune.[91]

The masking of humanitarian reason in this sense is twofold: it replaces political inequalities by humanitarian exigency while hiding its own political agenda. The track record of humanitarian interventions reveals that the politics of intervention included also a politics of restriction. In the Kosovo intervention, for instance, the intervening states were not only highly reluctant to accommodate Kosovar refugees in their territories;[92] rather, intervention policies also aimed at preventing people

89 European Commission, 'Proposal for a Regulation of the European Parliament and of the Council Amending Regulation (EC) No 539/2001 Listing the Third Countries whose Nationals Must be in Possession of Visas when Crossing the External Borders and those whose Nationals are Exempt from that Requirement' (COM/2016 290 final, 4 May 2016) 2.

90 Gregor Noll, 'Seeking Asylum at Embassies: A Right to Entry Under International Law?' (2005) 17(3) International Journal of Refugee Law 542.

91 Fassin, *Humanitarian Reason* (n 49) 6.

92 The U.S. government first proposed to resettle 20.000 Kosovar refugees to Guantanamo and subsequently, after protests from UNHCR, tracked back and proposed to issue temporary residence permits to the same number of Kosovar refugees – Philip Shenon, 'U.S. Chooses Guantanamo Bay Bases in Cuba for Refugee Site' (*New York Times*, 7 April 1999) <https://partners.nytimes.com/library/world/europe/040799kosovo-bases.html> accessed 29 July 2016.

from leaving and facilitating forced returns.[93] Iraq, a place where the U.S. and UK led intervention in 2003 produced a theatre of violence whose brutal consequences provide the justification of today's interventions,[94] provides an ample illustration. With the battle of Fallujah still raging, UK Home Secretary David Blunkett wrote to Prime Minister Tony Blair:

> As the conflict in Iraq moves to a successful conclusion, we need to look at the consequences for the tens of thousands of Iraqi asylum seekers currently in the United Kingdom. Once peace and stability have returned to Iraq I think it is right to press ahead with a substantial returns programme [...][95]

3.2 *Concreteness and Abstraction*

The absence of creating "asylum spaces" in the major overhaul of the European asylum system is supplemented by abstracting from 'war'. The terms 'war' or 'armed conflicts' are largely absent in the more than 65 EU legislative documents and instruments; where these terms appear, they appear as a 'root cause' of forced migration, as another issue to be addressed in migration management. Increase of the contribution and political engagement to stabilise the political situation in refugee send-

93 The employment of German armed forces in the Kosovo intervention was deliberately linked to facilitate the return of Kosovar refugees in Germany by effectively fulfilling civilian tasks of reconstruction – see Sahla, 'Between Fear and Compassion' (n 44). In the Iraq intervention in 1991, the British, U.S. and French armed forces induced Kurds to return. Turkey closed its borders to Kurdish refugees – Diana Jean Schemo: "Turkey closed its southern border yesterday to an estimated 200,000 Kurds fleeing an onslaught by Iraqi forces" quoted in Adelman, 'Humanitarian Intervention' (n 30) 9. Temporary protection was granted only under the condition of resettlement commitments, something other countries, including Canada and the U.S. were adamantly opposed to – see ibid. Also the US led and Security Council mandated intervention in Haiti in 1993 has to be viewed against the U.S. government's Migrant Interdiction Policy Haitian refugees. For a detailed analysis see Azadeh Dastyari, *United States Migrant Interdiction and the Detention of Refugees in Guantanamo Bay* (Cambridge University Press 2015).

94 Martin Chulov, 'Tony Blair is Right: Without the Iraq War there would be No Islamic State' (*The Guardian*, 25 October 2015) <https://www.theguardian.com/world/2015/oct/25/tony-blair-is-right-without-the-iraq-war-there-would-be-no-isis>. See also the voluminous Report of the Iraq Inquiry ("Chilcot Report") – The Iraq Inquiry, 'The Report of the Iraq Inquiry: The Executive Summary (6 July 2016) 109-110 <http://www.iraqinquiry.org.uk/the-report/> all accessed 29 July 2016.

95 Ibid., 503.

ing countries might acquire different meanings in specific contexts with each project inhibiting different chances of success, limitations, and effects. Promoting political stability in order to end conflicts in Niger, Libya, or, for that matter, Syria and its neighbouring countries might at the end of the day prove ineffective, might result in ending a conflict temporarily while increasing social and political discrepancies, or it might not be about ending a conflict at all in the first place, but might simply mean to enhance a country's capability (or rather of certain agencies and institutions of that country) to control its borders or strengthen the resilience of refugees.[96] Or it might mean bombing ISIS positions in Syria and Iraq.[97] Similarly, measures to combat the 'business model' of human smuggling is likely to increase its net worth, instead of curbing it.[98]

Considering abstraction and concreteness in a temporal frame, 'war' as a root cause is represented as long-term engagement, while immediate measures, e.g. to step up operations against human smuggling, increase return operations or enhance cooperation with third countries – largely measures that aim at containing or distributing refugees within the EU[99] – are given precedence as the European Commission points out:

> In the face of the current crisis, precedence is being given to actions that have greater immediate impact on migration flows. At the same time, long-term engagement on these matters is necessary to address root causes.[100]

---

96 For the various actions envisaged to prevent and tackle conflicts in Sub-Sahara Africa an EU Emergency Trust Fund for Africa was set up. Its operational framework lays out actions that are to be undertaken, with a stark focus on improving border management of African governments – see European Commission, 'Emergency Trust Fund for Stability' (2015) – and addressing root causes of irregular migration and displaced persons in Africa – European Commission, 'Operational Framework for the Sahel & Lake Chad Window' (13 June 2016) 7.

97 As the Communication on external actions in addressing the refugee crisis suggests: "In this context [of finding solutions to the Syrian conflict], the Commission and the High Representative have set out the policy framework for a regional strategy, including the fight against Da'esh […]"; European Commission, 'Addressing the Refugee Crisis in Europe: The Role of EU External Action' (JOIN/2015 40 final, 9 September 2015) 4.

98 Den Heijer and others, 'Coercion, Prohibition, and Great Expectations' (n 87).

99 European Commission, COM/2015 240 final (n 81) 3-6.

100 European Commission, JOIN/2015 40 final (n 96) 3; on the containment dimension of the immediate measures see European Commission, COM/2015 240 final (n 81) 4-6.

Thus, framing 'war' as a root cause represents not merely the aspirational *avénir* of the biblical gardens of peace, but also an abstraction that renders it an equal part in the duality of long-term and short-term measures, thereby abstracting from the context of migration management; from a context where combating human smuggling, enhancing return operations or financial assistance to enhance Turkey's border management capabilities feature not merely in semantic concreteness, but actually *are* realised. Abstracting from 'war' as a root cause of forced migration suggests that the 'refugee problem' would be solved at some point by addressing its root causes. This reflects in a way the image of the refugee as social and legal anomaly, pointed out at the outset of this chapter.

4 Concluding Remarks

The separation of the law of force from refugee law facilitates the continuing reduction of refugees to mere objects of intervention, be it benevolent (saving lives at sea) or securitarian (enhancing return operations). If under humanitarian intervention protection acquires a limited meaning and the current approaches of the EU and its Member States further curb the mobility of refugees, then, why does the changing narrative in the contemporary context of the Syrian conflict matter?

It matters for two reasons.

First, the way we define intervention matters for the way we see those fleeing the conflict. In humanitarian intervention, the refugee appears as passive victim whose life has to be saved, although the scope of protection remains limited. If we turn to the narrative of self-defence, the refugee disappears as an object of humanitarian concern and appears instead as the object of threat to national security, to the imagined body of the nation. Various EU Member States amended their domestic laws over the course of the year 2015 that severely curtailed rights of refuges in order to deter refugees from applying for protection on their territory.[101] And U.S. President Donald Trump signed an executive order that stops the admission of Syrian refugees to the U.S. indefinitely.[102] If the spatial coordinates of the spaces of intervention are ubiquitous, as I have

101 For an overview of various laws: Integrated Regional Information Network, EU laws designed to deter refugees (16 January 2016) <http://www.refworld.org/docid/56b1b6c54.html> accessed 29 July 2016.

102 *New York Times*, 'trump Targets Muslim Areas In Refugee Ban' (28 January 2017).

argued, then it might result in societies mimicking the characteristics of the violence they purport to combat. That might result in a radical, and surreal, logic of violence where self-proclaimed migrant hunters in military uniforms, official emblems and endorsed by state authorities 'arrest' refugees that irregularly cross the border,[103] and ISIS, in turn, offers USD 50.000 reward for the 'head' of these self-proclaimed migrant hunters.[104]

The second point is the extension of the first. Using law strategically does not merely change the law, but eventually results in shifting meanings of our ethical responsibilities towards others, facilitated by the shifting meanings of violence and conflict (self-defence narrative). As the confines of the 'other' are fluid, the other might always appear in different robes. It indeed came as no surprise that the UK referendum on leaving the EU was largely fuelled by anti-immigration angst. It is telling that the refugee as the disquieting figure that appears and claims her rights without belonging to the nation provokes such a crisis for a European project that is built upon that very same idea of including non-citizens and extending mobility. Focusing on the individual human beings might thus help in taking seriously the political claims and the global nature of mobility rights and thus overcome transcendental nonsense of *a priori* existing bounded communities.

103 Maria Cheresheva, 'Bulgaria Awards Vigilante Migrant-Hunters' (*Balkan Insight*, 08 April 2016) <http://www.balkaninsight.com/en/article/bulgaria-awards-vigilante-migrant-hunters-04-08-2016>; all accessed 29 July 2016.

104 On the mimesis of violence which is the logic that seems to be enacted here, see still: Rene Girard, *Violence and the Sacred* (John Hopkins University Press 1972) 79-80.

PART III

Forced Migration and the Sea

Human Security and Shared Responsibility to Fight Transnational Crimes: Resolution 2240 (2015) of the UN Security Council on Smuggling of Migrants and Human Trafficking off the Coast of Libya

*Vassilis P. Tzevelekos**

1 Introduction

On 9 October 2015, the United Nations Security Council (UNSC), acting under Chapter VII of the Charter, passed quasi-unanimously[1] Resolution 2240 (2015).[2] With it, it authorises for a certain period of time United Nations (UN) member states to inspect and seize vessels on the high seas off the coast of Libya when they reasonably suspect that these are being used for migrant smuggling or human trafficking.[3] As paragraph 12 of the resolution explains, its aim is to "disrupt the organised criminal enterprises engaged in migrant smuggling and human trafficking and prevent loss of life".[4] What is not intended with the resolution is to "undermine the human rights of individuals or prevent them from seeking protection under international human rights law and international refugee law."[5] Obviously, among other aspects of human rights protection,[6] this last quote

* The author is thankful to the editors of the book for their comments.

1 UN Security Council, 'Adopting Resolution 2240 (2015), Security Council Authorizes Member States to Intercept Vessels off Libyan Coast Suspected of Migrant Smuggling' (*UN, Meetings Coverage and Press Releases*, 9 October 2015) <http://www.un.org/press/en/2015/sc12072.doc.htm> accessed 20 April 2016.

2 UNSC, 'Resolution 2240' (9 October 2015) UN Doc S/RES/2240.

3 Ibid. [7] and [8]. But states must make "good faith efforts to obtain the consent of the vessel's flag prior to using the authority" given to them under [7] of the resolution. See also [5] regarding unflagged vessels. States are invited in [5] to inspect these vessels as is permitted under international law of the sea.

4 Ibid. [12].

5 Ibid.

6 For instance, the UNSC notes the vulnerability of migrants and expects states to treat them with humanity and dignity, but also protect their human rights "regardless of their migration status, including when implementing their specific migra-

Salomon, Heschl, *et al.* (eds.), *Blurring Boundaries: Human Security and Forced Migration*
 ISBN 978-90-04-32686-6. pp. 101-121.

implies non-refoulement,[7] the duty of states to duly consider individual applications for asylum and, in particular, the personal circumstances of each concerned person separately.[8] This guarantees that state authorities will avoid exposing migrants to risks of violation of their fundamental rights at the country to which they will be transferred/returned.

The resolution raises a considerable number of thought-provoking questions from various perspectives, including law of the sea, the limits of the powers of the UNSC, the implementation of UNSC resolutions by member states acting through regional organisations, such as the EU, transnational crimes and, of course, human rights. But what is of particular importance for the present study is the idea that transpires from this resolution that transnational phenomena, such as smuggling of migrants and human trafficking,[9] require (co-ordinated, as this study argues) action by *all* involved states and, more generally, international actors (although the focus here is on states). Because of their transnational nature, such situations involve a plurality of duty bearers, each one of which is partially connected to the situation and has an obligation to be pro-actively engaged – to the extent, of course, that its individual connection with the situation at issue justifies and requires it.[10] As the analysis that follows suggests, this leads to a situation of multiple duty bearers[11] who

---

tion and border security policies." ibid. [preamble]. See also para. 13 of the Resolution.

7 Non-refoulement is employed here in the widest possible way going beyond refugee protection law and, in particular, Article 33 of the 1951 Convention Relating to the Status of Refugees. It includes the case law of human rights institutions on the duty of states not to transfer (i.e. extradite, deport, expulse etc.) a person to a third state, where that person risks experiencing violations of her fundamental human rights. In that respect, see the concurring opinion of Judge Pinto de Albuquerque in *Hirsi Jamaa and others v Italy* App no 27765/09 (ECtHR, 23 February 2012).

8 Hence, the prohibition of collective expulsion of aliens. See, for instance, Article 4 of Protocol 4 to the European Convention on Human Rights.

9 Referring to the United Nations Convention against Transnational Organized Crime, the UNSC explains that, "although the crime of smuggling of migrants may share, in some cases, some common features with the crime of trafficking in persons, Member States need to recognise that they are distinct crimes". UNSC, 'Resolution 2240' (n 2) [preamble].

10 Ibid. The UNSC notes that different crimes require different "legal, operational, and policy responses".

11 On multiple duty bearers, see the collection of studies edited by Wouter Vandenhole, *Challenging Territoriality in Human Rights Law. Building Blocks for a Plural and Diverse Duty-Bearer Regime* (Routledge 2015).

exercise parallel and, possibly, also overlapping jurisdiction as a means to fulfil their duties under international law – especially regarding the so-called positive dimension of human rights, i.e. the duty to protect.[12] This implies that concurrent state responsibility (in the sense of liability) may arise, if more than one of these duty bearers break their duties.[13]

Furthermore, because human trafficking and smuggling raise issues of human security, the idea of multiple duty bearers and concurrent state responsibility advanced in this study can be associated with the UN human security policy framework.[14] The picture built in the analysis that follows sits comfortably within human security, but also indicates that this concept ought to be attuned to fully meet the particular needs, nature and features (which are discussed below) of transnational phenomena, such as trafficking and smuggling, that threaten the security and well-being of people.

Seen from the perspective of human security – which, as it will be explained in further detail below, places the accent on the protection of human beings and, primarily, of their lives – human smuggling and trafficking correspond to two separate sociolegal phenomena. These necessitate distinctive answers, policies and strategies by states – which, as will be argued below, have a duty to protect people found under their jurisdiction when their rights are threatened by other individuals, who are involved in smuggling and trafficking. Human security offers a unique lens enabling us to distinguish between trafficking and smuggling, but also build custom-made and context-specific reactions and remedies against these distinctive crimes. Be they different "animals", trafficking and smuggling are explored in this study within the confines and under

---

12 See Dinah Shelton and Ariel Goult, 'Positive and Negative Obligations' in Dinah Shelton (ed.), *The Oxford Handbook of International Human Rights Law* (Oxford University Press 2013) 562; Asbjørn Eide, 'Economic, Social and Cultural Rights as Human Rights' in Asbjørn Eide and others (eds.), *Economic, Social and Cultural Rights* (Brill-Nijhoff 2001) 9. See also Olivier De Schutter, *International Human Rights Law: Cases, Materials, Commentary* (Cambridge University Press 2010) 242ff; UN Office of the High Commissioner for Human Rights, 'Civil and Political Rights: The Human Rights Committee: Fact Sheet No 15 (Rev. 1)' (2005) 4-5.

13 See para. 3 of this chapter and Vassilis P Tzevelekos, 'Reconstructing the Effective Control Criterion in Extraterritorial Human Rights Breaches: Direct Attribution of Wrongfulness, Due Diligence, and Concurrent Responsibility' (2014) 36 Michigan Journal of International Law 129, 164ff.

14 UN Trust Fund for Human Security, <http://www.un.org/humansecurity/> accessed 20 April 2016. See also n 65.

the common "umbrella" of the UNSC resolution 2240 (2015), which deals with the situation in Libya. The focus of the study is not on trafficking and/or smuggling, *per se*, but on the named resolution. This is seen as an instance of human security objectives being served by the UNSC. With its resolution, the UNSC contributes to the idea of shared responsibility by multiple states to react against transnational social phenomena that raise concerns from the perspective of human rights and human security. UNSC resolution 2240 (2015) offers a solid basis for the analysis that follows. This is the reason why this chapter uses it as a case study.

The next Paragraph of the chapter identifies a number of "ingredients" within UNSC resolution 2240 (2015) that are necessary for and reinforce the argument about multiple duty bearers and concurrent state responsibility. That argument is developed in more detail in Paragraph 3. Paragraph 4 links previous analysis in the paper with human security and calls for "tweaking" that framework so that it can effectively address transnational threats. Paragraph 5 concludes by recapping.

2 Smuggling of Migrants and Human Trafficking: Who Shall do What According to the UNSC

As already explained, with its resolution, the UNSC primarily authorises states to go beyond what the law of the sea allows[15] and inspect/seize on the high seas any vessel that they have reasonable grounds to believe is

15 The key principle here is that of the exclusivity of the flag-state jurisdiction, according to which vessels on high seas are exclusively under the jurisdiction and authority of the state whose flag they lawfully fly. See e.g., Arts. 87, 105 and 110 of the UN Convention on the Law of the Sea. For a recent monograph on the topic, see Efthymios Papastavridis, *The Interception of Vessels on the High Seas. Contemporary Challenges to the Legal Order of the Oceans* (Hart 2013) 50-82. Obviously, outside inspection of foreign vessels engaged in human trafficking and migrant smuggling, a number of other questions arise as to the rights and duties of states for life endangering situations in the high seas, especially with regard to search and rescue at sea. For a brief but comprehensive overview, in the context of migration through seas, see Richard Barnes, 'Refugee Law at Sea' (2004) 53 International and Comparative Law Quarterly 47, 48-61. See also, Matteo Tondini, 'The Legality of Intercepting Boat People under Search and Rescue and Border Control Operations with Reference to Recent Italian Interventions in the Mediterranean Sea and the ECtHR Decision in the Hirsi Case' (2012) 18 Journal of International Maritime Law 59.

involved in migrant smuggling and human trafficking.[16] This is a means to an end. The rationale behind that authorisation is that these crimes are associated with losses of human lives in the Mediterranean.[17] The resolution's ultimate goal is to save these lives by fighting the sources of their endangerment, i.e. smuggling and trafficking. Among several other policy options that would serve that goal, the UNSC opts for the said authorisation. Thus, *all* UN member states may[18] inspect vessels in accordance with the resolution.

Human life protection in the context discussed here requires co-ordination and co-operation[19] between various circles of states. At the more general level, the SC calls "*all* flag States *involved* to cooperate with respect to their efforts"[20] in line with its resolution and urges all "Member States and regional organisations, in the spirit of international *solidarity* and *shared responsibility* to cooperate with the Libyan Government, and with each other".[21] In particular, the UNSC urges those "States and regional organisations whose naval vessels and aircraft operate on the high seas and airspace off the coast of Libya, to *be vigilant* for acts"[22] of smuggling and trafficking. Beyond that last category of states, which are willingly involved through their operations off the coast of Libya, co-operation and co-ordination are crucial for "*concerned* Member States"[23] and for "the *States in the region* affected by smuggling of migrants and human trafficking".[24] This will allow states to "strengthen an effective multidimensional response to these *common* challenges in the spirit of inter-

---

16 UNSC, 'Resolution 2240' (n 2) [7], [8].

17 Ibid. [7] – which explains that the authorisation is given "with a view to saving the threatened lives of migrants or of victims of human trafficking on board such vessels as mentioned above" – and, primarily, [12]. See also the preamble that starts by reminding a maritime tragedy in the Mediterranean Sea, but also the part in the preamble where the UNSC underlines the primary responsibility of Libya to prevent the endangerment of lives, and [1], [2] of the resolution.

18 As it will be argued below, a state might, under certain circumstances, have a duty to do so.

19 The preamble repeatedly uses these terms. See also UNSC, 'Resolution 2240' (n 2) [4], [9].

20 Ibid. [9] (emphasis added).

21 Ibid. [3] (emphasis added).

22 Ibid. [4] (emphasis added).

23 Ibid. [preamble] (emphasis added).

24 Ibid. (emphasis added).

national *solidarity* and *shared responsibility*".[25] But, if we want to narrow down the circle of involved states to a minimum, the problem is such that it "requires a coordinated *multidimensional* approach with States of *origin*, of *transit*, and of *destination*".[26]

The resolution can schematically be understood as drawing a number of homocentric circles. Ideally, for reaction to the crimes at issue to be effective, all states should join forces and be pro-actively engaged even if they are not connected with the problem. This (i.e. the problem) is of particular concern to the states in the region. These two groups of states, namely the international community of states as a whole and states in the near proximity, need to be juxtaposed to the states of origin, transit and destination. What places these three last states in a distinct category is that, unlike states in the previous groups, these are *directly* involved in a situation that requires from them to protect human life. Territory[27] and nationality[28] link smuggling and trafficking through seas with these states. And, because these crimes are life threatening and, more generally, raise concerns from the perspective of human rights, directly connected states have a *duty* to exercise jurisdiction with a view to grant protection. A big variety of actions fall under protection, spanning from *ex ante* preventive measures, to *ex post facto* punitive policies. Protection involves the executive, the legislature and the judicial authorities of the state. These are expected to exercise their respective powers vis-à-vis any aspect of trafficking and smuggling. The transnational nature of these phenomena results in plural states being involved. As is explained below in further detail, all involved states *share* the responsibility (in the sense of duty) to protect.[29]

As far as the nature of the required action is concerned, resolution 2240 (2015) authorises all states – that is, each one of them individually – to intercept vessels in the high seas. As already argued, this ought to be seen as a means towards life protection. Yet, vessel interception is one among several "tools" serving that end. States may adopt a plethora

25 Ibid. (emphasis added).

26 Ibid. (emphasis added).

27 That is, when trafficking and smuggling are taking place on the territory of a state.

28 That is, when the victims – passive personality – or the perpetrators – active personality – of the crime are the nationals of a state.

29 The term is not used here in the sense of the concept of Responsibility to Protect (R2P). Among several other publications on R2P, see Spencer Zifcak, 'The Responsibility to Protect' in Malcolm D Evans (ed.), *International Law* (4th edn, Oxford University Press 2014) 509.

of policies and take action in a variety of ways that are pertinent and lawful under international law. This is why the UNSC acknowledges that states in the region need assistance to develop "comprehensive and integrated regional and national strategies, legal frameworks, and institutions to counter terrorism [and] transnational organised crime [...]".[30] It, furthermore, acknowledges "the need to develop effective strategies to deter migrant smuggling and human trafficking in States of origin and transit".[31] UN Member states are called in the resolution "to assist Libya, upon request, in building needed capacity including to *secure its borders* and to *prevent, investigate* and *prosecute* acts of smuggling of migrants and human trafficking through its territory and in its territorial sea".[32] States operating on the high seas and airspace off the coast of Libya are urged "to *be vigilant*"[33] for acts of smuggling and trafficking and encouraged to "coordinate their efforts to *deter*"[34] such acts. Finally, "all States with relevant jurisdiction under international law and national legislation, [are called] to *investigate* and *prosecute* persons responsible for acts of migrant smuggling and human trafficking at sea".[35]

All these amount to means through which states may contribute to the goal of human life *protection*. The term protection implies that the situation under discussion corresponds to the second, positive[36] strand of the effect human rights rules develop, amounting to *protection*.[37] As opposed to *respect*, which sets obligations of result, protection is associated with the principle of due diligence.[38] This explains why protection establishes

30 UNSC, 'Resolution 2240' (n 2) [preamble].

31 Ibid.

32 Ibid. [2] (emphasis added).

33 Ibid. [4] (emphasis added).

34 Ibid. (emphasis added).

35 Ibid. [15] (emphasis added).

36 Among others, see Shelton and Goult, 'Positive and Negative Obligations' (n 12).

37 On the triptych respect-protect-fulfil, see Eide, 'Economic, Social and Cultural Rights' (n 12). See also De Schutter, *International Human Rights Law* (n 12); UN Office of the High Commissioner for Human Rights, 'Civil and Political Rights' (n 12).

38 Among others, see Riccardo Pisillo-Mazzeschi, 'The Due Diligence Rule and the Nature of the International Responsibility of States' (1992) 35 German Yearbook of international Law 9; Timo Koivurova, 'Due Diligence', *Max Planck Encyclopedia of Public International Law* (2013); Robert P Barnidge, 'The Due Diligence Principle under International Law' (2006) 8 International Community Law Review 81; Tzevelekos, 'Reconstructing the Effective Control Criterion' (n 13) 152-157; International Law Association, 'ILA Study Group on Due Diligence in International Law:

obligations of *means* or conduct.[39] States enjoy discretion in choosing, among various means that are available to them, the ones that they wish to employ in order to act in a diligent manner and offer the protection they are capable of offering given their resources and the particular circumstances of each individual case. The UNSC resolution suggests some pertinent means and authorises states to employ the "tool" of interference with foreign ships in the high seas. Finally, it explicitly refers to due diligence and to its content in the present context, the aim being to protect human lives endangered by human trafficking and the smuggling of migrants. Thus, the UNSC delivers its resolution,

> [b]earing in mind the obligations of States under applicable international law to exercise *due diligence* to *prevent* and *combat* migrant smuggling and human trafficking, to *investigate* and *punish* perpetrators, to identify and *provide effective assistance* to victims of trafficking and migrants and to *cooperate* to the fullest extent possible to *prevent* and *suppress* migrant smuggling and human trafficking.[40]

Inspection of foreign vessels in the high seas under the conditions surrounding its authorisation by resolution 2240 (2015) is a lawful means that the UNSC makes available to any state that may wish (i.e. is entitled) or is legally expected (i.e. has an obligation) to engage in protection. States that are directly linked (through nationality or territory, for instance, as discussed earlier) with a situation calling for protection are expected to exercise jurisdiction for human rights protection purposes. They enjoy discretion in choosing the appropriate means, but they need to show that they did the best they could do, given the circumstances of each case,

---

First Report' (Duncan French as Chair, Tim Stephens as Rapporteur, 7 March 2014); International Law Association, 'Due Diligence in International Law' (*International Law Association*, Committees, 2014) <http://www.ila-hq.org/en/committees/study_groups.cfm/cid/1045> accessed 20 April 2016. The International Court of Justice has in a number of instances employed due diligence. To give an example of explicit use, see Pulp Mills on the River Uruguay (*Argentina v Uruguay*) Judgment, ICJ Reports 2010, 14, [101].

39 André Tunk, 'La Distinction des Obligations de Résultat et des Obligations de Diligence" (1945) 449 La Semaine Juridique; Pierre-Marie Dupuy, 'Reviewing the Difficulties of Codification: On Ago's Classification of Obligations of Means and Obligations of Result in Relation to State Responsibility' (1999) 10 European Journal of International Law 371.

40 UNSC, 'Resolution 2240' (n 2) [preamble] (emphasis added).

to protect human life. Unconnected states do not have a duty, but are entitled, if they wish, to take action.

Both these scenarios raise complex questions regarding jurisdiction, especially concerning its bases[41] and the lawfulness of its exercise extraterritorially.[42] These issues extend beyond the limited scope of the present study. What, however, is of importance for the purposes of this paper is that a plurality of states may engage in protection, whereas few of them – namely the ones that are directly linked to the situation in a way that establishes their jurisdiction (either territorial or extraterritorial), and activates due diligence and (in the light of that principle) human rights' positive effect – have a duty to do so. Migration and human trafficking are transnational in their nature. This means that a number of states are connected – through territory and nationality, principally – with the situation. All connected states have a duty to engage in protection to the extent that they are linked and in ways justified by their connection to the situation. This leads to a plurality of duty bearers that are expected to exercise parallel jurisdiction. Quite often, there will be no overlap in the way these states exercise their jurisdiction. For instance, one state may act in a preventive manner, by conducting regular controls to secure that vessels under its flag are not engaging in trafficking, whilst another state may rescue migrants at sea and prosecute traffickers/smugglers it arrests on its territory. As argued below, co-operation (for example, search and rescue zones or extradition agreements) between states is crucial to ensure that "polyphony" owing to the exercise of parallel jurisdiction by a number of involved states does not result in "cacophony" that undermines the effectiveness of the efforts indertaken individually by each state. In similar terms, priorities can be established as to who shall exercise jurisdiction on the basis of the robustness and tangibility of

41 On the bases of jurisdiction see eg Christopher Staker, 'Jurisdiction' in Malcolm D Evans, *International Law* (4th edn, Oxford University Press 2014) 309. See also Rosalyn Higgins, *Themes and Theories* (Oxford University Press 2009) 801-810; Cedric Ryngaert, *Jurisdiction in International Law* (Oxford University Press 2008) chs. 3 and 4. Gavouneli examines that question with a special focus on the law of the sea – Maria Gavouneli, *Functional Jurisdiction in the Law of the Sea* (Martinus Nijhoff 2007) 5-32.

42 The literature on extraterritoriality (especially regarding human rights protection in Europe) is vast. Among others, Tzevelekos, 'Reconstructing the Effective Control Criterion' (n 13) and the case law and literature to which that study refers.

each state's connection with the situation calling for protection.[43] In that respect, after reaffirming its "strong commitment to the sovereignty [...] of Libya",[44] resolution 2240 underlines "the *primary responsibility* of the Libyan Government to take appropriate action to prevent the recent proliferation of and endangerment of lives by, the smuggling of migrants and human trafficking through the territory of Libya and its territorial sea."[45]

3 Concurrent State Responsibility Explained

Having, first, identified the "ingredients" in resolution 2240 that reveal that trafficking and smuggling of migrants require action by multiple states and, then, situated that scenario within the (interlinked) concepts of due diligence and human rights protection, the paper moves now to further explain why, in such cases, multiple duty bearers exist and how their failure to protect may lead to concurrent state responsibility. Space constraints do not permit a detailed discussion of jurisdiction[46] (its bases and limitations) and of how responsibility (in the sense of liability) for failure to demonstrate due diligence functions.[47] Admittedly, both these concepts (jurisdiction and responsibility) are essential elements of the argument built in the chapter. But for its needs, suffice it to explain that (outside enforcement jurisdiction, which is in principle territorial[48]) jurisdiction may have extraterritorial effects and be of course established on bases other than territory. Nationality, passive or active, is a characteristic example. These bases may result in the exercise of jurisdiction for conduct attributed to (in the case of active nationality) or suffered by (in the case of passive nationality) nationals extraterritorially.

---

43 See Ryngaert's idea about *reasonable jurisdiction* and the distinction he makes between primary and subsidiary jurisdictional bases. Ryngaert, *Jurisdiction* (n 41) 185ff.

44 UNSC, 'Resolution 2240' (n 2) [preamble].

45 Ibid. (emphasis added).

46 See n 41; n 42; n 43.

47 See n 38.

48 See e.g. para. 49 of the dissenting opinion of Judge Van den Wyngaert in the *Arrest Warrant* case, distinguishing between prescriptive jurisdiction and enforcement jurisdiction and arguing that, when the exercise of jurisdiction is permitted for states, it cannot lead to acts of extraterritorial enforcement. Arrest Warrant of 11 April 2000 (*Democratic Republic of Congo v Belgium*) Judgment, ICJ 14 February 2002, ICJ Reports 2002, 3.

As far as due diligence is concerned, as already mentioned, this is linked with the positive strand of protection in human rights law;[49] it establishes obligations of means (and not of result),[50] giving discretion to states as to how they pursue protection. States cannot be held liable unless they are proven negligent in their duty to protect. Negligence is assessed on the basis of criteria, such us the existence of knowledge by state authorities regarding the need to engage in prevention/protection (which involves risk assessment),[51] the particular circumstances of each case and the particular need for protection these raise, but also the ability of the state to effectively grant protection, given the means that are available to it.[52] This amounts to the so-called test of state fault for lack of diligence.[53]

Brief as they may be, these explanations provide the necessary theoretical basis to understand why multiple states are legally expected to fight trafficking off the coast of Libya, but also why failure to react to that crime may lead to the concurrent responsibility of these states. This is a conclusion supported by the case law of the European Court of Human Rights (ECtHR) on trafficking. In *Rantsev*,[54] human trafficking resulted in loss of life in Cyprus. What is particularly interesting in that case is that the ECtHR found liable both Cyprus, on the territory of which the victim died, and Russia, whose national the victim was and on the territory of which trafficking started.[55]

---

49 See n 36; n 37. See also *Velásquez-Rodriguez v Honduras*, Judgment, Inter-American Court of Human Rights Series C No 4 (29 July 1988) [172].

50 See n 39.

51 See e.g., Case Concerning United States Diplomatic and Consular Staff in Tehran (*United States of America v Iran*) Judgment, ICJ 24 May 1980, ICJ Reports 1980 [68].

52 Ibid.

53 Among others, Pierre-Marie Dupuy, 'Le fait générateur de la responsabilité internationale des États' (1984) 188 Recueil des Cours de l'Académie de Droit International 9, 102-103; Mazzeschi, 'The Due Diligence Rule' (n 38) 18-21, 49-50; Tzevelekos, 'Reconstructing the Effective Control Criterion' (n 13) 155-157; Andrea Gattini, 'La notion de faute à la lumière du projet de convention de la Commission du droit international sur la responsabilité internationale' (1992) 3 European Journal of International Law 253; Andrea Gattini, 'Smoking/No Smoking: Some Remarks on the Current Place of Fault in the ILC Draft Articles on State responsibility' (1999) 10 European Journal of International Law 397.

54 *Rantsev v Cyprus and Russia* App no 25965/04 (ECtHR, 07 January 2010).

55 Although the ECtHR established Russia's jurisdiction on the basis only of the territorial links that existed between it and trafficking. ibid., 207-208.

Transnational social phenomena, such as human trafficking, inevitably occur on the territory of multiple states. These are all expected to exercise territorial jurisdiction against human rights risks/violations. It would be a mistake to think that these states are called to exercise jurisdiction in a row, only when and for the part of wrongfulness that takes place on their territory. This is what would happen had territory been the only basis for jurisdiction. Yet, next to territory, other legal bases apply too, linking concomitantly several states with the same transnational situation. When the situation at issue falls under due diligence (as human rights do, developing a positive effect aiming at protection), all involved states are expected to exercise parallel jurisdiction as a means to grant protection, to the extent they are connected with the situation and in ways justified by its particular set of facts/circumstances. This is the case in *Rantsev*. The authors of the human rights breaches, that is, the persons who directly caused[56] these breaches (i.e. the traffickers), are unknown to the ECtHR and to the two respondent states. But both these states, because they are connected with the same transnational human rights issue, have a duty to demonstrate diligence with a view to protecting the victim's life. The ECtHR proceeded with a state fault test (although this is not a term employed by the Court) and found that Cyprus, on the territory of which the victim died, did not break its obligation to rescue the victim's life, as it could not have foreseen her death.[57] However, Cyprus was found to be

---

56 The term direct causation is used here in the sense of direct attribution, which is juxtaposed to the concept of indirect attribution that refers to indirect responsibility for lack of due diligence. See Jean Salmon (ed.), *Dictionnaire de Droit International Public* (Bruylant 2001) 996, defining indirect responsibility as "incurred by a subject of law because of the conduct of another subject of law" [our translation]. See also the Jan Arno Hessbruegge, 'The Historical Development of the Doctrines of Attribution and Due Diligence in International Law' (2004) 36 New York Journal of International Law and Politics 265, 268-269. For a more general discussion on causality and state responsibility, treating both direct attribution and indirect (omissions, fault, negligence etc), see Ilias Plakokefalos, 'Causation in the Law of State Responsibility and the Problem of Overdetermination: In Search of Clarity' (2015) 26 European Journal of International Law 471. See also Skogly who discusses causality (again with regard to both direct and indirect responsibility) and state responsibility in an area contiguous to the topic of this paper, namely extraterritorial violations of human rights. Sigrun I Skogly, 'Causality and Extraterritorial Human Rights Obligations' in Malcolm Langford and others (eds.), *Global Justice, State Duties. The Extraterritorial Scope of Economic, Social and Cultural Rights in International Law* (Cambridge University Press 2013) 233.

57 *Rantsev* (n 54) 223.

responsible, *inter alia*, because of its failure to effectively investigate that death[58] – which is part of the positive effect of the right to life in light of due diligence. In similar terms, that state was found liable for a breach of Article 4 (prohibition of slavery and forced labour) of the European Convention on Human Rights (ECHR) because of its failure to put in place an appropriate domestic legal framework to combat trafficking and to take suitable operational measures to protect the victim from trafficking.[59]

At the same time, the ECtHR also found liable the Russian state because of its failure to investigate the victim's recruitment in Russia, as it ought have done under Article 4 of the ECHR.[60] As a result, two states are connected through different grounds with one situation[61] of human rights protection. Aspects of that situation occur, respectively, on the territory of both states. This leads to both of them being held concurrently responsible for their failure to diligently react against a wrong (trafficking, falling under Article 4 of the ECHR) that is not directly[62] attributable to any of them. Each state was expected to demonstrate its own share of diligence, to the best of its ability, on the basis that connected it to the situation at issue, and for as long as and to the extent that it was connected.

The failure by more than one states to be sufficiently (i.e. duly) diligent leads to concurrent responsibility. The term means *individually* allocated responsibility to plural subjects for the same harmful situation (owing obviously to different wrongs which are either directly or indirectly attributable to different states).[63] In the context of the paper, this owes to the exercise of complementary, parallel and, possibly, also overlapping jurisdiction over the same situation. Concurrent responsibility may take various shapes. One state might be responsible for directly causing the wrongful result, i.e. in terms of human rights law, breaking a negative obligation. Next to that state, other states may break their obligation to demonstrate diligence, i.e. protect from the conduct of the former state. Another scenario would be that the author of the breach is an individu-

58 Ibid. [242].

59 Ibid. [293], [298].

60 Ibid. [309].

61 Which happens, in the present instance, to raise a number of human rights protection issues.

62 See n 56.

63 André Nollkaemper, 'Introduction' in André Nollkaemper, Ilias Plakokefalos (eds.), *Principles of Shared Responsibility in International Law. An Appraisal of the State of the Art* (Cambridge University Press 2014) 1, 9-10. See also, Tzevelekos, 'Reconstructing the Effective Control Criterion' (n 13) 136 fn 16, 169.

al/non-state actor whose conduct is not attributable to any state. What leads to concurrent responsibility in that case is that multiple states might be expected to demonstrate diligence against the illicit conduct of the author of the breach. In these scenarios, each state is breaking its own obligations. A plurality of distinguishable international law breaches exists. This is the reason why responsibility is not joint.[64] States may share responsibility over the same in essence (one single and common to all) harmful situation (for instance, human trafficking putting at risk human life), but responsibility can be individually allocated and apportioned.

4 Transnational Threats: What Role for Human Security?

Having finished with the first main point made in this paper concerning shared responsibility to protect, analysis now turns to the links between that idea (i.e. shared responsibility) and the UN framework of human security. Life-threatening social phenomena, such as the ones prompting the reaction of the UNSC with resolution 2240 (2015), raise issues of human security.[65] This is what makes that concept pertinent and the

---

64 See Article 47 of the International Law Commission Articles on the Responsibility of States for Internationally Wrongful Acts, annex to General Assembly resolution 56/83 of 12 December 2001, and corrected by document A/56/49(Vol. I)/Corr.4. Article 47 only deals with the scenario of a plurality of responsible states regarding the *same wrongful act*, which is clearly distinguished from that of a plurality of states contributing through *separate* internationally wrongful conduct to the same damage. See also, ILC, 'Draft Articles on Responsibility of States for Internationally Wrongful Acts, with Commentaries' <http://legal.un.org/ilc/texts/instruments/english/commentaries/9_6_2001.pdf> accessed 20 April 2016, 125. According to the ILC, "[i]n international law, the general principle in the case of a plurality of responsible States is that each State is separately responsible for conduct attributable to it in the sense of article 2", ibid. 124. "Paragraph 1 [of Article 47 ARSIWA] neither recognizes a general rule of joint *and several* responsibility, nor does it exclude the possibility that two or more States will be responsible for the same internationally wrongful act. Whether this is so will depend on the circumstances and on the international obligations of each of the States concerned" [emphasis added], ibid., 125.

65 See the four volumes edited by Owen – Taylor Owen, *Human Security* (Sage 2013). See also Mary Martin and Taylor Owen (eds.), *Routledge Handbook of Human Security* (Routledge 2014). For an overview, see Martin Wählisch, 'Human Security: Concept and Evolution in the United Nations' (2014) 18 Max Planck Yearbook of United Nations Law 1. For a more critical account, see, Alexandra Homolar, 'Human Secu-

relevant UN framework applicable in the context of trafficking and smuggling through seas. As is explained in the 2013 report of the UN Secretary General (UNSG) on human security, that concept "provides the people-centred approach by which to comprehensively address the totality of the challenges we face and to translate our efforts into actions that give rise to more effective and tangible improvements in the daily lives of people."[66] Human security aims at establishing a crosscutting framework (both at the national and at the international level, especially within the UN) to develop comprehensive, custom-made and context-specific strategies aiming to ensure human security. In the UNSG's words, it amounts to a

> dynamic and practical policy framework for addressing widespread and cross-cutting threats facing Governments and people. Recognizing that threats to human security vary considerably across countries and communities and at different points in time, the application of human security calls for an assessment of human insecurities that is both comprehensive and contextually relevant.[67]

Ultimately, human security suggests a new approach,[68] which signals a "paradigm shift because of its focus on the individual and individual wellbeing and livelihood."[69]

As a concept, human security counts more than two decades of life.[70] Originating from the 1994 "Human Development Report" of the UN

---

rity Benchmarks. Governing Human Wellbeing at a Distance' (2015) 41 Review of International Studies 843; Yaniv Roznai, 'The Insecurity of Human Security' (2014) 32 Wisconsin International Law Journal 95.

66 UN General Assembly, 'Follow-up to General Assembly Resolution 66/290 on Human Security' (2013) UN Doc A/68/685 [7].

67 UNGA, 'Follow-up to General Assembly Resolution 64/291 on Human Security' (2012) UN Doc A/66/763 [28].

68 UN Trust Fund for Human Security, 'Human Security Approach' <http://www.un.org/humansecurity/human-security-unit/human-security-approach> accessed 20 April 2016.

69 Wolfgang Benedek, 'The Role of the Human Security Perspective' in Hans-Joachim Heintze and Pierre Thielbörger (eds.), *From Cold War to Cyber War. The Evolution of the International Law of Peace and Armed Conflict over the last 25 Years* (Springer 2016) 139, 140.

70 For a brief but very comprehensive presentation of the evolution of human security and the role of the various actors and networks (such as the Human Security

Development Programme,[71] it found a place in the 2005 World Summit Outcome – paragraph 143 of which is entitled "human security".[72] There, the commitment of states is expressed to further discuss and develop the concept within the UN framework.[73] Indeed, in 2012, the UN General Assembly (UNGA) adopted resolution 66/290 on human security.[74] This is seen as "an approach to assist Member States in identifying and addressing widespread and cross-cutting challenges to the survival, livelihood and dignity of their people."[75] Human security is an ambitious concept with far reaching aims, encompassing threats stemming from poverty and, more generally, vulnerability.[76] But, human life is at the core of the concept and, in particular, the survival of people.[77] The link between human rights and human security is evident.[78] The two share common objectives, with the former (i.e. human rights) consisting in a legal vehicle towards policy goals set by human security. The latter should be seen as having no autonomous legal standing, as it "does not entail additional legal obligations on the part of States".[79] All families of human rights are important for human security,[80] and, because prevention falls within hu-

---

Network and the Friends of Human Security) involved see ibid 140-143. For milestones within the UN system, see UN Trust Fund for Human Security, 'Human Security Milestones' <http://www.un.org/humansecurity/content/human-security-milestones> accessed 20 April 2016.

71 UN Development Programme, 'Human Development Report 1994' <http://hdr.undp.org/sites/default/files/reports/255/hdr_1994_en_complete_nostats.pdf> accessed 20 April 2016. See in particular chapter 2 of the Report, 22-40.

72 UNGA, 'Resolution 60/1. 2005 Word Summit Outcome' (24 October 2005) UN Doc A/RES/60/1 [143].

73 Ibid.

74 UNGA, 'Resolution 66/290. Follow-up to paragraph 143 on Human Security of the 2005 World Summit Outcome' (25 October 2012) UN Doc A/RES/66/290. For the course of discussion at the UNGA before the adoption of its resolution, see UNGA, 'Follow-up to General Assembly Resolution 64/291' (n 67) [5]-[15].

75 UNGA, 'Resolution 66/290' (n 74) [3].

76 Ibid. [3(a)]. Freedom from want may have far-reaching consequences touching upon welfare state and socioeconomic policy.

77 Ibid. [3].

78 Ibid. [3(c)].

79 Ibid. [3(h)]. See also Benedek, 'The Role of the Human Security Perspective' (n 69) 147, who argues that "[h]uman security and human development are mainly political concepts, which can be strengthened and operationalized by legally binding human rights."

80 UNGA, 'Resolution 66/290' (n 74) [3(c)].

man security[81] – although this is not explicitly stated in the UNGA resolution – we can safely conclude that due diligence is relevant to it.

This concise outline of human security and, especially, the elements of the concept that have been highlighted here demonstrate that any (human rights) policy aiming to protect human life falls within human security. Seen from that perspective, resolution 2240 (2015) can be understood as an attempt of the UNSC to facilitate states in their efforts to safeguard and enhance human security. Of course, a more critical approach could reproach the UNSC for delivering a resolution that, altogether, protects human life imperfectly – even though life protection is the main preoccupation and goal of its resolution.[82] When it comes to life-saving measures, resolution 2240 is rather abstract, referring in quite broad terms to the duties various states already have under international law. The UNSC would/could serve human security much more effectively if it authorised/ordered more (ideally, equally concrete as the interference with foreign vessels in the high seas) measures associated with life protection in the specific context of trafficking and smuggling off the coast of Libya. Such measures would establish standards and concretise the expected conduct, diminishing thereby the margin of discretion states enjoy as to how to fulfil their duty to demonstrate diligence.

On the other hand, one cannot overlook the political nature of the UNSC and the impediments that often prevent it from reaching consensus (especially when it acts under Chapter VII). Besides, the introduction of this study has explained that what matters for its analysis is not the context (fight against trafficking and smuggling off the coast of Libya resulting in loss of life), but the UNSC resolution as a case study. By rendering permissible certain conduct (interference with foreign vessels in the high seas) that serves human security goals, the UNSC contributes and reinforces human security. This suffices to make the argument that resolution 2240 and the idea of concurrent responsibility to offer protection that transpires from it, sit comfortably within the human security framework.[83]

Nonetheless, there is one particular element of human security that the UNSC resolution discussed here has difficulties in satisfying. The

81 Ibid. [3(b)]. See also, UNGA, 'Follow-up to General Assembly Resolution 64/291' (n 67) [32].

82 See n 4; n 17.

83 Besides, trafficking is one of the areas where human security may apply – UN Trust Fund for Human Security, 'Human Security Approach' (n 68).

logic underpinning human security is that of subsidiarity. "The role of the international community is to complement and provide the necessary support to Governments, upon their request, so as to strengthen their capacity to respond to current and emerging threats."[84] Thus, the international community and third states may be seen as only having an auxiliary role, with governments "retain[ing] the primary role and responsibility for ensuring the survival, livelihood and dignity of their citizens."[85] This explains why the whole "project" of human security relies on "national ownership".[86] The authorities of each state are entrusted with the responsibility of promoting the goals of human security through strategies that they "own", that is, that they develop at the national level by taking into account the needs of their society, but also the particular circumstances and context of each situation. The rest of the word only has a complementary, i.e. subsidiary role.

Evidently, this is a point of divergence between the UNSC resolution discussed in this chapter and the concept of human security. But equally evident are the reasons why the UNSC – although it recognises the primary role of Libya[87] – invites the international community of states to contribute to the protection of human life off the coast of the named state. Arguably, at the present time, Libya is not in a position to effectively prevent and fight trafficking and smuggling, whilst the transnational nature of these activities renders necessary – for the reasons that have already been exposed – that multiple states be involved. This is exactly where the human security framework can make a very positive contribution, by co-ordinating and organising the role and actions of the involved actors.

For human security to be successful in the solutions it offers to problems like human trafficking and migration, it needs to take into account the transnational nature of these phenomena. Thus far, the main argument in this study has been that such phenomena involve plural states. These are mutually connected to the situation and have a duty to demonstrate diligence, i.e. take action and exercise jurisdiction with a view to protect human life. This raises a number of challenges for human security.

---

84 UNGA, 'Resolution 66/290' (n 74) [3(g)].

85 Ibid. See also, UNGA, 'Follow-up to General Assembly Resolution 64/291' (n 67) [2], [33].

86 UNGA, 'Resolution 66/290' (n 74) [3(f)].

87 UNSC, 'Resolution 2240' (n 2) [preamble].

First and foremost, it raises the issues of co-ordination of action, allocation of responsibilities (in the sense of duties) and avoidance of clash of jurisdiction. To play a meaningful role in case of transnational phenomena implicating multiple jurisdictions, human security needs to organise action and offer a specific and as detailed as possible framework for co-ordination of efforts by states in the light of the context of each particular case. Policies can be designed at the national level and "owned" by states. There are good reasons as to why this should be the case. National ownership has a number of advantages from the perspectives of democracy, popular sovereignty and accountability, but also legitimacy, subsidiarity and effectiveness. But, when planning their policies and course of action, states need to be cognizant of the international ramifications of their conduct in the context of social phenomena that transcend the borders of multiple states. This requires co-ordination. States ought to refrain from undermining the human security policies of other states, which are equally involved in the same situation. Sometimes, this might require from states to demonstrate self-restraint in the exercise of their powers and comity vis-à-vis other jurisdictions. But co-ordination can play a significant role in another direction too.

Beyond clash of jurisdictions, a different scenario that undermines human security is inaction by multiple involved states when they remain passive, expecting (or hoping) that, because of the transnational nature of a situation, their negligence will be covered by the pro-active engagement of another involved (and more diligent) state. Co-ordination is, finally, also important for less altruistic and more "self-help" (or state/national security, as opposed to human security) kind of purposes. Within our interconnected and increasingly globalised word, the insecurity of others is contagious. It can easily threaten our own security. Insulation from (what may be perceived as) a source of insecurity, but also from liability[88] for the reaction (or the lack thereof) against that perceived source of insecurity is implausible. By strengthening (or at least refraining from putting at risk) the human security of "others", states may strengthen their own security, thus the human security of their own people too. This is yet another incentive for states to co-ordinate action against transnational, hence common, dangers.

88 See, for instance, Thomas Gammeltoft-Hansen and James C Hathaway, 'Non-Refoulement in a World of Cooperative Deterrence' (2015) 53 Columbia Journal of Transnational Law 235. The authors discuss non-entrée policies in the context of refugee protection and the issues of state responsibility these policies raise.

In modern times, many of the risks we face are transnational in nature. Transnational organised crime (including trafficking), refugee protection, private military companies operating overseas, cyber crimes, trans-boundary environmental pollution, globalised corporate activities threatening human rights and the environment, epidemic communicable diseases – to name but a few of these transnational threats – all raise concerns from the perspective of human security. These situations menace the enjoyment of fundamental human rights and are, all, transnational in their nature. Human security cannot but take that very reality into account. Responses to transnational phenomena ought to be international. The minimum level of internationalisation is to agree on forms of co-ordination in the answers different nations give to these threats. Then, international law can set standards for states by prohibiting certain conduct or establishing obligations for them to pro-actively fight these phenomena. Ultimately, it can regulate and sanction directly at the international level the wrongful behaviour of non-state actors, as international criminal law does. Yet, the first step is co-ordination of state action. This is a precondition for action to reach its maximum potential, be efficient and effective.

To do justice to the UNGA resolution on human security, while it emphasises national ownership and assigns a primary role to the government whose citizens' security is endangered, it explicitly acknowledges the need for "greater collaboration and partnership among Governments, international and regional organizations and civil society".[89] With resolution 2240 (2015), the UNSC authorisation arms states with an important "tool" against human trafficking and smuggling of migrants. Human security's role is to follow up by suggesting a concrete, custom-made framework of co-ordination and co-operation so that involved states (but also international organisations and non-state actors)[90] can make the most out of the UNSC authorisation to the benefit of the victims of these crimes.

89 UNGA, 'Resolution 66/290' (n 74) [3(g)]. See also, UNGA, 'Follow-up to General Assembly Resolution 66/290 on Human Security' (n 66) [35]-[42].

90 For a collection of essays on human security and non-state actors, see Cedric Ryngaert and Math Noortmann (eds.), *Human Security and International Law. The Challenge of Non-State Actors* (Intersentia 2014).

5 Concluding Remarks

This chapter has focused on resolution 2240(2015), seeing in it an example of how the UNSC may empower states to take action against transnational social phenomena that raise serious concerns from the perspective of human rights – regarding especially the right to life. Resolution 2240 is a response to ongoing, life-threatening transnational crimes. It is also a case study that allowed making two main arguments in this chapter. *First*, in the case of transnational situations, such as transnational crimes, a plurality of states are involved. When such a situation raises concerns from the perspective of fundamental human rights or, more generally, falls under the principle of due diligence, states that are connected to the situation through the various bases that establish jurisdiction in international law are expected to be proactively engaged and strive to protect. This means that these states will be exercising parallel and, possibly, also overlapping jurisdiction, as well as that they may be held concurrently responsible for their failure to fulfil due diligence. *Second*, the framework of human security finds an application in these situations. But, for human security to be successful in its goals, it needs to be adjusted to the transnational nature of these phenomena. What is required when a situation necessitating protection exceeds or transcends the borders of a state, is establishing frameworks of co-operation and co-ordination between the various involved parties. This is an essential precondition for human security to deliver effective results and prosper in the era of inter-connection and globalisation.

The 2015 Andaman Sea Boat 'Crisis': Human Rights and Refugee Law Considerations

*Bríd Ní Ghráinne**

1 Introduction

At the nexus of state security and human security lies the concept of the 'refugee crisis' – persons fleeing their places of habitual residence to preserve their survival, and the state characterising the situation as a 'crisis' in order to shift the focus to, or at least to share the focus with, national security concerns.[1] While understandably, much of the recent literature has focused on what is termed a 'European crisis', the plight of persons fleeing Myanmar and Bangladesh by sea has been relatively under-studied. This crudely-termed game of 'human ping-pong' involved the Thai, Malaysian, and Indonesian authorities turning back boatloads of people, leaving about 8,000 people stranded at sea.[2] Many on board the ships were members of Myanmar's minority Rohingya population, who lack citizenship, endure systematic discrimination, have limited access to education and healthcare, and cannot move around freely.[3]

The scope of protection under international law to which these people are entitled is unclear. None of the states affected by this 'crisis' are party to the 1951 Refugee Convention which contains the refugee definition, sets out the rights associated with refugee status, and prohibits states

* The author is grateful to Dr Richard Collins and Stefan Salomon for comments on an earlier draft of this chapter. All errors and omissions remain the author's own.

1 Terming the situations in Europe and the Andaman Sea as crises can be problematic for numerous reasons. For example, it draws attention away from the problem in the countries from which the refugees have fled, it strips decision-makers of responsibility, and it presents certain decisions and injustices as unavoidable. See Heath Cabot, 'Crisis and Continuity: "A Critical Look at the European Refugee Crisis"' (*Allegra lab*, 10 November 2015) <http://allegralaboratory.net/crisis-and-continuity-a-critical-look-at-the-european-refugee-crisis/>.

2 BBC News, '"Thousands" of Rohingya and Bangladeshi Migrants Stranded at Sea' (11 May 2015) <http://www.bbc.co.uk/news/world-asia-32686328>.

3 Human Rights Watch, 'World Report 2015: Burma' <https://www.hrw.org/world-report/2015/country-chapters/burma>.

Salomon, Heschl, *et al.* (eds.), *Blurring Boundaries: Human Security and Forced Migration*
 ISBN 978-90-04-32686-6. pp. 123-134.

from engaging in refoulement.[4] The lack of these states' participation in the Refugee Convention is particularly regretful in this context, as the Rohingya are clearly victims of persecution based on race and would thus most likely qualify as refugees if the Refugee Convention were applicable.

In this instance, the concept of national security appeared to override the needs of these individuals to escape threats to their lives and dignity. However, international law provides that national security interests can be curtailed by considerations of human security and the purpose of this brief chapter is to map out the legal protection applicable to those who were affected by the 2015 Andaman sea boat 'crisis.' First, this chapter will set out the nature the migration problem in the Andaman Sea. Second, it will go on to reject the commonly-held perception that there is little or no legal protection available for refugees or migrants in the Andaman Sea. It will argue that the scope of the applicable Law of the Sea provisions is vague and that the customary prohibition of refoulement in Refugee Law was not breached in this instance. However, it will illustrate that human rights law forms the overarching framework within which interception activities may be carried out, and that the activities of Thailand, Malaysia, and Indonesia were in breach of Articles 6 and 7 of the 1966 International Covenant on Civil and Political Rights ('ICCPR').[5]

2 The 'Crisis' in the Andaman Sea

Migration by sea in Asia is not a new phenomenon. The term 'boat people' was coined in the 1970s to identify the tens of thousands of people who fled Indochina in fishing boats after the Vietnam War. The modern-day usage of the term 'boat people' more commonly refers to those leaving Myanmar and Bangladesh via the Andaman Sea and the Bay of Bengal towards Thailand, Malaysia, and Indonesia. Some of those on board the vessels are migrants from Bangladesh who are not fleeing persecution. However, many of them are Rohingya, who have been historically discriminated against on the basis of ethnicity.

The term 'Rohingya' commonly refers to Muslims from Northern Rakhine State in Myanmar. They are an ethnic minority descended from a merging of Arakanese Buddhists, Chittagonian Bengalis, and Arabian sea-traders. Their dialect is Bengali in origin, yet distinct, with influenc-

4 Convention Relating to the Status of Refugees [1951] 189 UNTS 13, Art 31.

5 International Covenant on Civil and Political Rights [1961] 999 UNTS 171.

es from Persian.[6] Repeated cycles of historical displacement, beginning with the Burmese invasion of Arakan and deportation of Arakanese in 1784, followed by returns and armed struggle in the British colonial era and further displacements after independence, formed a justification for the Myanmar government's labelling of Rohingya as 'illegal migrants' and forcing them out again on several occasions.[7] In 1982, the Burmese Government passed the Citizenship Act which rendered the Rohingya stateless.[8]

Today, the Rohingya are the worst treated group in Myanmar. An estimated 139,000 people – mostly Rohingya – remained displaced in Rakhine state for a third year after violent clashes erupted between Rakhine Buddhists, Rohingya and other Muslims in 2012.[9] In its most recent report on Myanmar, Human Rights Watch describes the 'systematic repression' of the Rohingya, estimating that one million people along the border with Bangladesh continue to face restrictions on movement, employment, and religious freedom.[10]

In October 2014, the government announced a new Rakhine State Action Plan, which if implemented, would further entrench the discrimination and segregation of the Rohingya population.[11] This plan triggered an increase in the number of people attempting to cross the Andaman Sea and the Bay of Bengal by boat, hoping to reach Indonesia, Malaysia, and Thailand. Many of these vessels had no, or limited, navigation aids or charts. They had unreliable engines and steering, and little by way of safety equipment. Women were raped, children were separated from their families and abused, and men were beaten and thrown overboard.[12]

---

6 David Scott Mathieson, 'Plight of the Damned: Burma's Rohingya' (2009) 4 Global Asia 86.

7 Samuel Cheung, 'Migration Control and the Solutions Impasse in South and Southeast Asia: Implications from the Rohingya Experience' (2011) 25(1) Journal of Refugee Studies 1.

8 David S Mathieson, 'Plight of the Damned: Burma's Rohingya' (2009) 4(1) Global Asia 86.

9 Amnesty International, 'Myanmar; Annual Report 2015/2016' <https://www.amnesty.org/en/countries/asia-and-the-pacific/myanmar/report-myanmar/>.

10 HRW, 'Burma' (n 3).

11 AI, 'Myanmar' (n 9).

12 UN Human Rights, 'Joint Statement by UNHCR, OHCHR, IOM and SRSG for Migration and Development: Joint Statement by UNHCR, OHCHR, IOM and SRSG for Migration and Development: Search and Rescue at Sea, Disembarkation, and Protection of the Human Rights of Refugees and Migrants Now Imperative to Save

The latest figures indicate that 88,000 people made the dangerous voyage by sea since 2014, including 25,000 who arrived in the first quarter of 2015 alone.[13]

Over 1,100 people are estimated to have died at sea along this route since 2014.[14] In addition, disease, severe malnourishment, and psychological distress affect many of those who have survived these voyages.[15] The situation has been worsened by the crudely-termed game of 'human ping-pong' involving the Thai, Malaysian, and Indonesian authorities turning back boatloads of people, leaving about 8,000 people stranded at sea in May 2015.[16] One report described a fishing boat of about 350 people being refused entry into Thailand after the crew abandoned them and disabled the engine. They were stranded without food and water, resulting in ten deaths.[17] Indonesian authorities have admitted to pushing back one boat on May 11 and directing it to Malaysia after providing food and water to those on board.[18] In Malaysia, Deputy Home Affairs Minister Wan Junaidi Tuanku Jaafar publicly stated that the government would turn back boats and deport those who land ashore.[19] Senior Thai officials announced the government adopted a policy of pushing away boats from Thai shores after providing them with fuel, food, and water.[20]

Following talks in Kuala Lumpur, Malaysia and Indonesia agreed to offer temporary shelter to 7,000 stranded migrants but they asked for international assistance to resettle them after a year. Thailand also said it

---

Lives in the Bay of Bengal and Andaman Sea' (*Office of the High Commissioner*, 19 May 2015) <http://www.ohchr.org/EN/NewsEvents/Pages/DisplayNews.aspx?NewsID=15976&LangID=E#sthash.TG48h6n4.dpuf>.

13 Ibid.

14 UNHCR, 'South-East Asia: Mixed Maritime Movements' (UNHCR April/June 2015) 2.

15 Michael Pugh, 'Drowning not Waving: Boat People and Humanitarianism at Sea' (2004) 17(1) Journal of Refugee Studies 50, 56.

16 BBC News, '"Ten Deaths" on Stranded Myanmar Migrant Boat' (14 May 2015) <http://www.bbc.co.uk/news/world-asia-32733963>.

17 Ibid.

18 Human Rights Watch, 'Southeast Asia: End Rohingya Pushbacks: Thailand, Malaysia, Indonesia Should Act Urgently to Save Lives' (14 May 2015) <http://www.hrw.org/news/2015/05/14/southeast-asia-end-rohingya-boat-pushbacks>.

19 Ibid.

20 Ibid.

would no longer push back the stranded boats.[21] Of the 8,000 stranded at sea in mid-May 2015, 4,500 were known to have returned to shore and the number of estimated deaths at sea during that period is unknown.

3 Applicable Law

3.1 *Law of the Sea*

It would be remiss to examine the human rights and refugee law frameworks applicable without briefly setting out how they relate to the Law of the Sea. This is because there is a tension between the rights of the individual to leave their state and seek asylum and the right of the state to control its borders and in certain circumstances, to intercept vessels at sea. There is also an obligation on states to render assistance to persons in distress at sea.

If we take the case in favour of the push-back regime at its strongest, i.e. if we accept that it is permissible to push back ships carrying migrants present in the territorial seas as they are not engaged in 'innocent passage',[22] the actions of the Thai, Malaysian, and Indonesian authorities are still not in compliance with international law. The *MV Saiga* case held that:

> [International law] requires that the use of force must be avoided as far as possible and, where force is inevitable, it must not go beyond what is reasonable and necessary in the circumstances. Considerations of humanity must apply in the law of the sea as they do in other areas.[23]

---

21 BBC News, 'Missing Migrant Boat Found as Countries Offer Shelter' (20 May 2015) <http://www.bbc.co.uk/news/world-asia-32806972>.

22 UN Convention on the Law of the Sea [1982] 1833 UNTS 3, Art 19. The vast majority of migrant smuggling vessels are stateless, and therefore UNCLOS Art 110(1)(d) grants official vessels an express right of visit (a right to board and inspect) over those vessels that are stateless, but it does not specify what further actions, if any, may be taken by a state.

23 The M/V "Saiga" (No. 2) Case (*St Vincent and the Grenadines v Guinea*) Judgement, ITLOS 1 July 1999, ICGJ 336 [155].

The use of force must also be proportionate to the objective in sight.[24] As force was the first response to many of these incoming migrant vessels, it is highly unlikely that the use of force was "avoided as far as possible", i.e. that all other options were considered and/or exhausted.[25] The loss of life resulting from the pushback operation probably entails that the means used (i.e. pushback operations involving life-threatening measures) were not proportionate to the objective (interfering with the passage of a ship that is not engaged in innocent passage as per Article 19 UNCLOS) and it is unclear from the facts whether the minimum force necessary was used. Most importantly, the actions were a clear violation of human rights law, as will be set out below, which forms the overarching framework within which interception activities may be carried out.

In addition, the states involved were under the obligation in both treaty and customary law to render assistance to any person found in distress at sea.[26] However it is problematic that international law does not stipulate the nature and scope of assistance to be provided. It was reported that in some instances refugees were given rice and water and pushed back out to sea.[27] Whether this would satisfy the obligation to render assistance is unlikely, as given the object and purpose of the obligation, which is to prevent the loss of life at sea, assistance which would only marginally prolong life would not be interpreting the obligation in good faith. In addition, it would fall foul of the principle of effectiveness, which provides that the obligation in a treaty is to produce an outcome which advances

24 Ibid. Proportionality is also a crucial factor for determining whether there has been a violation of the right to life under international human rights law. See the case of *McCann and Others v the United Kingdom* App no 18984/91 (ECtHR, 27 September 1995); UN Human Rights Committee, 'Camargo v Columbia: Communication No 45/1979' (31 March 1982) UN Doc CCPR/C/OP/1.

25 For example, in its concluding observations on Israel, the Human Rights Committee considered the targeted killing of suspected terrorists to be arbitrary since other measures to arrest the suspected person had not been exhausted – UN Human Rights Committee, 'Consideration of Reports Submitted by States Parties under Article 40 of the Covenant: Israel' (21 August 2003) UN Doc CCPR/CO/78/ISR, [15].

26 Guy S Goodwin-Gill and Jane McAdam, *The Refugee in International Law* (3rd edn, Oxford University Press 2011), 278; UNCLOS (n 22), Art 98.

27 HRW 'End Rohingya Pushbacks' (n 18).

the aim of the treaty.[28] This is further supported by the obligation to apply considerations of humanity as outlined in the *MV Saiga* case above.[29]

That said, the obligation to rescue persons in distress at sea is very much compromised by the lack of equally rigorous obligation with respect to the disembarkation of persons rescued at sea. States are obliged to 'cooperate and coordinate' to ensure that ships' masters are allowed to disembark rescued persons to a place of safety, irrespective of the nationality or status of those rescued, and with minimal disruption to the ship's planned itinerary (which implies that disembarkation should occur at the nearest coastal state). However, a refusal of disembarkation cannot be equated with a breach of non-refoulement, even though it may result in serious consequences.[30] Nonetheless, human rights law could be engaged where, for example, persons are subjected to protracted confinement to a vessel under deteriorating conditions. It has been suggested that in certain circumstances, this could compel a state with primary responsibility to accept disembarkation.[31]

3.2 *Non-Refoulement and Human Rights Law*

Notwithstanding the fact that the relevant states involved in the Andaman Sea migration 'crisis' are not bound by the 1951 Refugee Convention, Article 33 of the Refugee Convention, the prohibition of non-refoulement, is a customary norm.[32] This principle prohibits the expulsion of a refugee 'in any manner whatsoever to the frontiers of territories where his life or freedom would be threatened on account of his race, religion, nationality, membership of a particular social group or political opinion.'

---

28 Richard K Gardiner, *Treaty Interpretation* (Oxford University Press 2008) 190.

29 More generally, see Richard Barnes, 'Refugee Law at Sea' (2004) 53 International and Comparative Law Quarterly 47.

30 Goodwin-Gill and McAdam, *The Refugee in International Law* (n 26) 278.

31 Anne T Gallagher and Fiona David, *The International Law of Migrant Smuggling* (Cambridge University Press 2014) 456.

32 See e.g. Aoife Duffy, 'Expulsion to Face Torture? Non-Refoulement in International Law' (2008) 20(3) International Journal of Refugee Law 373, 383; Seline Trevisanut, 'The Principle of Non-Refoulement at Sea and the Effectiveness of Asylum Protection' in Armin von Bogdandy and Rüdiger Wolfrum, *Max Planck Yearbook of United Nations Law* (Brill 2008) 205-246, 215.

This provision also applies to asylum-seekers,[33] and applies extra-territorially.[34]

Goodwin-Gill and McAdam correctly argue that the simple denial of entry of ships to territorial waters cannot be equated with a breach of the principle of non-refoulement, which requires that state action have the effect or result of returning refugees to territories where their lives or freedoms would be in danger.[35] The key terms here are 'effect' and 'result', meaning that it is the outcome of the 'pushback' activities that will determine whether refoulement has occurred. It is argued here that the actions of the authorities on the Andaman Sea would not constitute refoulement. Although many of the refugees drowned, this was not 'on account of race, religion, nationality, membership of a particular social group or political opinion' as stipulated in the definition of refoulement, but rather because of the conditions at sea. In addition, the High Seas, to which they were sent, does not constitute the 'frontiers of territories', given that the High Seas are beyond the sovereignty of any one state,[36] and the nexus that exists between state sovereignty and territory.[37] This is distinguishable from the actual physical return of passengers to their country of origin, which would constitute refoulement.[38] However, if a pushback operation would leave refugees with no option but to return to their country of origin, or to a third state that would return them, this would constitute refoulement.[39] Those on board the vessels in the Anda-

33 UNHCR, 'Advisory Opinion on the Extraterritorial Application of Non-Refoulement Obligations under the 1951 Convention relating to the Status of Refugees and its 1976 Protocol' (26 January 2007) [6].

34 Mark Pallis, 'Obligations of States towards Asylum Seekers at Sea: Interactions and Conflicts Between Legal Regimes' (2002) 14(2, 3) International Journal of Refugee Law 329, 343.

35 Goodwin-Gill and McAdam, *The Refugee in International Law* (n 26) 277. This is supported by the convention's *travaux preparatoires*, which reads: '… the obligation not to return a refugee to a country where he was persecuted did not imply an obligation to admit him to the country where he seeks refuge. The return of a refugee-ship, for example, to the high seas could not be construed as a violation of this obligation.' See UN Economic and Social Council, 'UN Ad Hoc Committee on Statelessness and Related Problems, Comments of the Committee on the Draft Convention' (10 February 1950) UN Doc E/AC.32/L.32/Add.1, Comment on Draft Art 28 (expulsion to country of persecution).

36 UNCLOS (n 22) Art 89.

37 Pallis, 'Obligations of States towards Asylum Seekers at Sea' (n 34) 343.

38 *Hirsi Jamaa and others v Italy* App no 27765/09 (ECtHR, 23 February 2012).

39 Pallis, 'Obligations of States towards Asylum Seekers at Sea' (n 34) 349.

man Sea, were not able to reach any territory, as every state that they tried to reach attempted to push them back out to sea and those that eventually survived remained stranded until Malaysia and Indonesia agreed to allow them to come ashore as a temporary solution.

The ICCPR is also applicable to the situation in the Andaman Sea.[40] The most relevant rights in the ICCPR are Article 6, which protects the right to life; and Article 7, which prohibits cruel, inhuman or degrading treatment. Thailand and Indonesia are a party to the ICCPR, whereas Myanmar and Malaysia are not. However the latter states are also bound by these articles as they represent customary international law.[41]

These provisions may be applicable in two respects. First, there is a significant amount of jurisprudence setting out that where a state exercises control outside of its territory in a way that could have an impact on the enjoyment of human rights, that state is bound by human rights provisions.[42] There can be little doubt that interdiction of a ship which involves conduct such as boarding the vessel or pushback operations fall within this test.[43] Coercive actions that threaten or result in loss of life whether deliberate (such as the pushback of an unseaworthy vessel) or accidental would appear to be in violation of the positive obligation attached to the right to life in Article 6. Where migrants are subject to deteriorating conditions on board, pushback operations could also be a violation of Article 7. More controversially, read together with the provisions of the Law of the Sea as outlined above regarding the assistance of those in distress at sea, an argument could be made that Article 7 would be violated through the failure of a state that is in a position to come to the aid of migrants who are at risk of physical harm.[44] However, as the state would not be in effective control of the migrants, this chapter does not assert that Article 7 would be violated in such circumstances.

Secondly, there is an implied obligation of non-removal under the ICCPR which has been emphasised repeatedly by the Human Rights Com-

---

40 ICCPR (n 5).

41 UN Human Rights Committee, 'General Comment No. 24: General Comment on Issues Relating to Reservations Made Upon Ratification or Accession to the Covenant or the Optional Protocols thereto, or in Relation to Declarations Under Article 41 of the Covenant' (4 November 1994) CCPR/C/21/Rev.1/Add.6, [8].

42 See e.g. *Al-Jedda v United Kingdom*, App no 27021/08 (ECtHR, 7 July 2011); *Hirsi* (n 38).

43 Gallagher and David, *The International Law of Migrant Smuggling* (n 31) 471.

44 Pallis, 'Obligations of States towards Asylum Seekers at Sea' (n 34) 335.

mittee. In General Comment 31, the Committee stated that states are obliged:

> [...] not to extradite, deport, expel or otherwise remove a person from their territory [...] where there are substantial grounds for believing that there is a real risk of irreparable harm, such as that contemplated by articles 6 and 7 of the Covenant, either in the country to which removal is to be effected or in any country to which the person may subsequently be removed.[45]

The use of the phrase 'such as' implies that the non-removal obligation is not limited to violations of Article 6 and 7. It is argued that this non-removal obligation also applies to pushback operations conducted at sea. The underlying rationale of non-removal obligations as developed in numerous cases is that states cannot turn a blind eye to the consequences of their removal decisions where it exposes individuals to treatment in violation of international human rights norms. This is in line with the object and purpose of the ICCPR, which is inter alia to recognise "the inherent dignity and ... the equal and inalienable rights of all members of the human family." It is irrelevant that the quoted extract from General Comment 31 refers to removal from one territory to another (as opposed to removal from one area of the seas to another). The fact that the Human Rights Committee is primarily concerned with the potential harm at issue (rather than geographical location) is evident from the fact that the terms 'territory' and 'country' are used interchangeably to elaborate on the same principle, whereas the phrase 'real risk' is used consistently in its General Comment and jurisprudence.[46] Thus the proposition that a state can remove an individual to the High Seas to face terrible conditions and possibly death is permitted by international law is unsustainable, and moreover, highly undesirable, as it would create a dangerous loophole for states wishing to prevent aliens from entering their territory.

---

45 UN Human Rights Committee, 'General Comment No. 31: The Nature of the General Legal Obligation Imposed on States Parties to the Covenant' (29 March 2004) CCPR/C/21/Rev.1/Add. 13, [12].

46 UN Human Rights Committee, 'Kindler v Canada: Communication No 470/1991' (11 November 1993) UN Doc CCPR/C/48/D/470/1991.

4 Conclusion

The discussion in this brief chapter reveals that Articles 6 and 7 of the ICCPR have most probably been violated by the authorities of the states involved with respect to their pushback policies. The practical impact of the findings of this research suffers from many of the shortcomings of the system of international law as a whole, namely, the lack of enforcement at an international level. This is due to a general lack of standing of individuals in the international judicial system and the lack of regional human rights court in Asia. However, the arguments put forward in this piece can nonetheless be of valuable assistance to those who have been treated unlawfully by the Thai, Malaysian, and/or Indonesian authorities. First, the issue could be raised by individual states, the UN, and/or NGOs during Thailand, Indonesia or Malaysia's Universal Periodic Review before the Human Rights Council. Second, the arguments put forward in this piece can be employed at a domestic level. For states such as Indonesia and Thailand that operate a dualist legal system, the national legislature must 'transform' the international obligation into a rule of national law, and the national judge will then apply it as a rule of domestic law.[47] However, a domestic judge should interpret that domestic rule in accordance with its original source as an international instrument.[48] Third, the arguments put forward in this piece can be used to put diplomatic pressure on Indonesia, Malaysia, and Thailand to change their policies toward migrants at sea. By condemning their actions within the framework of international law, it puts significant weight behind the argument that these actions were wrong and should never be repeated. Finally, on a more general theoretical or epistemological level, the arguments put forward in this piece form part of the "remarkable revival" of the concept of human security.[49] Although the state remains the fundamental purveyor

47 Eileen Denza, 'The Relationship Between International and National Law' in Malcolm D Evans (ed.), *International Law* (2nd edn, Oxford University Press 2006), 429. It is unclear whether Indonesia operates a monist or dualist system, as its Constitution is silent on the matter. See Simon Butt, 'The Position of International Law within the Indonesian Legal System' (2014) 28(1) Emory International Law Review 1.

48 See the discussion of Lord Bingham in *Horvath v Secretary of State for the Home Department* [2000] UKHL 37 with regards to the 1951 Convention Relating to the Status of Refugees (n 4).

49 Amaratya Sen, 'Birth of a Discourse' in Mary Martin and Taylor Owen (eds.), *Routledge Handbook of Human Security* (Routledge 2014) 17.

of security, discussion surrounding the plight of those who flee by sea bolster the shift in attention from the security of the state to the security of people,[50] and thus provides a theoretical underpinning for legal accountability and enforcement.

50 Ibid. 27.

PART IV

Climate Change, Environmental Degradation and People on the Move

Just Relocation? Planned Relocation from Climate Change, Human Rights and Justice

Daniel Petz

1 Conceptualizing Planned Relocation

Statistics show that the number of disasters caused by natural hazards has been rising in recent decades and that many of those disasters have led to forced displacement. In 2015, more than 19 million persons affected by disasters were displaced by natural hazards, with an average of 26.4 million persons displaced every year since 2008.[1] Climate change is expected to exacerbate these human mobility impacts, by increasing the frequency and ferocity of hydro-meteorological sudden-onset disasters, exacerbating the negative effects of disasters, as well as through direct climate change impacts, eroding the habitability of certain areas through slow-onset effects such as sea-level rise, salinization and desertification.[2] Larger numbers of displaced persons are likely to be only one of the consequences of climate change. Research shows that it will also have other human mobility impacts in terms of changing scope and patterns of migration, creating the need for governments and other actors to support individuals and communities to relocate.[3] The international community has acknowledged the challenges that climate change poses for human mobility, particularly through a call to enhance action on adaption under the Cancun Adaptation Framework:

---

1 See Internal Displacement Monitoring Centre and Norwegian Refugee Council, 'People Displaced by Disasters: Global Estimates for 2015' (Internal Displacement Monitoring Centre and Norwegian Refugee Council 2015).

2 See Christopher B Field and others (eds.), 'Managing the Risks of Extreme Events and Disasters to Advance Climate Change Adaptation: A Special Report of Working Groups I and II of the Intergovernmental Panel on Climate Change' (Intergovernmental Panel on Climate Change, Cambridge University Press 2012). See also Walter Kälin, 'Conceptualising Climate-Induced Displacement' in Jane McAdam (ed.), *Climate Change and Displacement: Multidisciplinary Perspectives* (Hart Publishing Ltd 2010).

3 See United Kingdom Government Office for Science, 'Foresight: Migration and Global Environmental Change' (Final Project Report, Government Office for Science 2011). See also Alex De Sherbinin and others, 'Preparing for Resettlement Associated with Climate Change' (2011) 334(6055) Science 456.

Salomon, Heschl, *et al.* (eds.), *Blurring Boundaries: Human Security and Forced Migration*
 ISBN 978-90-04-32686-6. pp. 137-160.

> The Conference of Parties [...] invites all Parties to enhance action on adaptation under the Cancun Adaptation Framework, taking into account their common but differentiated responsibilities and respective capabilities, and specific national and regional development priorities, objectives and circumstances, by undertaking, inter alia, the following:
> [...]
> (f) Measures to enhance understanding, coordination and cooperation with regard to climate change induced displacement, migration and planned relocation, where appropriate, at the national, regional and international levels.[4]

As can be seen, the framework conceptualizes human mobility in terms of displacement, migration and planned relocation and as a form of climate change adaptation. It further can be interpreted to encourage States to engage more closely with issues of human mobility connected to climate change. So what is the difference between planned relocation and the other forms of human mobility? To answer this question, let me look at one recent definition of planned relocation. The 'Guidance on Protecting People from Disasters and Environmental Change through Planned Relocation' (in the following: 'Guidance') defines planned relocation as:

> A planned process in which persons or groups of persons move or are assisted to move away from their homes or places of temporary residence, are settled in a new location, and provided with the conditions for rebuilding their lives. Planned Relocation is carried out under the authority of the State, takes place within national borders, and is undertaken to protect people from risks and impacts related to disasters and environmental change, including the effects of climate change. Such Planned Relocation may be carried out at the individual, household, and/or community levels.[5]

4 UN Framework Convention on Climate Change, 'Report of the Conference of the Parties on its Sixteenth Session, held in Cancun from 29 November to 10 December 2010' (UNFCCC 15 March 2011) FCCC/CP/2010/7/Add.1:4.

5 Brookings Institution and others, 'Guidance on Protecting People from Disasters and Environmental Change through Planned Relocations' (Brookings Institution, Georgetown University, UNHCR 2015) 5.

The conceptual distinction between planned relocation and displacement is not easy. Standard definitions of displacement highlight the element of coercion.[6] While planned relocation from climate change involves at least an element of coercion caused by climate impacts, it is yet debated if people, who are subject to planned relocation, are also displaced, particularly in situations where communities voluntarily choose to relocate.[7] In regards to differentiate planned relocation from migration, one can first argue with the element of coercion, which is absent in some definitions of migration. Second, the large role of State authorities in the planned relocation process might also be a distinction to the common conceptualization of labor migration.[8] While a clear definitional boundary from other terms of human mobility is not clear-cut, it seems nonetheless sensible to conceptualize planned relocation as distinct from migration and displacement, as it poses a distinct set

6 The Guiding Principles on Internal Displacement – UN Office for the Coordination of Humanitarian Affairs, 'Guiding Principles on Internal Displacement' (United Nations Publications 1998) E/CN.4/1998/53/Add.2.1 – define the term internally displaced person as: "Internally displaced persons are persons or groups of persons who have been forced or obliged to flee or to leave their homes or places of habitual residence, in particular as a result of or in order to avoid the effects of armed conflict, situations of generalized violence, violations of human rights or natural or human-made disasters, and who have not crossed an internationally recognized State border."

7 For a more detailed discussion see Jane McAdam and Elizabeth Ferris, 'Planned Relocations in the Context of Climate Change: Unpacking the Legal and Conceptual Issues' (2015) 4(1) Cambridge Journal of International and Comparative Law 143.

8 There are many definitions of migration. The Foresight Report on Migration and Global Environmental Change (n 3, 35) defines migration and displacement as: "[…] the term 'migrant' or 'migration' […] refer[s] to individuals who have changed their place of residence either by crossing an international border […] or by moving within their country of origin to another region, district or municipality […]. People are normally considered to be 'migrants' if they remain outside their original place of residence for a period of at least 3 months. Displacement is a particular form of migration, in which individuals are forced to move against their will." This is a very broad definition of migration. UNESCO based on the UN Commission on Human Rights – UN Commission of Human Rights, 'Measures to Improve the Situation and Ensure the Human Rights and Dignity of all Migrant Workers' (UNHCR 1998) E/CN.4/1998/76 – provides a definition of migrant that highlights the elements of voluntariness and missing coercion as part of the definition of migrant: "The term 'migrant' […] should be understood as covering all cases where the decision to migrate is taken freely by the individual concerned, for reasons of 'personal convenience' and without intervention of an external compelling factor."

of challenges in regards to the relation and interaction between State authorities and affected persons and groups.

This inquiry will use the 'Guidance' definition provided above when discussing planned relocation. This has a number of reasons. First, it is one of the most fitting and comprehensive definitions currently available and second, as will be discussed in the following, it makes sense in terms of coherence to use this particular definition.

A number of specifics about the 'Guidance' definition have to be pointed out before proceeding. First, it defines planned relocation only as taking place within national borders and under the authority of the State. While it is likely that most cases of planned relocation will take place within the borders of a country,[9] there clearly is a case to be made that planned relocation could also take place between countries. Given extra layers of complexity in terms of possible international relocation in terms of international law, politics, coordination or logistics, it seems a viable step to conceptualize the term planned relocation in terms of in-country relocation at this stage. Second, the definition does not only focus on climate change, but also on disasters and environmental change. I think this step is also sensitive, given the frequent overlap of these three causes in terms of triggering planned relocation and the difficulties we still face in clearly attributing single disasters to climate change. Third, the definition leaves very broad space in terms of determining the scope of planned relocations, including relocations of either individual, household and/or community levels, which makes sense given the many shapes that planned relocation has taken in the past.[10]

One major distinction regarding planned relocation needs to be made in terms of at which point in time relocation takes place. While the distinction is often not clear-cut, one can distinguish two major modes of planned relocation: one in anticipation of disasters or climate change impacts, for example, as a pre-emptive response to rising sea levels, the other one in response to disaster or climate change impacts often when people cannot safely return to their previous homes or places of resi-

9 This follows assessment about migration from environmental change and displacement from climate change. See United Kingdom Government Office for Science, 'Foresight' (n 3) 37; McAdam and Ferris, 'Planned Relocations' (n 7) 142.

10 See Daniel Petz, 'Planned Relocations in the Context of Natural Disasters and Climate Change. A Review of the Literature' (Brookings-LSE Project on Internal Displacement 2015) for a review of case studies literature on planned relocation.

dence.[11] This paper will use the terms 'anticipatory' and 'reactive' relocation to distinguish between these forms of planned relocation.

2 Exploring some of the Challenges to Planned Relocation

Planned relocation, while not necessarily used in this exact terminology, is not a new phenomenon, as governments in many countries have relocated at-risk populations before. Only in recent years has it begun to be framed in terms of climate change adaptation.[12]

While, given the relatively small amount of research on planned relocation there is no conclusive evidence about the long-term outcomes of planned relocation (particularly when discussed in terms of climate change), there is enough evidence to claim that planned relocation is problematic in terms of the human rights of affected persons. The IPCC states that "most practice to date, learning from other resettlement programs, demonstrates negative social outcomes for those resettled, often analyzed as breaches in individual human rights."[13] Evidence from the development-induced displacement and resettlement (DIDR) literature based on millions of people who have been resettled because of development projects and which have many similarities with planned relocation from climate change, shows a large number of negative consequences for resettled persons and communities. These consequences are described and discussed in detail in Cernea's Impoverishment Risk and Reconstruction model, which identifies the common risks as landlessness, joblessness, homelessness, marginalization, food insecurity, increased morbidity and mortality, loss of access to common property, and social

11 E.g. Robin Bronen, 'Climate-Induced Community Relocations: Creating an Adaptive Governance Framework Based in Human Rights Doctrine' (2011) 35 NYU Review of Law & Social Change 357. For the case of Typhoon Haiyan see Alice R Thomas, 'Resettlement in the Wake of Typhoon Hayian in the Philippines: A Strategy to Mitigate Risk or a Risky Strategy?' (Brookings-LSE Project on Internal Displacement 2015).

12 See Petz, 'Planned Relocations' (n 10).

13 Christopher B Field and others (eds.), 'Climate Change 2014: Impacts, Adaptation, and Vulnerability. Part A: Global and Sectoral Aspects. Contribution of Working Group II to the Fifth Assessment Report of the Intergovernmental Panel on Climate Change' (Intergovernmental Panel on Climate Change, Cambridge University Press 2014) 771.

disintegration.[14] While a number of issues differ between planned relocation and DIDR, such as, particularly in terms of climate change, questions of at what time planned relocation should take place and likely different sources of funding, both areas share a number of contentious issues like questions of compensation, access to land, employment and livelihoods, and relations with host communities.[15]

A recent literature review of the case studies literature on planned relocation provides a glimpse on what researchers and affected communities see as problematic in regards to planned relocation.[16] A first set of issues is about the politics of planned relocation, emphasizing that planned relocations cannot be simple seen as a technical issue. In several cases, planned relocation is seen by affected persons as connected to previous relocation and/or resettlement attempts. Past experiences with or narratives of resettlement can be seen as precedents for people seeing authorities acting in good faith, really focusing on protecting lives and reducing risk or seeing relocation tied to ulterior political and economic

14 Michael M Cernea, 'Compensation and Investment in Resettlement: Theory, Practice, Pitfalls, and Needed Policy Reform' in Michael M Cernea and Hari M Mathur (eds.), *Can Compensation Prevent Impoverishment?* (Oxford University 2009); Michael M Cernea, 'Impoverishment Risks, Safeguards, and Reconstruction: A Model for Population Displacement and Resettlement' in Michael M Cernea (ed.), *Risk and Reconstruction: Experiences of Resettlers and Refugees* (World Bank 2000). See also Anthony Oliver-Smith (ed.), *Development & Dispossession: The Crisis of Forced Displacement and Resettlement* (School for Advanced Research Press 2009) for a broad discussion of these challenges.

15 Other major differences are that while DIDR projects are undertaken by private entities in planned relocation State authorities are likely responsible for planned relocation. As many DIDR projects are for-profit ventures there is also the likelihood that funds will be scarcer for planned relocations. Planned relocation (particularly reactive) will also take place on different time scales than DIDR projects, leaving less time for detailed planning. For additional discussion on the differences see UNHCR, Brookings Institution and Georgetown University, 'Planned Relocations, Disasters and Climate Change: Consolidating Good Practices and Preparing for the Future' (Background Document, Sanremo Consultation, 12-14 March 2014); Daniel Petz, 'Operational Guidance and Frameworks Relevant to Planned Relocations Caused by Natural Hazards, Environmental Change, and Climate Change' (Brookings-LSE Project on Internal Displacement 2015) 22.

16 Petz, 'Planned Relocations' (n 10).

motives. In addition, the debate is often also framed in terms of elite or scientific knowledge versus local knowledge.[17]

Another set of research studies focuses on legal and political issues. Particularly prevalent in case studies about planned relocation in the developed world, they concern themselves mainly on how government structures can assist relocated persons and how legal and policy gaps can be addressed, with land- and property rights being a frequently addressed sub-issue.

Human rights issues are also prevalent in research about planned relocation, with research focusing on which rights are impacted by planned relocations and if and how international human rights law and frameworks can assist with minimizing the possible negative effects of planned relocation.

Another set of issues concerns planning and technical issues. In terms of anticipatory relocations, questions of community participation get more importance, as on average those cases have a longer planning horizon, while case studies on reactive relocation often have an evaluative character, identifying good practices and problematic areas. The main areas of analysis are participation of the affected population, as well as planning and execution (housing, land and property, livelihood, etc.) of the relocation process. Other issues of importance in the literature are socio-cultural aspects of planned relocation. Existing literature shows that planned relocations can have severe impacts on the social fabric of families and communities, particular if socio-cultural issues are not taken into account in the planning process, with those effects often compounded by changes in livelihoods.[18]

3 Planned Relocation and a Human Rights-Based Approach (HRBA)

There are many ways of conceptualizing human rights, among others, in terms of their philosophical foundations, as a frame of analysis, in terms of their status as international or domestic legal rights, and in

---

17 Jane McAdam, 'Relocation and Resettlement from Colonisation to Climate Change: The Perennial Solution to "Danger Zones"' (2015) 3(1) London Review of International Law 93 provides a good overview about some of the historical conceptual and political debates in regards to relocation and resettlement.

18 Petz, 'Planned Relocations' (n 10) 8.

terms of their operationalization through a rights-based approach. This contribution focuses on a rights-based approach. Given the numerous risks of violations of rights planned relocations pose for affected persons, this paper looks at one recent international attempt to devise human rights-based guidance on planned relocation. Before analyzing the guidance document based on a number of critical issues for planned relocation, first, merits and problems of rights-based approaches are discussed. It is argued that notwithstanding some challenges, a rights-based frame and approach are likely to be helpful in minimizing negative effects of planned relocation.

The human rights-based approach has grown out of shortcomings of the pre-eminent needs-based approach that was used by international development and humanitarian actors after World War II and has been promoted and mainstreamed by the United Nations (UN) since the late 1990's as part of its reform agenda. In a needs-based approach people were often seen as passive recipients of aid and assistance, lacking agency and it was also often identified with a lack of identification of duty – bearers for needs – fulfillment. A shift from needs to rights led to an important change of perspective, while needs can be fulfilled through charity, rights are based on legal and moral obligations, as rights claims are addressed to certain identifiable duty-bearers. Moreover, the rights-perspective furthers people's agency making them active participants in the process, thereby empowering them in the process.[19] With the UN as one of the leading proponents of such an approach, the orientation of the HRBA focuses on international human rights treaties and conventions. These treaties and conventions are the cornerstones within a rather broad array of different interpretations and implementations of the HRBA.

Facing the impacts of climate change, a HRBA, based on the normative strength of human rights can particularly help in providing a comprehensive framework for dealing with human mobility issues.[20] It allows for a clear conceptualization of different vulnerabilities based on cultural, social, economic or any other status and focuses on the agency of affected persons. Gromilova highlights that the Office of the High Commissioner of Human Rights in 2009 "has called for increased State action on adaptation and has emphasized the importance of applying

19 For a discussion, see e.g. Urban Jonsson, *Human Rights Approach to Development Programming* (UNICEF 2003).

20 They can provide guidance in both humanitarian crisis as well as in regards to more long-term, developmental processes.

a human rights-based approach in guiding policies and measures of climate change mitigation and adaptation."[21]

While, as discussed, a HRBA has a number of merits, the approach also faces some challenges.[22] First, particularly among non-democratic countries human rights-language is often viewed critically and at times connected to the possible interference into the sovereignty of States.[23] Second, even for the most developed countries in the world the fulfillment of their human rights obligations has proven to be difficult.[24] There might therefore be an argument to be made that a HRBA is overly demanding, particularly for less developed countries. Third, a HRBA could also be affected by some general criticisms of human rights, such as doubts on their universality, particularly regarding cultural specifics, or the claim that they are too individualistic and do not sufficiently represent group rights. Fourth, there is the problem of conflicts of rights, e.g. there might be either disagreement of which right or group of rights has priority in a genuine conflict of rights (for example socio-economic vs. political rights) or different persons and groups might disagree on which rights are more important (for example relocated persons vs. State).[25]

---

21 Mariya Gromilova, 'Revisiting Planned Relocation as a Climate Change Adaptation Strategy: The Added Value of a Human Rights-Based Approach' (2014) 10(1) Utrecht Law Review, 76, 91. As a more recent example of the importance that the United Nations gives a rights-based approach is the 'Rights up Front' Initiative, which was launched by the Secretary General of the United Nations in 2013. It aims at making human rights and the protection of civilians a system-wide core responsibility of the UN System. See United Nations, '"Human Rights up Front" Initiative' (*Secretary-General Ban Ki-Moon*, 2014) <www.un.org/sg/humanrightsupfront/>.

22 For a detailed debate on some of the criticisms towards human rights see Peter Jones, *Rights* (Palgrave Macmillan 1994).

23 The case of Typhoon Nargis and Myanmar might count as an example. See e.g. Alan Collins, *Building a People-Oriented Security Community the ASEAN Way* (Routledge 2003); Julie Belanger and Richard Horsey, 'Negotiating Humanitarian Access to Cyclone-Affected Areas of Myanmar: a Review' (2008) 41 Humanitarian Exchange 2.

24 In terms of human rights law, not all countries have ratified all UN conventions. Further there are regional and national differences in applying human rights law.

25 See e.g. Roger Zetter and James Morrissey, 'Environmental Stress, Displacement and the Challenge of Rights Protection' (2014) 45 Forced Migration Review 67, who for the case of resettlement in Vietnam highlight that while the government focuses on the restoration of the economic basis of the resettled population, the more political rights regarding participation and decision-making of relocated persons are not addressed.

While this paper lacks the space to comprehensively argue each point, I nonetheless want to comment on a number of them. Regarding the first point, while some countries are critical towards human rights language, the fact remains that almost all countries have signed and ratified at least a number of human rights treaties and conventions.[26] Further, a rights-based approach clearly states that the main responsibility of protecting human rights lies with the affected State. While the approach implores States to seek outside assistance, particularly if their capacities are insufficient, it does not promote coerced intervention except in cases of genocide and egregious human rights violations.[27] It is highly unlikely that these questions will ever arise in regards to planned relocation.

For the issue of over demandingness particularly in terms of a HRBA one can see the approach as aspiring and action-guiding. This means that, while given the complex challenges of a planned relocation, it is unlikely that all human rights can be fulfilled, the authorities organizing a planned relocation should at least aspire to fulfill as many rights as possible. By conceptualizing the process through a human rights lens, they are hopefully able to guarantee more human rights than without having used a rights-based approach. A HRBA can be seen, to a certain extent, quite similar as the concept of disaster risk reduction, as by using the approach actors reduces the risk of rights violations. One might be enticed to call the approach 'human rights violation risk reduction' to highlight this similarity.

There has been a wide debate about the third point in regards to cultural relativity and also the question of group rights, with some critique of human rights as supporting values coming from a particular Western tradition that are not suitable for other cultures.[28] Nonetheless, in arguing for human rights in regards to disaster risk management, there

26 E.g. the International Covenant on Civil and Political Rights has currently 168 State Parties and 7 signatories, while the International Covenant on Economic, Social and Cultural Rights has 164 State Parties and 6 signatories. Data from Office of the High Commissioner for Human Rights, 'Status of Ratification Interactive Dashboard' (*United Nations, Human Rights*, 1996-2014) <http://indicators.ohchr.org/> accessed 17 November 2015.

27 For a discussion of the issue see Cecil A J Coady, *The Ethics of Armed Humanitarian Intervention* (Peaceworks, United States Institute of Peace 2002).

28 See e.g. Jack Donnelly, 'Cultural Relativism and Human Rights' (1984) 6(4) Human Rights Quarterly 400; Michael C Davis, 'Constitutionalism and Political Culture: The Debate over Human Rights and Asian Values' (1998) 11 Harvard Human Rights Journal 109.

seem few issues that might be that contentious to override the basic usefulness of a HRBA.[29]

The fourth argument regarding rights-conflicts is indeed a difficult challenge. Still, without a HRBA we might not even realize that there are conflicting rights and cannot try to resolve such conflicts in the sphere of the political. I would see it as a particular advantage of a HRBA that it can make such conflicts visible and engage the affected persons in having a stake and say in resolving such rights conflicts. In planned relocation scenarios risks to the right to life or health are often pitted versus risks to a whole range of other rights. There is however not a patented way to resolve these possible conflicts once and for all for all possible cases – which further points towards the importance of case-to-case solutions based on inclusive dialogue of all impacted actors.

One way in which international actors have engaged with States and other actors involved in humanitarian and/or development to promote a HRBA was through the development of human-rights based guidance documents. Those documents, on the one hand, provide affected persons and their advocates with knowledge about human rights and their possible application in certain situations/fields and on the other hand engage States in developing laws, policies and projects based on human rights obligations and/or human rights considerations. One successful example for such a guidance are the UN Guiding Principles on Internal Displacement[30] which are a collection of the human rights of persons who are displaced within their own country or country of residence based on international human rights law. The principles provide an important frame through which questions on internal displacement are discussed globally and have been incorporated into national laws and policies as well as into regional conventions (the African Union's Kampala Convention).[31]

Not dissimilar to the Guiding Principles, the 'Guidance on Protecting People from Disasters and Environmental Change through Planned Relocation' was developed as the outcome of a multi-year consultative process including representatives of States, international organizations

29 See e.g. Alan J Milne, *Human Rights and Human Diversity* (Palgrave Macmillan 1986), for some of the discussions.

30 UN Office for the Coordination of Humanitarian Affairs, 'Guiding Principles' (n 6).

31 Another example for rights-based guidance are the Guiding Principles on Business and Human Rights, which were endorsed by the UN Human Rights council in 2011.

and experts from a wide range of disciplines.[32] It was based on a wide array of background research, including an analysis of more than 30 guidance documents (most of which focusing on rights-based guidance) from related fields such as displacement, development-induced displacement and resettlement, evacuations, evictions, land, housing and property rights issues. The research showed that while many of those documents had something valuable to say in terms of planned relocation, no guidance existed that focused entirely and comprehensively on planned relocation and climate change issues.[33] There has also been a blind-spot or reluctance of States to engage with the issue of planned relocation, which likely at least in part has to do with the many risks and difficulties connected to planned relocation. An analysis of National Adaptation Plans of Action from Pacific countries for example shows that there are almost no references to planned relocation in regards to climate change adaptation.[34] Other research shows the difficulties that the United States, one of the most affluent countries in the world, faces in coordinating and funding the relocation of indigenous communities in Alaska.[35] Given that planned relocation is very likely to be inevitable in a large number of countries if sea-level rise projections are correct, it might not bode well if States are not prepared to face the many challenges of planned relocation. Human rights-based guidance might therefore provide important input for State and non-state actors in regards to planned relocation.

4 The 'Guidance on Protecting People from Disasters and Environmental Change through Planned Relocation'

Having discussed the merits and challenges of a HRBA in the previous section, this section takes a closer look at the Guidance. The first aim is to see how the authors of the Guidance apply a rights-based approach as

32 Disclosure: The author of this paper was involved as an expert in the drafting process of the Guidance.

33 For a discussion see Petz, 'Operational Guidance' (n 15).

34 Daniel Petz, 'Neglected Displacement: Human Mobility in Pacific Disaster Risk Management and Climate Change Adaptation Mechanisms' (Internal Displacement Monitoring Centre and Norwegian Refugee Council 2013).

35 Bronen, 'Climate-Induced Community Relocations' (n 11); Julie K Maldonado and others, 'The Impact of Climate Change on Tribal Communities in the U.S.: Displacement, Relocation, and Human Rights' (2013) 120 Climatic Change 601.

the normative framework in the Guidance. I will discuss this by looking at how the Guidance ascribes rights and duties to different actors engaged in the planned relocation process, followed by a discussion how it fares in regards to some of the strengths and weaknesses of a HRBA. This will be followed by a discussion on if and how the Guidance applies a justice-based approach and if a justice-based approach would provide some added benefit to rights-based guidance on planned relocation.

Fully in line with being a rights-based guidance, the document highlights in its overarching principles that States have the primary responsibility to respect, protect and fulfill the rights of people within their territory and that in some cases these responsibilities might require planned relocation in order to protect persons or groups.[36] It further notes that States need to have "compelling reasons, robust evidence, and a sound legal basis for undertaking planned relocation".[37] While States carry the main responsibility, the Guidance acknowledges that likely not all States will be able nor should undertake planned relocation on their own, highlighting that "States will normally need, and should accept, support and assistance from other actors throughout a Planned Relocation."[38] After pointing out the main responsibility, the Guidance develops a whole set of points on how States should develop comprehensive legal and policy frameworks for planned relocation.[39] They also should provide the basis for when the States' involvement and authority over a planned relocation has ended.[40] The Guidance further discusses a whole range of obligations of States throughout the process of planned relocation. For example

36 Brookings Institution and others, 'Guidance' (n 5) §6.

37 Ibid. §7.

38 "Such actors may include other States; regional bodies; inter-governmental organizations; development banks; funders/funding mechanisms; community leaders; the private sectors; and other experts.", ibid. §26.

39 As noted in McAdam and Ferris, 'Planned Relocations' (n 7) 159, planned relocation is likely to have impacts on a wide range of laws and policies. "Since relocation has implications for a whole range of rights – civil, political, economic, social and cultural – it necessarily concerns a wide range of domestic laws relating to such apparently disparate issues as land, housing, property, insurance, employment, anti-discrimination, minorities, restitution, and so on. Laws relating to evictions, for instance, may be highly relevant."

40 In regards to this question the Guidance notes that planned relocation ends when "Relocated Persons no longer have needs or vulnerabilities related to the Planned Relocation and can enjoy their rights at least at the same level as pre-Planned Relocation, before the impacts of disaster sand environmental change affected

in regards to livelihood restoration, which often plays a crucial part in determining the success of planned relocation, the Guidance highlights the need to provide adequate support, resources and services to address the main impoverishment risks associated with settlement.[41]

As can be seen from these parts of the Guidance, the document lays a lot of emphasis on the duties of the State as the main duty-bearer for the planned relocation process. Still, it encourages the State to seek support with the planned relocation from other actors, if necessary. It discusses the role of the State comprehensively, in that it discusses the entire relocation process from the risk assessment, the development of laws, policies and institutions, technical details within the relocation process such as compensation and livelihood restoration, as well as questions of monitoring and evaluation.

Aside from the State, at-risk or affected persons and groups feature prominently in the Guidance. Here, it also follows important premises of a rights-based approach, which seeks to engage affected persons as active and participative actors within the relocation process and also comprehensively speaks out to protect the rights of those affected. To that respect, one important cross-cutting statement of the Guidance is that planned relocations should be undertaken for the benefit of relocated persons and in a manner that respects and protects their rights and dignity.[42] Further, the Guidance states in its overarching principles that planned relocation should be carried out within a rights-based framework that "safeguards both individual and collective civil, political, economic, social, and cultural rights of relocated persons and other affected persons throughout all phases."

The Guidance pays detailed attention to the question of participation in all stages of the relocation process, from deciding if and when a planned relocation is necessary to issues of livelihood restoration.[43] It

---

the enjoyment of such rights, and at a level that is at least equal to that of Host Populations" – Brookings Institution and others, 'Guidance' (n 5) §57.

41 Based for example on "landlessness, joblessness, homelessness, marginalization, food insecurity, morbidity and mortality, loss of access to common property and services and social and cultural disarticulation", ibid. §42.

42 Ibid. §5.

43 E.g., concerning when a planned relocation is necessary, the Guidance suggests a number of steps that should be taken to determine when planned relocation is needed, all of which ascribe a participatory process between the State and affected persons. Here, it notes that the decision for planned relocation should be based on a participatory analysis of certain factors that involves both persons

further highlights that the agency, resilience and empowerment of those relocated should be recognized, promoted and enhanced.[44] Part of a participatory process of planned relocation is the provision of mechanisms to address grievances, as well as the provision of conflict resolution and redress mechanisms.[45]

Another important principle of the HRBA is a special focus on those who are particularly vulnerable because they are the most likely victims of rights violations throughout the relocation process. The Guidance takes this into account by highlighting that the specific needs, circumstances and vulnerabilities of those affected by planned relocation based on a broad range of criteria should be taken into consideration during all stages of the planned relocation.[46]

In laying out the rights of those affected by the planned relocation, the Guidance differentiates between different groups which are impacted differently during the relocation process. These are the persons that are actually relocated, host communities, those who choose not to take part in planned relocation and persons who live in close proximity.[47] As those different groups might be differently affected by the planned relocation process the Guidance takes the position that they should be therefore entitled to different degrees of support, protection, but also participation, which according to a rights-based approach can be argued for in terms of differentiated vulnerabilities.[48]

---

that live in the area considered for planned relocation and the State and could be initiated by either of those actors. It also notes that those affected have the right to request a risk assessment and/or have the right to undertake a risk assessment and risk monitoring by themselves and inform State based structures through those activities. See ibid. §28-30 for more details.

44 Ibid. §13.

45 Ibid. §27.

46 Ibid. §14. While the Guidance does not discuss questions of vulnerable groups in detail in each section, there are a number of other, more specific provisions regarding certain persons and groups, like persons without formal land titles or indigenous communities.

47 The latter three at times referred to as 'other affected persons'.

48 The differentiation can for example be seen in regards to socio-economic rights or in on how much planned relocation can impact the socio-economic status of relocated persons, host communities and other affected persons. Here, the Guidance notes that planned relocation should improve, but at least at a minimum restore the living standards of relocated persons. For host communities they should at least maintain their pre-existing standard or attain the standard of relocated persons, depending on which is higher.

As the previous paragraphs have shown, the Guidance does not only address the State and those persons or groups that are relocated, but also considers the rights of host communities and even other persons and groups that are affected by the relocation. It points out that regarding to different categories of persons States might have different obligations throughout the relocation process, based on how the planned relocation impacts the rights of each of those categories of persons. The Guidance however focuses almost exclusively on the State's obligations, while leaving out possible duties of affected persons in the process. It addresses this point in the preamble, noting that:

> While this Guidance focuses on the obligations of States, it is important to recognize that individuals, households, and communities have responsibilities as well. They may be primary agents initiating Planned Relocation, and should be provided with the latitude to take charge of decisions and the process.[49]

While some more detailed discussion on obligations of affected persons might have certainly enriched the document, it is within the tradition of rights-based guidance that those documents are mainly addressed towards the State, as the State has the primary responsibility to uphold human rights and is therefore the main duty-bearer. Moreover, the definition of the relevant duties or responsibilities of affected persons should probably be part of the political process surrounding the development of laws, policies and plans for planned relocation because than those responsibilities can be tailored to the problem at hand. Human rights documents have largely refrained from formulating duties of individuals as there is open debate if such duties exist and/or about what those duties would entail (one notable exception is the 1981 African (Banjul) Charter on Human and People's Rights) and therefore one can argue that the Guidance stays within the mainstream of rights-based documents by leaving out that discussion.[50]

In respect to how detailed the Guidance discusses rights and duties a close reading of the document shows a certain vagueness in a number of areas. One could contest that this weakens the document as a rights-based guidance. A contrary opinion though could state that by laying out

---

49 Brookings Institution and others, 'Guidance' (n 5) 6.

50 It is debatable if citizens have duties. See e.g. Dimitry Kochenov, 'EU Citizenship Without Duties' (2014) 20(4) European Law Journal 482.

more general principles and suggestions, the document provides guidance on the one hand, while on the other hand allowing enough space for States and affected people to tailor the process to local needs and circumstances (and to allow for a political process to decide on the specific criteria). As can also be seen with the detailed discussion of legal, policy and institutional frameworks, the Guidance puts a strong focus on the development of the right procedural enabling environment for planned relocation based on human rights obligations, rather than prescribing ready-made solutions. Given the inherent complexity in planned relocation, as well as sensitivities regarding human rights approaches, this paper is critical that such a paternalistic approach based on ready-made solutions could succeed.

Further, in terms of comprehensiveness, one might argue that the Guidance is not very explicit in regards to the protection of rights of vulnerable groups. While it highlights them clearly among the overarching principles, there are only few provisions regarding rights protection for specific persons or groups based on vulnerabilities throughout the document. Here, likely the goal to keep the document short and legible collided with the goal to highlight this issue stronger. To address this issue, the authors are planning to develop more operational guidance based on real-world examples and best practices, which would allow discussing these issues in the amount of detail they deserve.

On the question of demandingness, already discussed earlier, the Guidance does not demand anything from States that is not based on already existing international human rights obligations. While also advocating for the implementation of specific redress mechanisms, the Guidance is a proactive instrument in terms of preventing human rights violations before they occur. It further takes a clear normative stance that States should seek assistance from other actors, if needed.

5 Is a Justice Perspective Complementing a Rights-Based Approach to Planned Relocation?

While there is an emerging human rights discourse surrounding planned relocation, questions of justice regarding planned relocation have so far received relatively little systematic attention. Justice considerations however might be important when conceptualizing and implementing planned relocations. Next, and possibly even complementary, to a human rights perspective, a justice perspective can provide important inputs. I particularly want to look at issues of distributive justice.[51]

Theories of distributive justice concern themselves with the question what a just distribution of a certain currency (resources, capabilities, welfare) is and which distributive rules it should follow. While I do not have the space to develop a comprehensive theory of distributive justice in this paper, it is, in my view of interest to raise a number of distributive justice issues that are posed by planned relocation. Let me start with considering a quote by McAdam and Ferris, who are one of the few authors writing about planned relocation and climate change that directly allude to (distributive) justice, noting that planned relocations also raise questions of justice:

> Finally, planned relocation is an issue of justice. Those who are able to migrate will likely do so before the situation becomes desperate, while those without the necessary financial or social means will be dependent on governmental assistance to support their relocation. If that is not forthcoming, then they will be stuck.[52]

As this quote alludes, moving out of the way will be easier for those who have enough means rather than for the less and least well-off, who might even get stuck without outside assistance. Even if we do not assume that the majority of those relocated will be the less or least well-off, planned relocation poses a number of distributive justice issues. Key among the questions is to what level of a metric of justice (well-being, wealth, resources, capabilities, etc.) those relocated are entitled to and how that level relates to the entitlements of other persons or groups (those left behind, host communities, the wider population). The positions to this question could range from 'nothing much as relocated persons should be happy that they receive some help and survive' to 'they should be much better off after the relocation'.[53] Most persons (and most philosophers too, no matter if following egalitarian, prioritarian or sufficientarian

---

51 There are also issues of intergenerational justice that are worthy discussing surrounding the issue of planned relocation, but have to be left out due to space constraints.

52 McAdam and Ferris, 'Planned Relocations' (n 7) 166.

53 On the other side of the scale of justice one might argue about the question whether people who are sufficiently wealthy and live in coastal areas should be entitled to assistance regarding relocation (for example in the case an entire community is

conceptions)[54] would intuitively subscribe to some notion that people should at least be entitled to certain minimum standards and if they are not well off or even among the least well-off that they should be entitled to an improvement of their conditions or at the very least not be worse off than before. While those principles are easy to defend under ideal circumstances, once we get to real relocation cases it might be more difficult to fulfill circumstances of justice as those responsible for planned relocation might have to deal with limited resources which might not allow for fulfilling such ideals for everybody involved in the relocation process. Nonetheless, this is not a reason to discard discussion about justice, because the setting of standards based on considerations of justice might set important benchmarks for the relocation process and a process based on justice considerations might also have a larger chance of success than one that does not take such considerations in concern. As this paper discusses rights-based guidance to planned relocation it might be interesting to see if and if yes how the Guidance incorporates issues of distributive justice.

While the Guidance does not explicitly use justice-based language, it deals with issues of distributive justice. For example §44 of the Relocation Guidelines points out that "States should ensure at a minimum the restoration, but ideally the improvement of livelihoods of relocated persons".[55] The Guidance further highlights that States need to provide adequate support, resources and services to address the main impoverishment risks associated with settlement.[56] Part of the

relocated), here it is questionable if a government would find it reasonable to pay fully for the relocation of villas of very wealthy people.

54 Egalitarians in regards to distributive justice usually subscribe to measures that at least foster more equality in distribution. Prioritarians support the principle that those worse off should profit more from a distributive scheme than those already well off. Sufficientarians believe that those below the threshold of sufficiency should have strong priority until they reach the threshold and that priority ends once the threshold is reached. See e.g. Larry Temkin, 'Equality, Priority or What?' (2003) 19 Economics and Philosophy 61; Derek Parfit, 'Equality or Priority?' (Lindley Lecture, University of Kansas 1991) reprinted in Matthew Clayton and Andrew Williams (eds.), *The Ideal of Equality* (Palgrave Macmillan 2002). See also Harry Frankfurt, 'Equality as a Moral Ideal' (1987) 98 Ethics 21.

55 Brookings Institution and others, 'Guidance' (n 5) §43.

56 Based for example on "landlessness, joblessness, homelessness, marginalization, food insecurity, morbidity and mortality, loss of access to common property and services and social and cultural disarticulation", ibid. §42.

distributive justice debate can also be framed in terms of compensatory issues, for example if the relocated persons are entitled for compensation for their land and possessions that remain behind. Here, the Guidance highlights that State resources, including compensation, services and/or financial assistance should be provided to those relocated and other affected persons. Should compensation be provided, the eligibility criteria should be equitable and address barriers that might limit certain people to receive fair compensation.[57] If States acquire the land left behind by relocated persons, those persons should have the rights to equitable compensation. In this process also the particular needs of persons with non-formal land rights should be taken into consideration, as well as those of landless, or unlawful occupants.[58]

There are also further issues regarding distributive justice, for example, regarding how relocated communities fare compared to host communities and how differences between those communities might influence the distribution of assistance (who receives it and how much). Here, the Guidance notes that host communities should at least maintain their pre-existing standard or attain the standard of relocated persons, depending on which is higher. According to the Guidance, the planned relocation process should also mitigate negative effects on other people who may be affected by the relocation.[59]

There is also a question if planned relocations should aim at making communities more equal, by for example providing ownership of housing for those who were landless or renters before the relocation or by providing livelihood opportunities and/or training for those who were un- or underemployed before the relocation. Here, the Guidance while acknowledging the need to address such questions, particularly in regards to land, property and compensation, does not take any explicit position. The Guidance though highlights that States should provide the necessary conditions to enable those who are relocated to "build a sustainable life of dignity" at the settlement sites.[60] This seems an indicator that the authors suggest the facilitation of at least some basic threshold of welfare for those relocated.

Another set of questions arise in terms of global (distributive) justice. As many of those countries that will have to relocate the largest amount of

57 Ibid. §47.
58 Ibid. §48.
59 Ibid. §15.
60 Ibid. §42.

people are among the less well-off countries in the world, considerations of justice might show that wealthier countries have duties of justice to support countries with planned relocation. The debate on global justice is much contested between those who argue that duties of justice only apply within a State and those that argue for global duties of justice.[61] In terms of climate change, at least it seems that there is some political agreement based on the common but differentiated responsibilities, which countries have agreed under the UNFCCC process, that wealthier countries should provide a regular amount of adaptation funding for less well-off countries which might also be used for planned relocation. Still, commitments by rich countries have been less forthcoming than promised.[62]

In addition, one can also connect planned relocation to questions of compensatory justice.[63] Considerations of justice are likely to show that countries that bear more responsibility for climate change could be liable for compensating those countries that have to cope with negative climate change impacts, for example through the need to do planned relocation. If one accepts this argument, a case might be made that planned relocation rather than being considered exclusively as an adaptation measure might fall under what is now discussed as loss and damage from climate

61 John Rawls, *The Law of Peoples: with "The Idea of Public Reason Revisited"* (Harvard University Press 1999) as well as Richard W Miller, *Globalizing Justice: The Ethics of Poverty and Power* (Oxford University Press 2010) making the former case; Thomas W Pogge, 'Cosmopolitanism and Sovereignty' (1992) 103(1) Ethics 48, making the latter.

62 Developed countries have promised US$ 100 billion of climate finance for developing countries per year by 2020. Tracking of climate finance is difficult as often donor's do not disclose if they pledge additional money or if former pledges gets 'recycled' from earlier pledges. In addition, only a small percentage of all climate funding goes to climate change adaptation. See for some discussions Maria Galucci, 'UN Climate Summit: Countries Promise To Give Billions in Climate Change Financing, but Road from Promise to Project Uncertain' (*International Business Times*, 24 September 2014) <www.ibtimes.com/un-climate-summit-countries-promise-give-billions-climate-change-financing-road-1694608>; Barbara Bucher and others, 'The Global Landscape of Climate Finance 2014' (Climate Policy Initiative Report 2014).

63 If and in how far this is the case is an open debate among philosophers. See e.g. Eric A Posner and Cass R Sunstein, 'Climate Change Justice' (2008) 96 Georgetown Law Journal 1565; Daniel A Farber, 'The Case for Climate Compensation: Justice for Climate Change Victims in a Complex World' (2008) Utah Law Review 377.

change.[64] Of course the issue of attribution of individual disasters to climate change is still problematic and legal claims for compensations have so far been rejected by courts. This does not mean though that such claims might not be successful in the future.[65]

Looking at the Guidance, one can see that certain justice aspects are addressed (albeit not framed in justice terms), particularly regarding distributive justice for relocated persons, host communities and other affected persons. One would expect a human rights based guidance to have certain egalitarian tendencies as it strives for the fulfillment of human rights of all affected persons, part of which will be the fulfillment of socio-economic rights of those persons and the above discussion about the Guidance shows that those elements can be found within the Guidance. Nonetheless, one can argue that the Guidance is rather vague and cautious in arguing about distributive justice, not aiming at certain absolute levels (above a certain threshold as for example the poverty line, average income, etc.). Obviously, circumstances on the ground will vary significantly from planned relocation to planned relocation and hence a certain vagueness of language might have been seen as useful in terms of guaranteeing universality of the Guidance by the drafters. Nonetheless distributive justice aspects might have benefitted from clearer and particularly more comprehensive language. Still, where it argues about distributive justice, the Guidance makes the strong point that the planned relocation process should not be at the detriment of relocated persons, host communities and other affected persons and that there should be an aspiration to improve living standards. Much of the discussion about justice will need to take place at the country and/or local level and include those affected by the relocation process, here the Guidance puts an important focus on procedural justice.[66] In terms

64 See for a discussion on loss and damage from climate change impacts Linta M Mathew and Sonia Akter, 'Loss and Damage Associated with Climate Change Impacts' (2015) in Wei-Yin Chen and others (eds.), *Handbook of Climate Change Mitigation and Adaptation* (1st edition, Springer New York 2015).

65 See e.g. Randall S Abate, 'Public Nuisance Suits for the Climate Justice Movement: The Right Thing and the Right Time' (2010) 85 Washington Law Review 197.

66 The term procedural justice has been framed by John Rawls. It can be interpreted in the sense that in situations where there is no criterion for what constitutes a just outcome at least a just procedure should be followed (pure procedural justice). In John Rawls, *A Theory of Justice* (Harvard University Press 1971) 86, Rawls uses the term pure procedural justice which obtains "when there is no independent criterion for the right result: instead there is a correct or fair procedure such that

of planned relocation questions of participation of affected persons play an important role in determining the outcomes of the planned relocation and while justice considerations might differ too much from one case of relocation to the next to come up with reliable principles of what a just planned relocation would entail, one could see the achievement of at least procedural justice as an important aim regarding planned relocation.[67] The relocation Guidance, for example, seems to take elements related to procedural justice as important when discussing the necessity of developing legal and institutional frameworks and the participation of affected persons in detail.

While taking into account a number of justice-related issues on the micro-level, the Guidance largely fails to address justice issues on the macro level (national, global and intergenerational justice). Given that it is very focused on the scope of the relocation project as such this does not necessarily mean that it has been an oversight, but that rather it is a question of choosing the scope of engagement with the issue. Nonetheless, a successful relocation policy will very likely need to engage with a wider set of justice-related issues than the Guidance offers.

This short analysis of several aspects related to considerations of distributive justice regarding planned relocation shows that such considerations are certainly relevant for the issue of planned relocation. The question however is if a justice perspective is beneficial to or even necessary for the 'success' of planned relocation.[68] I believe that looking at planned relocation through the justice lens provides one with an angle that is not fully covered by a rights-based approach, as laid out in the Guidance, as justice questions can provide both a micro (justice

---

the outcome is likewise correct or fair, whatever it is, provided that the procedure has been properly followed." He then adds that pure procedural justice in terms of distributive shares need to be based on a just system of institutions.

67 See Brookings Institution and others, 'Guidance' (n 5) Section IV and §35 for more details.

68 It is of course up for debate what success for a planned relocation means as definitions of enacting agencies and relocated persons might differ. I am inclined to follow the definition of the Guidance for when relocation ends, where it states that those relocated should have no more needs and vulnerabilities that are directly related to the relocation process and can enjoy their rights at least at the same level as before the planned relocation. ibid. §57. To make the term of success broader, I would likely add some kind of satisfaction with the relocation process as such and some measure of satisfaction with life at the new location which can be expressed in many different terms (economically, socially, less fear, etc.).

consideration concerning the relocation project) and macro (national, global justice and intergenerational considerations) lens for evaluating planned relocation. Particularly on the macro level, a focus on justice can help to connect one relocation project to broader societal, global and even intergenerational questions of justice.

6 Concluding Thoughts

Human rights guidance is an important part of a rights-based approach as it applies human rights to detailed real-world problems, contextualizing rights and so facilitating the application of human rights into laws, policies and actual on the ground projects. Given that planned relocation is likely to occur more frequently due to the negative effects of climate change and a large number States have so far been timid in engaging with the issue the Guidance on Protecting People from Disasters and Environmental Change Through Planned Relocation as the first comprehensive rights-based guidance document on planned relocation has the potential to provide important input to that process. Overall, a human rights-based approach seems to provide a valid frame to conceptualize planned relocation, particularly through comprehensively highlighting the wide array of considerations in regards to political, cultural and socio-economic rights of affected persons and through also highlighting the importance of agency of affected persons and groups. In addition, while discussing only cursory, this paper has shown that considerations of justice, particularly distributive justice, can play an important role regarding planned relocation and should therefore be considered to supplement a rights-based approach to planned relocation.

The EU's Strategy to Tackle Environmentally Induced Migration while Protecting Human Security

Susanna Villani

1 Introduction

Natural disasters have been increasing dramatically over the last thirty years. As the 2011 Great Eastern Japan Earthquake, as well as the 2010 Pakistani floods made clear, natural disasters are very difficult to predict and thus to fully prepare against, which exacerbates the impacts on people and society in affected areas. Such catastrophes tend to aggravate pre-existing inequalities, poverty, exclusions and rights violations, with vulnerable parts of the population often disproportionately affected. All these represent insecurities for the persons affected. Moreover, these disasters may result in large groups of people being displaced within their countries or abroad. Since 2008 an average of 26,4 million people have been displaced from their homes each year by natural disasters – equivalent to one person displaced every second.[1] As natural disasters often result in the destruction of public structures and institutions, the insecurity of those concerned is further exacerbated as it cannot be properly addressed by national authorities.

Against this background, the notion of human security and its implications in terms of political strategies play a relevant role. Actually, the concept of human security is used in different ways, varying from discipline to discipline.[2] It is however possible to identify some common features that refer to the content of the 1994 UNDP Annual Report on

---

1 See Internal Displacement Monitoring Centre and Norwegian Refugee Council, 'People Displaced by Disasters: Global Estimates for 2015' (Internal Displacement Monitoring Centre and Norwegian Refugee Council 2015).

2 For such conceptual overviews on the notion of Human Security see Mary Martin and Taylor Owen (eds.), *Routledge Handbook of Human Security* (Routledge 2014); Peter H Liotta and Taylor Owen, 'Why Human Security?' (2006) The Whitehead Journal of Diplomacy and International Relations 3(1), 37; Sabina Alkire, 'Concepts of Human Security' in Lincoln C Chen and others (eds.), *Human Insecurity in a Global World* (The Global Equity Initiative, Asia Center, Harvard University 2003).

Salomon, Heschl, *et al.* (eds.), *Blurring Boundaries: Human Security and Forced Migration*
 ISBN 978-90-04-32686-6. pp. 161-183.

Human Development.[3] For the UNDP, following the original wording of the 1945 United Nations Charter, fostering human security means to ensure freedom from fear and freedom from want.[4] The report initially identifies four essential characteristics of human security: it is deemed to be a universal concern relevant to people everywhere; its components are interdependent; it prioritizes early prevention to later intervention; it is people-centred. Later, the Commission on Human Security specified the core of human security by reporting that

> human security means protecting people from critical (severe) and pervasive (widespread) threats and situations.[5] It means using processes that build on people's strengths and aspirations. It means creating political, social, environmental, economic, military and cultural systems that together give people the building blocks of survival, livelihood and dignity.[6]

Hence, human security rejects the traditional prioritization of State security, and instead identifies the individual as the primary reference object of security. Furthermore, it offers a way of broadening perspectives that undergird subsequent strategic choices. Adopting human security thus implies recognizing that the most pressing threats to individuals derive from insecurities that affect people every day, such as famine, disease, displacement, civil conflict and environmental degradation. Although 'environmental security' was identified as component of the definition of human security outlined in UNDP's 1994 report, debates and policies around this notion have tended to focus more on human-made disasters, such as armed conflicts and human rights abuses, rather than on natural disasters. Recent catastrophes like the earthquakes in Haiti and Japan clearly illustrate that the actual threats people struggle with, following a natural disaster, such as aftershocks and deteriorating social order,

---

3 See UN Development Programme, 'Human Development Report 1994' <http://hdr.undp.org/sites/default/files/reports/255/hdr_1994_en_complete_nostats.pdf>.

4 See ibid. chapter 2, 24. According to Owen, while these categorizations are rather simplistic in their labels, they do prove useful in illustrating how different advocates of human security follow quite different paths in pushing for human security action. See Liotta and Owen, 'Why Human Security?' (n 2) 41.

5 The Commission on Human Security was established in January 2001 in response to the UN Secretary-General's call at the 2000 Millennium Summit for a world "free from want" and "free from fear".

6 See Commission on Human Security, 'Human Security Now' (Final Report, 2003) 4.

lack of food, water and shelter, or displacement are similar to those of a human-made crisis. While human security has progressively acquired relevance in the context of natural disasters, *inter alia* by offering a direct route towards integrating human rights issues in disaster response,[7] it has been rarely invoked in the context of environmental migrants.

The present work focuses on those migrants who flee so-called sudden-onset disasters, such as hurricanes, earthquakes, floods, volcano eruptions,[8] and aims at investigating the approaches taken by the international community and in particular the European Union (EU) towards environmental migration. In particular, the analysis will explore how traditional concepts of state security can be balanced with that of human security. Those who are forced to move in the aftermath of a disaster are in a state of human insecurity due to both the immediate impact of the disaster that makes them leave and the limited protection they receive. Unequal access to assistance, discrimination in aid provision, enforced relocation, sexual and gender-based violence, unsafe or involuntary re-

7 See Inter-Agency Standing Committee, 2010, 481-482.

8 For the sake of clarity, it is essential to distinguish between rapid-onset events and slow-onset events. The group of the Nansen Initiative defines "rapid-onset disasters" or "sudden-onset disasters" as hydro-meteorological hazards such as flooding, windstorms or mudslides, and geophysical hazards including earthquakes, tsunamis or volcano eruptions. *Par contre*, drought, desertification and land degradation are the main slow-onset events which are exacerbated by climate change and may have an impact on the mobility of people. Since the links between drought, desertification and migration are complex and difficult to identify, and there is no consensus on the impact of slow-onset events on migration, the present work takes into account just those movements arising from sudden-onset events. For further details on the distinction between slow/rapid-onset disasters and migration, see The Nensen Initiative <https://www.nanseninitiative.org/secretariat/>. In addition, see The Johns Hopkins and the International Federation of Red Cross and Red Crescent Societies, 'Public Health Guide for Emergencies' (2nd edn, 2008) 25; IDMC, 'People Displaced' (n 1). On the debate on what "disaster" means, see Ronald W Perry and Enrico L Quarantelli (eds.), *What is a disaster? New Answers to Old Questions* (Xlibris 2005); Etienne Piguet, 'Climate Change and Forced Migration' (New Issues in Refugee Research, Research Paper No. 153, UNHCR 2008); Etienne Piguet and others, 'Introduction: Migration and Climate Change' in Etienne Piguet and others (eds.), *Migration and Climate change* (UNESCO 2011); Koko Warner, 'Climate and Environmental Change, Human Migration and Displacement: Recent Policy Developments and Research Gaps' (9th Coordination Meeting on International Migration, UN/POP/MIG-9CM/2011/10, United Nations University – Institute for Environment and Human Security 2011).

turn or resettlement, and issues of property restitution are just some of the problems people displaced by a natural disaster often encounter. However, the movement of large groups of migrants not only challenges their individual human security, but may impact on the internal stability of hosting States, thereby creating human insecurities of host societies as well. It is therefore worth to illustrate the political and legal instruments elaborated to tackle environmental migration, by exploring, on the one hand, how they impact on Human Security of individuals and what may be the contribution of Human Security to political and legal discourses in this field, on the other. Indeed, since human security encourages considering the needs of the most vulnerable parts of the population, including those who are forced to migrate, it might offer an added-value for and contribute to a change of the international legal order that *de lege lata* only provides limited protection to environmental migrants. Therefore, this chapter employs human security as counter-concept to traditional approaches of security with the goal to enrich the existing EU legal regime on environmental migrants. Against this background, the EU, even though it is not universally considered as major player in *subjecta materia*, could become a forerunner and positive example by using human security as point of reference in defining political strategies. Indeed, as it will be reported, even though the current Common European Asylum Policy provides no legal regime regulating the entry of environmental migrants, its efforts in terms of budget and support programmes reveal that its policy could serve as example of an application of human security in situations of natural disaster that produce environmental-induced migration.

2 Environmental Migrants: Which Protection?

Between 2000 and 2008 an average of 38,8 million people was affected annually by cyclones and storms annually, while 99,2 million people were affected by flooding. In 2014 alone, 17,5 million people were displaced by disasters brought on by weather-related hazards and 1,7 million by geophysical hazards.[9] In many cases, these kind of events force people to leave their homes and move to other areas to avoid physical harm or loss of life. In addition, during and after sudden-onset disasters, livelihoods like crops, productive assets and homes are destroyed in

9 See IDMC, 'People Displaced' (n 1) chapter 3, 19.

some cases, making temporary shelter necessary.[10] Generally, these movements are overwhelmingly short-term internal displacements, as a largest proportion of the affected population returns to their previous homes. The ability to migrate over long distances is frequently further limited due to a lack of financial resources. Indeed, the real and ultimate impact of extreme weather events depends on the level of vulnerability of the affected population and the way disasters are managed. As a high frequency of disasters increases the vulnerability of a population and simultaneously decreases the capacity of governments to develop and implement effective coping strategies, this double predicament encourages people to move away permanently.[11] The low numbers of out-migration and the rapid reconstruction after the Indian Ocean Tsunami in 2004, for instance, can be explained by the rapid humanitarian response and the mobilisation of diaspora groups to support their affected families at home.[12] By contrast, several years after the 1991 Mount Pinatubu eruption in the Philippines many affected people were still living in temporary camps or squatter settlements.

Whereas environmental migration mainly concerns in-country migration,[13] peoples can be forced to leave their country becoming thereby cross border displaced people. For instance, in 1995, in order to escape the eruption of the volcano Montserrat in the West Indies that

10 See Koko Warner, 'Assessing Institutional and Governance Needs Related to Environmental Change and Human Migration' (The German Marshall Fund of the United States 2010).

11 See Wim Naudé, 'Conflict, Disasters and No Jobs: Reasons for International Migration from Sub-Saharan Africa' (Research Paper No. 2008/85, United Nations University, World Institute for Development Economics Research 2008).

12 See Cecilia Tacoli, 'Crisis or Adaptation? Migration and Climate Change in a Context of High Mobility' (2009) Environment & Urbanization 21(2) 513, 519.

13 According to the Internal Displacement Monitoring Center (IDMC) and the Norwegian Refugee Council, the number of people internally displaced by disasters in 2015 was 19.2 million in 113 countries, see IDMC, 'Global Report on International Displacement 2016' (Internal Displacement Monitoring Centre and Norwegian Refugee Council 2016) 5. Evidence gathered by the Nansen Initiative on cross-border displacement is strongest for people displaced across borders in Africa in relation to drought and floods, and in the Americas in relation to earthquakes and hurricanes in particular. Examples from Asia are rarer, though disasters and environmental degradation have been linked to people migrating abroad. See IDMC, 'People Displaced' (n 1).

devastated much of the island, a large group of people migrated to the United Kingdom.

Situations of natural disasters create operational, institutional and security challenges, not only for the affected countries but also for those welcoming and hosting those fleeing them. Security is an important human value, but also a right recognised by a number of international and regional conventions as well as national constitutions.[14] In addition, security is the normative core of the protection of rights that include the right to life, the right to physical integrity, the right to freedom and the right to the use and enjoyment of one's property.[15] Therefore, providing security and the protection of the rights linked to it is one of the core purposes of the legal system; hence, law is one of the major instruments for the pursuit of security.[16] Still, legal frameworks may sometimes not suffice to ensure the protection of people in general and environmental migrants in particular. As matter of fact, current international responses are not yet sufficient and protection for people forced to move within national borders or beyond remains inadequate.

Indeed, while environmental factors can contribute to prompting movements across international borders, they are not grounds for the granting of refugee status under international refugee law. The 1951 Convention relating to the Status of Refugees defines a refugee as

> any person who [...] owing to a well-founded fear of being persecuted for reasons of race, religion, nationality, membership of a particular social group, or political opinion, is outside the country of

---

14 States have the obligation to guarantee the security of the individual, as set forth in many international legal instruments: Article 3 of the Universal Declaration of Human Rights: "Everyone has the right to life, liberty and security of person"; Article 1 of the American Declaration of the Rights and Duties of Man: "Every human being has the right to life, liberty and the security of his person"; Article 7 of the American Convention on Human Rights: "Every person has the right to personal liberty and security"; Article 9 of the International Covenant on Civil and Political Rights: "Everyone has the right to liberty and security of person"; Article 5 of the European Convention on Human Rights: "Everyone has the right to liberty and security of person".

15 See Inter-American Commission on Human Rights, 'Report on Citizen Security and Human Rights' (Organization of American States, IACHR 50 Years Defending Human Rights, OEA/Ser.L/V/II. DOC. 57, 2009) chapter II, para. 18.

16 See Barbara von Tigerstrom, *Human Security and International Law: Prospects and Problems* (Bloomsbury Publishing 2007) 3.

> his nationality, and is unable, or owing to such fear, is unwilling to avail himself of the protection of that country.[17]

Extreme weather events are not included in the list of causes that can be invoked to receive the refugee status according to international law[18] and therefore the term "environmental refugee" accordingly has no legal basis under contemporary international refugee law.[19] Only those migrants fleeing persecution or conflict in addition to natural hazards, and who cross international borders, can qualify as refugees and receive the protections that this recognition entails.[20] To remedy these shortcoming, it has been suggested that the 1951 Refugee Convention should be amended to include environmental displacement.[21] In the current political situation, however, to open discussion of amendments to the refugee definition carries the risk of a total renegotiation of Convention

---

17 The 1951 Refugee Convention – Convention Relating to the Status of Refugees (GRC) [1951] – is the key legal document of today's international refugee protection. The Convention defines who is a refugee and the kind of legal protection, other assistance and social rights refugees should receive from the states that have signed up to it. A key provision of the Convention makes clear that refugees should not be returned to a country where they fear persecution. The Convention also defines refugees' obligations towards their host government and spells out that certain categories of people such as war criminals, shall not qualify for refugee status.

18 See Gaim Kibreab, 'Environmental Causes and Impact of Refugee Movements: a Critique of the Current Debate' (1997) Disasters 21(1), 20; Richard Black, 'Environmental Refugees: Myth or Reality?' (New Issues in Refugee Research, Working Paper No. 34, UNHCR 2001).

19 See Lauren Nishimura, '"Climate Change Migrants": Impediments to a Protection Framework and the Need to Incorporate Migration into Climate Change Adaptation Strategies' (2015) International Journal of Refugee Law 27(1), 107.

20 See Inter-Agency Standing Committee, 'Climate Change, Migration and Displacement: Who will be Affected?' (Working Paper, 31 October 2008) 4.

21 See, Roger Zetter, 'Protecting Environmentally Displaced People: Developing the Capacity of Legal and Normative Frameworks' (Research Report, Refugee Studies Centre, University of Oxford 2011); UNHCR, 'Climate Change, Natural Disasters and Human Displacement: a UNHCR Perspective' (Policy Paper, 2008) 9; Frank Biermann and Ingrid Boas, 'Protecting Climate Refugees: The Case for a Global Protocol' (2008) Environment: Science and Policy for Sustainable Development 50(6) 8; Bonnie Docherty and Tyler Giannini, 'Confronting a Rising Tide: a Proposal for a Convention on Climate Change Refugees" (2009) Harvard Environmental Law Review 33, 349; Angela Williams, 'Turning the Tide: Recognizing Climate Change Refugees in International Law' (2008) Law & Policy 30(4), 502.

and the lowering the standards of protection for all forcibly displaced persons. In addition, key stakeholders such as e UNHCR have voiced major reservations regarding the notion of "environmental refugees". According to the UNHCR, 'refugee' should be seen as essentially a legal term directly linked to the Geneva Convention.[22] Still, as long as no international legally binding solutions to guarantee protection to these groups of people are found, States remain the major decision-makers for welcoming migrants in their territories according to the traditional logic of state sovereignty, reflecting a traditional understanding of state security. Indeed, the right to admit or not third country nationals is one of the most evident manifestation of the classical notion of security.[23] Against this background, EU Member States have accepted that the EU should have common immigration and visa rules valid all across the EU. Therefore, to have a comprehensive view of the legal instruments available, it is necessary to analyse the current the EU legislative framework concerning migration to EU in order to verify the existence of some steps forward in guaranteeing protection to environmental migrants.

Since the 1980s, cooperation on asylum and migration matters has steadily developed and the Treaty of Maastricht granted the European Community its first, albeit modest, competences in the field of asylum and migration.[24] In 1999, the Treaty of Amsterdam granted the EU institutions certain powers to draw up legislation in the area of asylum to determine criteria and mechanisms for finding out which Member State was responsible for considering an application for asylum made by a third-country national within the EU.[25] In addition, the Treaty appointed

---

22 See Fabrice G Renaud and others, 'A Decision Framework for Environmentally Induced Migration' (2011) International Migration 49, 5.

23 See Ian Brownlie, *Principles of Public International Law* (6th edn, Oxford University Press 2003); Richard B Lillich, *The Human Rights of Aliens in Contemporary International Law* (Manchester University Press 1984); David Martin, 'The Authority and Responsibility of States' in Thomas Alexander Aleinikoff and Vincent Chetail, *Migration and International Legal Norms* (T.M.C. Asser Press 2003) 31-45; Susan Martin, 'The Legal and Normative Framework of International Migration' (Policy Analysis and Research Programme, Global Commission on International Migration, September 2005); David Fisher and others, 'Migration and Security in International Law' in Thomas Alexander Aleinikoff and Vincent Chetail, *Migration and International Legal Norms* (T.M.C. Asser Press 2003), 97-99.

24 See Treaty on European Union (Treaty of Maastricht) [1992] OJ C 191.

25 See Treaty of Amsterdam [1997] OJ C 340.

the Council to determine a "uniform status" for people in need of international protection as well as a common system of temporary protection for displaced persons in the event of a massive inflow.[26] However, the very notion of a "Common European Asylum System" (CEAS) was not mentioned in the Amsterdam Treaty, but introduced at the Tampere European Council in 1999, where the EU Member States announced their ambition to develop a "Common European Asylum System".[27] The Lisbon Treaty accomplished the Communitarisation process of asylum by finally providing the Union with additional competences to develop and revise a common policy on asylum, subsidiary protection and temporary protection with a view to offering an appropriate status to any third-country national requiring international protection and ensuring compliance with the principle of *non-refoulement*.[28] The influence of the EU over national policies thus is set to grow even stronger as the EU attempts to move beyond minimum standards to adopt common asylum standards. As already stressed, it is not common that cross-border environmentally displaced persons arrive in the EU territory, but, in theory, the Lisbon Treaty could provide the necessary legal basis for a uniform subsidiary protection regime for them. Yet, currently there are no instruments specifically regulating the protection of environmentally-induced migrants at EU level, whether for the scarcity of cases to be tackled or for security reasons that discourage Member States to find an agreement on their inclusion within special categories of protection. As a consequence, since they are neither refugees according to the 1951 Refugee Convention nor economic migrants in possession of the legal permits required, they could be considered "irregular migrants" and therefore expelled. Apparently, they do not benefit from any particular procedure that could ensure their protection. Despite this legal *vacuum*, literature has referred to some available instruments providing complementary protection standards at EU level, namely subsidiary and temporary protection, that could

---

26 Ibid. Art 73k.

27 See European Council, 'Tampere European Council 15-16 October 1999: Presidency Conclusions' in European Commission, *Bulletin of the European Union* (10/1999) 7ff.

28 See Consolidated version of the Treaty on the Functioning of the European Union [2012] OJ C 326/47, Article 78. For further details, see Jane McAdam, *Complementary Protection in International Refugee Law* (Oxford University Press 2007); Jane McAdam and Ben Saul, 'An Insecure Climate for Human Security? Climate-Induced Displacement and International Law' in Alice Edwards and Carla Ferstman (eds.), *Human Security and Non-Citizens: Law, Policy and International Affairs* (Cambridge University Press 2010) 378ff.

be applicable to this case as their scope of application seems reasonably broad.

In 2011, the European Parliament and the Council adopted Directive 2011/95/EU[29] recasting Directive 2004/83/EC.[30] The recast Qualification Directive, aims at harmonising national criteria for the qualification of third country nationals or stateless persons as refugees or as persons who otherwise need subsidiary protection laying down minimum common standards. The recast Directive constitutes an important step forward in harmonizing eligibility criteria and the content of protection at European level. However, although the scope of protection granted by Directive 2011/95/EU in Article 2(f)[31] is broader than that of the Geneva Convention, the list stipulated in Article 15[32] explicitly limits the notion of "serious harm" by establishing an exhaustive enumeration of situations that cannot be directly applied to environmentally displaced individuals.[33]

29 See Directive 2011/95/EU of the European Parliament and of the Council of 13 December 2011 on Standards for the Qualification of Third-Country Nationals or Stateless Persons as Beneficiaries of International Protection, for a Uniform Status for Refugees or for Persons Eligible for Subsidiary Protection, and for the Content of the Protection Granted [2011] OJ L 337/9 (Qualification Directive).

30 For a more detailed illustration of the Qualification Directive (n 29), see Jane McAdam, 'The European Union Qualification Directive: The Creation of a Subsidiary Protection Regime' (2005) International Journal of Refugee Law 17(3), 461.

31 See Qualification Directive 2011/95/EU (n 29) Art 2(f): "*person eligible for subsidiary protection' means a third country national or a stateless person who does not qualify as a refugee but in respect of whom substantial grounds have been shown for believing that the person concerned, if returned to his or her country of origin, or in the case of a stateless person, to his or her country of former habitual residence, would face a real risk of suffering serious harm as defined in Article 15, and to whom Article 17(1) and (2) does not apply, and is unable, or, owing to such risk, unwilling to avail himself or herself of the protection of that country*".

32 See ibid. Art 15: "*Serious harm consists of: (a) death penalty or execution; or (b) torture or inhuman or degrading treatment or punishment of an applicant in the country of origin; or (c) serious and individual threat to a civilian's life or person by reason of indiscriminate violence in situations of international or internal armed conflict*".

33 Paragraph 'a' of Article 15 is not applicable, as the death penalty or execution should be perceived as "legal, administrative, police and/or judicial measures which are either persecutory in themselves or have the appearance of legality and are misused for the purposes of persecution, or are carried out in breach of the law and are sufficiently serious to make return to the country of origin untenable" and therefore cannot be linked to the environmental circumstances (See European Commission, Proposal for a Council Directive on Minimum Standards for the Qualification and Status of Third Country Nationals and Stateless Persons as Refugees or as Persons

Thus, it seems to be rather unlikely that the Directive can be applied to environmentally-induced migrants. The internal flight alternative as enshrined by Article 8 of Directive 2011/95/EU has to be mentioned. Accordingly, subsidiary protection cannot be granted if protection can be found elsewhere.[34] Although States must take into consideration the personal circumstances of the applicant and assess technical obstacles to return to the country of origin, as long as protection is available in at least a part of the country, the application for protection by an environmentally displaced individual might be rejected.

In 2001, the Council adopted the Temporary Protection Directive,[35] which has been designed in particular for those who have fled areas of armed conflict or endemic violence being at serious risk of or who have been victims of systematic or generalised violations of their human rights.[36] The Temporary Protection Directive establishes "a procedure of exceptional character"[37] as it serves to tackle urgent protection needs in the case of an actual mass influx of displaced persons or when a mass influx is imminent until individual asylum applications can be handled. The reasoning behind minimum standards on temporary protection at EU level on this issue is twofold. First, disparities between the policies of EU States on the reception and treatment of displaced persons in a situation of mass influx should been reduced. Second, it had the aim of promoting solidarity and burden-sharing among EU States with respect

---

who Otherwise Need International Protection [2001] OJ 051 E, 0510 final, 19. In regard to the application of Article 15(c) the European Court of Justice has clarified that the existence of an armed conflict is the sole criterion for assessing the existence of a serious and individual threat. See Case C-465/07 *Meki Elgafaji, Noor Elgafaji v Staatssecretaris van Justitie* [2009] ECR I-00921.

34 See Qualification Directive **2011/95/EU (n 29)** Art 8(1): "*As part of the assessment of the application for international protection, Member States may determine that an applicant is not in need of international protection if in a part of the country of origin he or she (a) has no well-founded fear of being persecuted or is not at real risk of suffering serious harm; or (b) has access to protection against persecution or serious harm as defined in Article 7 and he or she can safely and legally travel to and gain admittance to that part of the country and can reasonably be expected to settle there*".

35 See Council Directive 2001/55/EC of 20 July 2001 on Minimum Standards for Giving Temporary Protection in the Event of a Mass Influx of Displaced Persons and on Measures Promoting a Balance of Efforts Between Member States in Receiving such Persons and Bearing the Consequences thereof [2001] OJ L 212/12.

36 Ibid. Article 2.

37 Ibid. Article 2(a).

to receiving large numbers of potential refugees at one time. *Prima facie*, the scope of application of the Temporary Protection Directive seems to be broader than that regarding subsidiary protection and, thus, could be potentially activated for environmentally displaced persons. However, the concept has not been deeply described and, even if it could make the provision flexible, it has never been applied so far.

After the 2004 Tsunami, the European Union proposed offering temporary asylum to child victims of the disaster to allow them several months medical stay in Europe to recover from trauma.[38] This proposal required an extension of current EU regulations on temporary asylum and thus was never realized. What is even more relevant is that the Temporary Protection Directive does not provide for a clear mechanism of protection, but leaves it up to States free to make a voluntary offer and to consent to the relocation. As long as State consent remains the leading principle of the migration policy at the EU level, it will be very complex to balance national interests with the solidarity principle of burden sharing between the Member States, as enshrined in Chapter VI of the Temporary Protection Directive.

Some Northern Member States have extended their refugee-type protection provisions by including categories of people who may be unable to return home in the aftermath of a disaster. For example, under Swedish law, a person "unable to return to the country of origin because of an environmental disaster" may also qualify for asylum.[39] In addition, the Finnish humanitarian protection framework set that "an alien residing in Finland is issued with a residence permit on the basis of humanitarian protection, if (…) he or she cannot return to his or her country of origin or country of former habitual residence as a result of an environmental

38 See Frank Laczko and Elizabeth Collett, 'Assessing the Tsunami's Effects on Migration' (2005) The Online Journal of the Migration Policy Institute <http://www.migrationpolicy.org/article/assessing-tsunamis-effects-migration>.

39 See Swedish Aliens Act (2009) chapter 4, section 2a. The drafting history reveals that the *travail préparatoire* covered also environmental displacement from sinking island states and longer-term solutions. The commentary on the finally adopted provision clarified that these suggestions were only intended to apply in cases of sudden disaster and would only be available if there were no internal flight alternatives. See European Commission, 'Climate change, environmental degradation, and migration' (Staff Working Document, 2013) 138 final, 18. In addition, see Vikram Kolmannskog and Finn Myrstad, 'Environmental Displacement in European Asylum Law' (2009) European Journal of Migration and Law 11(4), 313, 323.

catastrophe".[40] This opportunity is available both in individual cases – which results in permanent residence – as well as in cases of mass influx, where applicants can receive a residence permit valid up to three years. Denmark, on the contrary, does not refer to environmental migrants in its official asylum policy but adopted a rather pragmatic approach. It grants, on discretionary grounds, asylum to individuals from areas where a disaster occurred or where living conditions are considered to be very difficult because of famine and drought.[41] For example, it issued residence permits on humanitarian grounds to families with minor children from certain areas in Afghanistan particularly affected by as well as to poor Afghans without land coming from areas suffering from food insecurity.[42]

Despite the existence of such legal instruments, correlating permits have never been issued,[43] and in any case they could be issued only upon a specific assessment of the individual circumstances and, more importantly, according to the discretion of national authorities since no harmonised protection standards or coordination measures among Member States and the EU can be found.

Environmental migrants are unlikely to benefit from the existing EU legal tools relating to migration since they are not elaborated enough to accommodate their protection needs. Neither the EU institutions have perceived the necessity to strive to guarantee a certain level of protection to those fleeing their home territories in the aftermath of sudden-onset disasters, nor EU Member States have supported the idea to introduce a new category of migrants comparable to refugees in the EU protection framework. As a consequence, forced environmental migrants have been left in a kind of limbo since they are in an emergency situation, but without special *status*.[44] Two arguments have been brought forward

---

40 See Finnish Aliens Act (2010) chapter 6, section 88a(1). In comparison to the Swedish law, the Finnish one appears less restrictive, as the preparatory papers state that both natural and human-induced disasters are covered by this provision.

41 See Danish Aliens Act (2013) section 9b.

42 See International Centre for Migration Policy Development, 'Comparative Study on Categorized Protection: Comparative Study on the Existence and Application of Categorized Protection in Selected European Countries' (prepared by the ICMPD Vienna, commissioned and funded by the Advisory Committee on Aliens Affairs, 2006).

43 See Kolmannskog and Myrstad, 'Environmental Displacement' (n 39).

44 See Walter Kälin, 'Conceptualising Climate-Induced Displacement' in Jane McAdam (ed.), *Climate Change and Displacement: Multidisciplinary Perspectives* (Hart Publishing Ltd 2010) 81-103.

by States in this context. First, by designating environmentally-induced migrants as refugees the distribution of resources to those fleeing acute political violence and serious violations of human rights could be prejudiced.[45] The second argument is largely driven by national security considerations based on the misleading perception that the acceptance of anyone would be impossible and would, moreover, become dangerous for the internal stability of a country. As sub-category of migration, environmental migration has always been assessed on grounds of its implications on state security and the state prerogative to control migration. The arrival of large numbers of migrants, especially from very different social or cultural backgrounds than the receiving communities, can pose serious challenges to social cohesion and have practical implications for States, in terms of allocation of resources as well as of integration and protection of national identity.[46] Therefore, EU Member States still face the traditional dilemma, that is whether to guarantee protection or securitisation in managing immigration.[47] However, both stances follow the rationale to securitize State interests rather than to protect the human dimension of security. Immigrants, asylum seekers and refugees are framed as a security problem which is different from an approach by means of a policy which emphasizes that asylum is a human rights question and/or which proposes human rights instruments to deal with the issue. Such a self-interest approach can be explained best by analysing current migration flows to Europe. To allow third country nationals to reach European borders without planned and coordinated schemes is a threat to public security by placing a strain on public services, especially health and education, as well as exposing cities to social tensions. This creates human insecurities also for host societies that must face challenges to social and

---

45 See Pablo Bose and Elizabeth Lunstrum, 'Introduction Environmentally Induced Displacement and Forced Migration' (2014) Refuge 29(2), 5, 6. In addition, see Olivia Dun and François Gemenne, 'Defining Environmental Migration' (2008) Forced Migration Review 31, 10.

46 See Fiona Adamson, 'International Immigration in a Globalising World: Assessing Impacts on National Security' in Jonathan Kirshner (ed.), *Globalization and National Security* (Routledge 2006) 35-73; Elspeth Guild and Joanne van Selm, *International Immigration and Security: Opportunities and Challenges* (Routledge 2005); Myron Weiner, 'Security, Stability, and International Immigration' (1992) International Security 17(3), 91.

47 See Ingrid Boccardi, 'Confronting a False Dilemma: EU Asylum Policy between "Protection" and "Securitization"' (2007) Current Legal Problems 60(1), 204.

political integration, cultural identity and labour market stability.[48] As a consequence, security considerations permeate migration policies justifying rigid admission policies and give precedence to the interests of the people in the EU over the protection needs of environmental migrants.

Even though there is some room for manoeuvre to extend the scope of application of certain provisions to environmental migrants including them in the legal instruments mentioned, also the current EU legal framework cannot provide protection to environmental migrants. Against this background, human security could contribute to integrate the legal framework by countering the prerogatives of State sovereignty and in particular those concerning national security. Indeed, the people-centred and common concern elements of a human security approach clearly rise with regard to central issues of international law, such as State sovereignty, human rights and international cooperation to solve problems of common concern. In this perspective, the EU seems to be in the right direction, by promoting cooperation in order to develop regional adaptation strategies and to help people become more resilient thus limiting their need to migrate.

3 EU Political Strategies to Cope with Environmental Migrants in the Light of Human Security

The EU started dealing with the notion of human security in the 2000s. The endorsement of the concept by the Barcelona Report of the Study Group on European Security Capabilities represented a qualitative change in the conduct of European Union foreign and security policy.[49] The Barcelona Report declared that the most appropriate approach for Europe in the twenty-first century would be to promote human security. Therefore, the EU recognised the promotion of human security as a way

---

48 See Jef Huysmans, 'The European Union and the Securitization of Migration' (2000) Journal of Common Market Studies 38(5), 751. In addition, see Didier Bigo, 'Europe Passoire, Europe Fortresse. La Sécurisation et Humanitarisation de l'Immigration' in Andrea Rea (ed.), *Immigration et Racisme en Europe* (Complexe Bruxelles 1998) 203-241.

49 See 'A Human Security Doctrine for Europe: The Barcelona Report of the Study Group on Europe's Security Capabilities, presented to EU High Representative for Common Foreign and Security Policy Javier Solana' (15 September 2004) <http://www.lse.ac.uk/internationalDevelopment/research/CSHS/humanSecurity/doctrineForEurope.aspx>.

to improve its effectiveness and visibility as a collective global actor. In 2007 the Human Security Study Group published the Madrid report[50] as a follow-up to the Barcelona report with the aim to further develop the human security approach for the EU and offer ways to institutionalize the concept within the context of the European Security and Defence Policy (EDSP). Despite it can be questionable whether the EU lives up to it and whether it is realising such an ambitious project, the EU perspective towards human security can be thus seen in terms of a pro-active strategic narrative as part of its action to foster human development and human rights issues. Therefore, human security has animated the EU's willingness to intervene in difficult and dangerous locations, to deal with crises and to respond to urgent physical or material threat to individuals and communities. According to the Madrid Report, "human security is about the European Union helping to meet human need at moments of crisis, when people suffer not only because of wars but from natural and human-made disasters – famines, tsunamis, hurricanes".[51] In other words, it is about the objectives of EU actions as well as the methods to build its external policy. It is, therefore, "an organising frame that specifies how external intervention and engagement should be implemented",[52] and that is guided by a set of principles, developed by the Barcelona Report, based on the primacy of human rights, respect of political authority, consultation with local population, effective multilateralism, regional dialogue and transparent strategic direction.[53] Those principles, being mutually reinforcing and interdependent, give substance to the concept of human security as applied by the EU and serve as an operational methodology to guide and evaluate EU international operations. Although the notion of human security has been generally used to combine many of the concepts and ideas that have been developed in the ESDP,[54] it may also start being relevant in contexts of disaster response and in dealing with environmental migrants.

50 See 'A European Way of Security: The Madrid Report of the Human Security Study Group Comprising a Proposal and Background Report' (8 November 2007) <http://eprints.lse.ac.uk/40207/>.

51 Ibid. 8.

52 Ibid.

53 Ibid. 9-10.

54 See Mary Kaldor and others, 'Human Security: A European Strategic Narrative' (International Policy Analysis, Friedrich Ebert Stiftung, February 2008) <http://library.fes.de/pdf-files/id/ipa/05172.pdf>.

The European Parliament was the first to do some groundwork in this regard by including the issue in its 1999 Resolution on *The Environment, Security and Foreign Policy*,[55] where it warned for the first time about increasing numbers of so-called "environmental refugees". The engagement of the European Parliament was spurred by the spread of alarming claims about millions of people displaced by environmental disasters pushing the gates of the developed world.[56] In light of the security paradigm to migration as already described above, environmental migrants became seen as perpetrators rather than as victims in need of protection and, overall, environmental migration as a problem rather than a fact encouraging an adaptation strategy. Accordingly, as revealed by EU Strategy on adaptation to climate change adopted in 2013,[57] the main policy objective of the EU in this field is to contain migration triggered by environmental hazards by cooperating with third countries in climate change mitigation and adaptation, good governance, natural resource management and technology transfer. Therefore, the EU acts in all the phases of disaster management cycle, from prevention of to recovery from natural disasters, in order to keep people in their original locations without promoting migration.

In regard to prevention, the Commission supports numerous measures throughout the developing world in disaster risk reduction and adaptation to fast-onset events. In particular, Disaster Risk Reduction (DRR) is an increasing priority to address the alarming disaster trends and reduce vulnerability, by promoting a holistic strategy for all natural and man-made risks. From an initial focus on piloting and replicating a community based disaster risk management approach, the EU has developed a more comprehensive people-centred approach, including engaging with institutions at all levels. The European action consists in risk assessments and planning, sharing of good practices between countries, improving the know-how and early warning systems as well as strengthening capacities through training and other preparedness actions. The European Commission's Humanitarian Aid and Civil

55 See Maj B Theorin, Report on the Environment, Security and Foreign Policy (European Parliament, Committee on Foreign Affairs, Security and Defence Policy, A4-0005/99, 14 January 1999).

56 See Norman Myers, 'Environmental Refugees: a Growing Phenomenon of the 21st Century' (1997) Population and Environment 19(2), 167.

57 See European Commission, 'Communication on an EU Strategy on Adaptation to Climate Change' (COM/2013 216 final, 16 April 2013).

Protection department (ECHO) started funding the DRR activities in 1996 with the launch of the Disaster Preparedness ECHO Programme (DIPECHO Programme).

Currently, the Programme is implemented in nine disaster-prone regions throughout the world and it is aimed at helping the most vulnerable communities in rural and urban areas to be better prepared for and more resilient to natural hazards. It works through activities such as setting up disaster committees, developing contingency plans, early warning systems and evacuation routes, and identifying safe places to evacuate to. Projects also promote coordination between disaster management institutions at all levels, from local to national and supranational, in order to ensure that legislation is adopted or adapted and budgets are foreseen for preparedness and timely response.[58] On 23 February 2009, the Commission adopted the Communication "EU Strategy for Supporting Disaster Risk Reduction in Developing Countries"[59] aimed at ensuring that the EU works more closely and more effectively when supporting developing countries efforts for reducing the risk of disasters. Indeed, investing in disaster risk reduction means to strengthen the resilience and coping capacities in disaster-prone regions, minimising the need for environmentally-induced displacement when disasters occur.

Despite the EU collaborates with third countries to improve preventive measures, in many cases emergency response is needed to assist and protect victims of natural disasters. During and after rapid-onset events humanitarian organizations lead the efforts to assist people affected and possibly displaced by environmental hazards, in coordination with national governments and donors. Against this background, the EU provides significant humanitarian aid to persons displaced by natural disasters according to the humanitarian principles of neutrality, humanity, impartiality and independence.[60] In addition, the EU has progressively established a mechanism of intervention in order to

58 For a deeper analysis of the European action for Disaster Risk Reduction, see European Commission, 'Disaster Risk Reduction: Increasing Resilience by Reo 5, 2013.

59 See European Commission, 'Communication on EU Strategy for Supporting Disaster Risk Reduction in Developing Countries' (COM/2009 84 final, 23 February 2009).

60 See Joint Declarations: European Consensus on Humanitarian Aid [2007] OJ C 25/1.

provide disaster response in a timely and efficient manner and to ensure the EU assistance meets the real needs of the population. In 2001, the Community Civil Protection Mechanism[61] was established, fostering cooperation among national civil protection authorities across Europe. This mechanism, renewed and improved in 2013, gives the opportunity to any country inside or outside the EU whose capacities are overstretched by a disaster to request assistance through the Emergency Response Coordination Centre (ERCC). This structure located in Bruxelles collects and analyses real-time information on disasters, monitors hazards, prepares plans for the deployment of experts, teams and equipment, and works with Member States to map available assets and coordinate the EU's disaster response efforts by matching offers of assistance to the needs of the disaster stricken country. Such mechanism acquires particular relevance for the present field of analysis since it provides immediate assistance to environmentally displaced persons according to a rights-based approach. However, this policy instrument is mostly oriented towards the aftermath of a disaster, and a prompt and effective response to an occasional calamity cannot be sufficient to discourage people from leaving their country, in particular when the frequency of disaster increases. This is the reason why apart from providing humanitarian assistance, the EU also supports the provision of durable solutions for persons who are displaced permanently or for a longer term by granting humanitarian aid and promoting special programmes, such as the Regional Protection Programmes (RPPs) and Mobility Partnerships. The former, introduced by the European Commission in 2005[62] and

61 Since its launch in 2001, the EU Civil Protection Mechanism has monitored over 300 disasters and has received more than 180 requests for assistance. It intervened in some of the most devastating disasters the world has faced, like the earthquake in Haiti (2010), the triple-disaster in Japan (2011), typhoon Haiyan that hit the Philippines (2013), the floods in Serbia and Bosnia and Herzegovina (2014), the Ebola outbreak (2014), the conflict in Ukraine (2014), the earthquake in Nepal (2015), and the displacement crisis in Europe (2015). The EU Civil Protection legislation was revised at the end of 2013 to ensure better response to natural and man-made. It places a greater emphasis on disaster prevention, risk management and disaster preparedness, including a voluntary pool of pre-committed response capacities by the participating states. See Decision 1313/2013/EU of the European Parliament and of the Council of 17 December 2013 on a Union Civil Protection Mechanism [2013] OJ L 347/924.

62 See European Commission, 'Communication on Migration and Development: Some Concrete Orientations' (COM/2005 390 final, 1 September 2005).

subsequently integrated into the Global Approach to Migration and Mobility,[63] could be extended to include also environmental migrants. According to the Communication on Global Approach to Migration and Mobility, the RPPs are designed to enhance the protection capacity of the regions involved and to improve the protection of refugees through long-lasting solutions, namely return, local integration and resettlement in third countries of origin, transit and first asylum. The current RPPs are carried out in Tanzania and Ukraine, Belarus and Moldova, as well as in the Horn of Africa (including Kenya, Yemen and Djibouti) and in eastern North Africa (Egypt, Libya and Tunisia). They involve practical actions supported through EU financing, delivering real benefits both in terms of protection offered to refugees and arrangements with non-EU countries in support of refugees.[64] In particular, planned relocation measures could be a potential durable solution for communities which are at risk from environmental degradation. Moreover, the Mobility Partnerships might provide for the necessary framework to establish a structured dialogue on migration, mobility and security between the EU and third countries. Under this framework, the EU could provide assistance in strengthening the domestic capacities of the third countries in dealing with the internal displaced individuals, while keeping the cooperation in assuring stability, respect for human rights, democracy and good governance within concerned countries.

The EU has therefore progressively adopted a political approach aimed at strengthening responsive mechanisms to enhance protection of environmental displaced persons in third countries. Indeed, these movements are overwhelmingly temporary internal displacements as a high proportion of the affected population returns home as soon as possible to reconstruct their daily lives. Moreover, the ability to migrate over long distances is frequently limited because of the lack of necessary resources. From a legal point of view, the fact that these victims have not crossed an international border makes the State the first and foremost responsible to provide protection and humanitarian assistance to these people. Therefore, the EU's strategy has been to dialogue and work with origin and transit countries in order to reduce migration by promoting "local integration" over resettlement outside the region. Local

63 See European Commission, 'Communication on Global Approach to Migration and Mobility' (COM/2011 0743 final, 18 November 2011).

64 See European Commission, 'Climate Change, Environmental Degradation, and Migration' (SWD/2013 138 final, 16 April 2013) 30.

integration is indeed a long-term solution that let to permanently settle environmental migrants in host communities and, in principle, is a good solution because they enjoy the protection of their own governments or of neighbouring countries. Promoting intra-State and intra-regional mobility is thus seen as the solution for environmental migration by providing a practical support in the respect of human rights.

4 Concluding Remarks

Environmental events and risks of hazards are starting to play a bigger role in human movement worldwide.[65] The present analysis demonstrated that international and regional legal frameworks, apart from requiring the respect of basic human rights, do not guarantee full protection to environmental migrants. As only minimal legal protection is available for them, this results in a further decline of human security of migrants in the process of migrating. Also the EU legal framework concerning the common asylum policy reveals a number of shortcomings that are still permeated and oriented by the classical concept of State security thereby clashing with the necessity to meet the protection needs of those who are forced to move in the aftermath of a disaster. Against this background, human security may play a relevant role by integrating the legal framework and countering the traditional idea of national security. Indeed, the human security approach has much to offer by facilitating a focus on human vulnerabilities, thereby reducing the grave consequences of natural disasters for human safety and wellbeing. In situations of natural disasters human security should be the strategic objective, that guides solution seeking, encourages systematic information sharing, common action plans, needs assessment and better coordination of responses. During the rebuilding phase it should be used to suggest a bottom-up approach and consideration of the voices of all those affected, and, in disaster preparedness, to assist in guiding policy development by ensuring resilience measures and scenarios include consideration of human and community needs.

Against this background, the EU approach to environmental migration has a double face. On the one hand, both the EU institutions and

65 See Mark Mulligan and others, 'Environmental Change and Migration Between Europe and Its Neighbours" in Etienne Piguet and Frank Laczko (eds.), *People on the Move in a Changing Climate* (Springer 2014) 49-79.

Member States do not have seriously dealt with issues of how protect those who flee from natural disasters. This short-sighted vision of EU Member States gives prevalence to national security concerns over human security. However, best practices of Member States consisting in significant legislative adjustments introducing complementary forms of protection for those affected by natural disasters could lead to a revision of EU legislation. Against this background, the EU Court of Justice could play a relevant role. In particular, it could be called upon by the national courts to answer a preliminary question of interpretation of the provisions of Directive 2011/95/EU as well as of Directive 2011/55/EU and may determine whether these Directives can be interpreted so as to grant protection also to forced migration induced by environmental disasters. In this kind of situations, the judges in Luxembourg should promote a teleological and systematic interpretation of the relevant provisions of the Directives by taking into account the principles enshrined in the Charter of Fundamental Rights of the EU. There is no doubt that it would be the first step to ensure protection to the growing number of environmental migrants and to cope with this challenge by balancing traditional State security and human security.

On the other hand, the EU is demonstrating the intention to act as a global actor at international level by moving financial resources and promoting development and humanitarian projects aimed at addressing the root causes of environmental migration.[66] This commitment seems inspired but also guided, from a methodological point of view, by human security and by the guiding principles of the EU approach to human security set out in the Barcelona Report. As global actor the EU is developing instruments – such as the Civil Protection Mechanism – that in better assistance of those who are threatened by rapid-onset emergencies and to limit the necessity to move. In addition, it is negotiating with third countries specific programmes to managing environmental migration throughout planned strategies, the effective dialogue with local authorities and the involvement of regional actors.

66 See European Commission, 'Action Plan on the Sendai Framework for Disaster Risk Reduction 2015-2030: A Disaster Risk-Informed Approach for all EU Policies (SWD/2016 205 final/2, 17 June 2016). For useful examples concerning the EU projects related to Disaster Risk Reduction, visit the following webpage: <http://ec.europa.eu/echo/what/humanitarian-aid/risk-reduction_en>. For additional information concerning the EU efforts to promote resilience, visit the webpage: <http://ec.europa.eu/echo/what/humanitarian-aid/resilience_en>.

The preferred solution has been thus to direct the EU efforts towards the external dimension, by cooperating with third countries exposed to major risks for managing the impact of sudden environmental events on migratory flows. This approach takes into account the necessity to foster strategies of adaptation and resilience in an effective and concrete manner. Viewing migration through the human security lens highlights the social, political and economic dimensions of those on the move and of the communities that host them to live free from fear, want and indignity.

PART V

Human trafficking

Trafficking in Human Beings and Human Security: A Comprehensive Approach

Marco Borraccetti

1 Introduction

'Human security' was first embraced by the 1994 UNDP Development Report;[1] 'human' means a focus on the individual as a shift from a State-centred approach towards placing the individual in the centre and 'security' encompasses the protection from threats as well as the provision of a safe environment. Thereby, the concept is concerned with the security of people and the individual in terms of "survival, daily life and dignity of human beings" rather than with the security of a territorial state. Poverty, human development, and human rights as core elements of human security are closely connected with protecting 'the vital core' of human life. But while poverty and human rights focus on absolute levels of deprivation, human security focuses on the risks of sudden change for the worse.[2]

As for its content, human security is closely linked with human rights law, as it is about individual safety, integrity of the person and protection from structural as well as direct violence. It is also about the freedom from fear and freedom from want. On a general level, a 'rights-based ap-

1 The concept of human security has largely been created and shaped by Mahbub ul Haq. See Gerd Oberleitner, 'Human Security and Human Rights' (2002) ETC Human Rights Series 8. According to the Human Security Initiative the 1994 UN Development Programme Report "first popularized" it – HIS, 'Definition of Human Security' (28 February 2011) <http://www.humansecurityinitiative.org/definition-human-security>.

2 Sakiko Fukuda-Parr, 'New Threats to Human Security in the Era of Globalization' (2003) Journal of Human Development 4(2) 167. According to Shahrbanou Tadjbakhsh, 'Human Security: Concepts and Implications' (2005) Les Études du CERI 117-118, 5 – "Although the definition of human security remains an open question there is consensus among its advocates that there should be a shift of attention from a state-centered to a people-centered approach to security". In particular, human security "means helping victims cope with the consequences of the widespread insecurity resulting from armed conflict, human rights violations and massive underdevelopment".

Salomon, Heschl, *et al.* (eds.), *Blurring Boundaries: Human Security and Forced Migration*
 ISBN 978-90-04-32686-6. pp. 187-210.

proach' can provide a useful framework for the promotion of human security, enriching the concept. Human rights violations are often the root causes of conflict, insecurity and instability and are thereby a central element of a threat-based approach to explaining human security; in turn, respect for human rights prevents conflict and insecurity.[3] Therefore, human rights and human security are not used interchangeably. Hence, the respect of human rights is a mean to guarantee human security. To this effect, in addition, as highlighted by the Office of the High Commissioner for Human Rights "the human rights of trafficked persons shall be at the centre of all efforts to prevent and combat trafficking and to protect, assist and provide redress to victims."[4]

According to the 2005 Human Security Report, trafficking in human beings is "so widespread and so damaging to its victims that it has become a cause of human insecurity"[5] on a global scale.[6] Being linked with the exploitation of vulnerable persons, human security has implications and is related to the greater discourse on mobility, irregular and regular migration, within and to the EU. Vulnerable migrants – i.e. women, children[7] and persons in poor economic conditions or undocumented[8] – are at heightened risk to be trafficked, to be exploited in domestic work, in the agricultural sector or in the sex industry[9] because of their particu-

3 Bertrand Ramcharan, 'Human Rights and Human Security' (2004) Disarmament Forum 1, 39.

4 UN Office of the High Commissioner for Human Rights, 'Recommended Principles and Guidelines on Human Rights and Human Trafficking' (Commentary, UN-OHCHR 2010).

5 Human Security Centre, 'Human Security Report 2005: War and Peace in the 21st Century' (University of British Columbia, Oxford University Press 2005).

6 Richard H Friman and Simon Reich (eds.), *Human Trafficking, Human Security and the Balkans* (University of Pittsburgh Press 2007) 154. Friman and Reich are pointing out that the human security approach to human trafficking "remains underutilized and its potential underrealized".

7 See European Parliament, 'Press Release: Fate of 10,000 Missing Refugee Children Debated in Civil Liberties Committee' (21 April 2016).

8 See also Friman and Reich, *Human Trafficking* (n 6) 143.

9 Khalid Koser, 'Irregular Migration, State Security and Human Security' (Policy Analysis and Research Programme of the Global Commission on International Migration 2005).

lar conditions.[10] In the current context of the 'migration crisis',[11] part of the migrants that reached the EU territory have been confronted with human trafficking by becoming victims or experiencing violence during their journey.[12] The importance of the topic has also been highlighted by Commissioner for Migration, Home Affairs and Citizenship, Dimitris Avramopoulos, who stated that the EU action against trafficking continues to be a priority on the EU Agenda and will be so in the future.[13]

The realization of a human security approach to trafficking in human beings could have the effect to enhance measures of prevention, protection and prosecution in the fight against this serious crime, addressing freedom from want, freedom from fear and strengthening the rule of law.

The European Union approach is – in theory – characterized by the abovementioned elements[14] and the general analysis of the paper will be on the comprehensive approach promoted by EU legislation to human trafficking not only from a law enforcement perspective, but also considering the victims' position and their rights.

In particular, the central question touches upon the extent the approach in EU legislation and policy promotes and enables a human security approach to trafficking in human beings or if, in practice, a lack of human security still continues to exist. To that effect, the analysis will focus, on the one hand, on the 'access to victims' rights' in relation to the possession of a residence permit; on the other, on the consequences of the problematic definition of 'exploitation'.

---

10 According to Ramcharan, 'Human Rights and Human Security' (n 3), regarding the factors that contribute to the expansion of THB, a distinction can be made between: 1) economic factors (poverty, inequality, unemployment and indebtedness); 2) socio cultural factors (violence against women and children, ethnic and gender discrimination); 3) political and legal factors (armed conflict, weak and corrupt governments; 4) international factors (sex trade, restrictive migration policies).

11 European Commission, 'Report from the Commission to the European Parliament and the Council: Report on the Progress Made in the Fight Against Trafficking in Human Beings' (COM/2016 267 final, 19 May 2016).

12 Violence along the trip is not an 'exclusive' of trafficking; in fact, migrants can be victims of violence also in the case of smuggling. The important distinction of the two phenomena is not simple.

13 Dimitris Avramopoulos, 'Speech of Commissioner Avramopoulos in the Plenary Session of the European Parliament on the Trafficking of Human Beings' (10 September 2015).

14 See section 3 below: Trafficking in human beings in the EU legal order.

2 Human Trafficking and Human Security

Multiple aspects and factors of insecurity within countries of origin, transit and destination make trafficking in persons a human security issue.[15] Vulnerability, the use of violence – physical and psychological – and exploitation are characteristics of this phenomenon.[16]

Despite the recent legislative and political developments to prevent, fight and prosecute trafficking in human beings, a comprehensive framework embracing human security aspects is still lacking. Especially the lack of legislation, on one hand, and the effects of interpretation of the existing norms, on the other hand, put the protection of victims at risk, foremost their access to rights and the prosecution of their exploiters.

This particularly egregious criminal activity is characterised by the intention of perpetrators to exploit the vulnerabilities of potential victims for personal gain, frequently by exploiting conditions of poverty or forced migration due to civil unrest or the collapse of economic systems: economic, political and social factors can all contribute to creating a heightened status of insecurity among certain segments of a population. Strategies of traffickers aim at identifying and targeting these individuals who can be characterised as vulnerable, thereby ensuring greater success for themselves.

In a human security framework, both national and international dimensions have to be considered. The States are fully expected to maintain the security not only of their national borders, but also of the individuals living within those borders. They are held responsible for protecting the people living in their territory from external conflict and harm and they are also expected to ensure that those citizens enjoy a wide range of rights and are able to live their lives with a sense of dignity and an absence of fear. A human security framework will therefore provide a basis for specific policy and institutional changes necessary to protect vulner-

---

15 Friman and Reich, *Human Trafficking* (n 6); Alex Kreidenweis and Natalie Hudson, 'More than a Crime: Human Trafficking as Human (In)Security' (2015) International Studies Perspectives 16(1), 67.

16 See Michelle Anne Clark, 'Trafficking in Persons: An issue of human security' (2003) Journal of Human Development 4(2), 247 where she pointed out the importance to include trafficking in persons because of the fact that the growth of trafficking in human beings has reached such proportions as to present a significant human rights crisis in countries of origin, transit and destination. Second, because certain populations are specifically at risk for being exploited because of their particular vulnerabilities.

able populations from the risk of being trafficked in their countries of origin as well as in countries of transit and destination. Hence, in Europe, EU actions and the legal framework on trafficking in human beings has undoubtedly an added value, since trafficking is a transnational threat to human security.
The international community decided to implement actions against smugglers and traffickers with two Protocols to the Convention of Palermo on organised crime.[17] In particular, according to the *Protocol to Prevent, Suppress and Punish Trafficking in Persons Especially Women and Children,*[18] trafficking in persons shall mean

> the recruitment, transportation, transfer, harbouring or receipt of persons, by means of the threat or use of force or other forms of coercion, of abduction, of fraud, of deception, of the abuse of power or of a position of vulnerability or of the giving or receiving of payments or benefits to achieve the consent of a person having control over another person, for the purpose of exploitation. Exploitation shall include, at a minimum, the exploitation of the prostitution of others or other forms of sexual exploitation, forced labour or services, slavery or practices similar to slavery, servitude or the removal of organs.[19]

The approach adopted by the Protocol does not require only the use of force as a constitutive element of the crime of human trafficking, but leaves space for other forms of so called "means" such as traffickers taking advantage of the vulnerability of their victims using psychological violence or deception. The definition is comprehensive in its description of the three main characteristics: what are the acts, as recruitment, transportation, transfer, harbouring, receipt; what are the means, as threat, use of force, other forms of coercion, abduction, fraud, deception,

---

17 UN Convention against Transnational Organized Crime [2001] A/RES/55/25.

18 UN General Assembly, 'Protocol to Prevent, Suppress and Punish Trafficking in Persons Especially Women and Children, supplementing the Palermo Convention on Organised Crime' (15 November 2000). According to Ruggeri – Damien Ruggeri, *The European Legal and Policy Framework: Impacts on Human Trafficking: A Case Study on Albania* (Lambert Academic Publishing 2014) – the Protocol is using both a human rights approach and a criminal justice approach to define trafficking in human beings; however, the two theories are not considering the prevention approach.

19 UNGA, 'Palermo Protocol on Trafficking in Persons' (n 18) Art 3(a).

abuse of power, abuse of a position of vulnerability, receiving or paying of benefits; what are the purposes, as exploitation, in particular of the prostitution of others, other forms of sexual exploitation, forced labour or services, slavery or practices similar to slavery, servitude and removal of organs.[20] Punishing not only traffickers, but also exploiters that are not part of the organisation but are benefitting of their activity is crucial. For example, in countries where prostitution is legal, women victims of trafficking are marketed through the legalized sex industry. An action against the exploiters would complete in a reasonable way the legal framework.

Effective anti-trafficking legislation should be based upon two core principles. The first is the criminalization of the act of trafficking, and the second is the victims' protection. The recognition of trafficked persons as victims of a crime is a necessary step to ensuring their protection. The fact that victims are frequently criminalized for being in possession of illegal papers or for having been involved in prostitution, and that their families and communities will no longer accept them, helps us to point out the importance of a human security approach, where a victim is at the core of the legislation, irrespective of the status in the receiving country.

In particular, the need of better access to rights and to justice – clearly not requiring victims to testify against their alleged traffickers – is a key factor for the victims that – in theory – should not have to decide between deportation and protection. In this respect, the lack of unconditional access to support and protection puts victims at risk of criminalization and potential deportation, thereby denying them right of access to an effective remedy.[21] Furthermore, access to effective and appropriate remedies is an obligation on States,[22] confirmed by United Nations organs and a

---

20 Paula Banerjee, *Borders, Histories, Existences: Gender and Beyond* (Sage 2010), said that age and gender are the primary variables in identifying individuals at risk of being trafficked.

21 As stressed by the UNOHCHR, 'Recommended Principles and Guidelines' (n 4), the Human Rights Committee has noted that for trafficked women who "are likely to be penalized for their illegal presence […] by deportation," apprehension "effectively prevents these women from pursuing a remedy for the violation of their rights under article 8 of the Covenant" – UN Human Rights Committee, 'Concluding Observations of the Human Rights Committee: Israel' (18 August 1998) CCPR/C/79/Add.93, para. 16.

22 Recognizing the multifaceted nature of this right, guideline 9 of the UN Office of the High Commissioner for Human Rights, 'Recommended Principles and Guidelines on Human Rights and Human Trafficking (UNOHCHR 2002), recommends

range of regional and international policy instruments.[23] In a nutshell, unconditional assistance to victims would constitute a fundamental element for a trafficking approach to correlate with the notion of human security.

3 Trafficking in Human Beings in the EU Legal Order

Human security is intrinsic to the characteristics of trafficking in human beings. Where there is exploitation, where there is physical and psychological violence, the importance of victim protection is clearly arising. Only a safe environment is the place where a victim could have the possibility, could have the chance, to restore her or his own life. First of all to guarantee and to give back to the victims their dignity and their own freedom; secondly, to help and to cooperate to prosecute traffickers and criminal organisations. However, the cooperation with police and judiciary has to be put in a secondary place and it would be the added value of a system that has human protection, and therefore human security, as the main goal.

The importance of the fight against trafficking is part of the EU legal order: according to the EU Charter of Fundamental Rights, art. 5, trafficking in human beings is prohibited; the principle has to be seen in connection with the prohibition of forced or compulsory labour, slavery and servitude. It confirms that fighting against human trafficking is a way to respect and to protect human dignity and – in the case – to restore the dignity of the victims.

Furthermore, included in the Treaty of the European Union, the fight against human trafficking is a part of the EU general aims: in particular of the respect of human dignity and human rights (art. 2), and of the existence of an area of freedom, security and justice, with appropriate

---

the States to consider "[e]nsuring that victims of trafficking have an enforceable right to fair and adequate remedies, including the means for as full a rehabilitation as possible". See further *Rantsev v Cyprus and Russia* App no 25965/04 (ECtHR, 7 January 2010).

23 E.g., see also European Conference on Preventing and Combating Trafficking in Human Beings, 'Brussels Declaration on Preventing and Combating Trafficking in Human Beings' (14981/02, EU 29 November 2002) para. 16; Economic Community of West African States, 'Initial Plan of Action Against Trafficking in Persons 2002-2003' (2001) 3, para. 6.

measures for a common action in prevention and combating of crime (art. 3.2).

The Treaty on the Functioning of European Union (TFEU) includes the fight against human trafficking in the group of actions to develop an area of freedom, security and justice. In this case, it has to be seen from a double perspective: first, it is expressly included in art. 79 TFEU, the legal basis to counteract irregular migration, as a migration management measure with a particular attention to victims as vulnerable persons, in particular women and children.[24]

From a second perspective, trafficking in human beings (THB) and sexual exploitation of women and children – as serious forms of crime – are recognised as areas where to develop the cooperation in criminal matters: in that case, art. 83 TFEU recognizes the EU competence to establish common rules concerning the definition of criminal offences and sanctions to counteract particularly serious crimes with a cross-border dimension.

EU primary law is implemented by dir. 2011/36,[25] which aims at a more rigorous prevention of the phenomenon, the prosecution of traffickers and the protection of victims' rights: it establishes minimum rules concerning the definitions of criminal offences and sanctions in the area of human trafficking; it applies to the victims and it recognizes the gender-specific nature of trafficking.

Dir. 2011/36 adopts a gender-specific approach to trafficking in human beings, recognising that women and men, girls and boys, are trafficked into different situations and that they require gender-specific assistance and support. It further highlights that "the 'push' and 'pull' factors may be different for women and men depending on the sectors concerned, such as trafficking in human beings into the sex industry or for labour exploitation in, for example, construction work, the agricultural sector or domestic servitude". It further recognises gender as one of the factors contributing to vulnerability and urges Member States to establish and/or strengthen policies to prevent trafficking in human beings, including measures to discourage and reduce the demand that fosters all forms of

---

24 See Consolidated Version of the Treaty on the Functioning of the European Union [2012] OJ C 326/47, Art 79(2d).

25 Directive 2011/36/EU of the European Parliament and of the Council of 5 April 2011 on Preventing and Combating Trafficking in Human Beings and Protecting its Victims, and Replacing Council Framework Decision 2002/629/JHA [2011] OJ L101/1 (Trafficking Directive).

exploitation, and measures to reduce the risk of people becoming victims of trafficking in human beings, always by adopting a gender perspective.

The EU Strategy towards the Eradication of Trafficking in Human Beings 2012-2016 identified violence against women and gender inequalities as a root cause of trafficking and sets out a series of actions to address the gender dimensions thereof, as vulnerability to trafficking for different forms of exploitation is shaped by gender.

Member States of the European Union, in the October 2012 Council Conclusions on the new EU Strategy, acknowledged the gender-specific nature of trafficking in human beings and affirmed that it needs to be addressed in an integrated, multidisciplinary way and that measures should be human rights based, victim-centered, and gender specific, taking into account also the best interest of the child.[26]

For that reason, the European action can be classified as characterized by fundamental rights, victims' protection and gender approaches.[27] Furthermore, victims have to be protected from prosecution of crimes committed as a direct consequence of being subject to trafficking: the results are, first, the safeguards of the human rights of victims and, second, the fact of encouraging them to act as witnesses.[28]

Even if the directive follows the definition of the crime of the Palermo Protocol on trafficking in persons, it develops and specifies the meaning of vulnerability and exploitation. 'Position of vulnerability' means "a situation in which the person concerned has no real or acceptable alternative but to submit to the abuse involved"; whereas, 'exploitation' "shall include, as a minimum, the exploitation of the prostitution of others or other forms of sexual exploitation, forced labour or services, including

---

26 Council of the EU, 'Council Conclusions on the New EU Strategy Towards the Eradication of Trafficking in Human Beings 2012-2016' (3195th Justice and Home Affairs Council Meeting, Luxembourg, 25 October 2012).

27 On gender issues in trafficking in human beings, see Sylvia Walby and others, 'Study on the Gender Dimension of Trafficking in Human Beings: Executive Summary' (Migration and Home Affairs, European Commission 2016).

28 A critical analysis to the practical efficacy of the system was done by Magdalena Ionescu, 'A Human Security Approach to Anti-Trafficking Policies in the EU: Tackling the Structural Sources of Vulnerability' (2007), highlighting how "the protection responsibility is almost invariably left up to the civil society actors. This approach also limits the meaning of prevention, which is reduced to stopping, or managing, at best, the flow of immigration".

begging, slavery or practices similar to slavery, servitude, or the exploitation of criminal activities, or the removal of organs".[29]

Different pillars characterize the approach taken by the directive 2011/36 with a horizontal approach including particular attention in the case victims are women or children, pointing out the fundamental importance of a victims centred approach in the eradication of the phenomenon. In prosecution, because of the situation of weakness and vulnerability and the abuse thereof by the traffickers, the consent of victims to the exploitation shall be irrelevant (art. 2). Moreover, competent authorities are entitled not to prosecute victims for their involvement in criminal activities, which they have been compelled to commit (art. 8); last, to safeguard victims' lives from pressures inflicted to themselves and/or to members of their families also in the country of origin, investigation or prosecution have to be not dependent on reporting or accusation by a victim and a criminal proceeding may continue even if the victim has withdrawn his or her statement (art. 9). A rule justified by the fact that the position of vulnerability of the victim makes them more hesitant to initiate criminal proceedings, with a high risk of threat from traffickers to put the victims or their families under pressure, in order to make them withdraw what they had reported to the authorities.

In protection, the directive focused on the guarantee to assist and support the victims before, during and for an appropriate period of time after the conclusion of criminal proceedings, in order to enable them to exercise the rights set out both in trafficking and victims directives.[30]

---

29 Trafficking Directive 2011/36/EU (n 25) Art 2(2), Art 2(3), respectively. It should be noted that the definition of exploitation includes some particular forms of exploitation, but not a definition *per se* of the term. According to the European Commission, 'Report on the Progress Made in the Fight Against Trafficking in Human Beings' (n 11) 7, "Other forms of exploitation reported by the Member States include trafficking for the purpose of forced begging, criminal activity, forced marriage, sham marriage, or organ removal, trafficking of infants and young children for adoption, trafficking of pregnant women to sell their new-born babies, trafficking for the production of cannabis and trafficking for drug smuggling or the selling of drugs". There are also cases in which "people fall victim to multiple forms of exploitation".

30 Directive 2012/29/EU of the European Parliament and of the Council of October 2012 Establishing Minimum Standards on the Rights, Support and Protection of Victims of Crime, and replacing Council Framework Decision 2001/220/JHA [2012] OJ L315/57 (Victims Directive).

Assistance and support for victims have to be provided as soon as the authorities have a reasonable-grounds indication for believing that the person might have been subject to any of the offences typical of the THB.[31] In particular, assistance and support mean an adequate standard of living, safe accommodation, material assistance, medical treatment, translation and interpretation.

This assistance and protection are not made conditional on the victim's willingness to cooperate in the criminal investigation, prosecution or trial. However, according to Article 11, para. 3, this applies without prejudice to dir. 2004/81,[32] which could potentially affect the real benefit to victims. This is because, as stipulated in recital 18, "in cases where the victim does not reside lawfully in the Member State concerned, assistance and support should be provided unconditionally at least during the reflection period. If, after completion of the identification process or expiry of the reflection period, the victim is not considered eligible for a residence permit or does not otherwise have lawful residence in that Member State, or if the victim has left the territory of that Member State, the Member State concerned is not obliged to continue providing assistance and support to that person on the basis of this Directive." Therefore, the fact of not having access to a residence permit raises the questions as to whether the end of a regular stay in the territory of the Member State means the end of assistance measures.

Assistance has also a protective implication in the case of criminal investigation and proceedings; without delay, legal counselling and legal representation have to be guaranteed in any case, if necessary free of charge. In that situation, access to a scheme of compensation for victims of violent crimes has to be included.

For that reason, States shall ensure that investigation into or prosecution of offences is not dependent on reporting or accusation by a victim, that consent is irrelevant and that criminal proceedings may continue

---

31 Trafficking Directive 2011/36/EU (n 25) Art 11; according to recital 18, "A person should be provided with assistance and support as soon as there is a reasonable-grounds indication for believing that he or she might have been trafficked and irrespective of his or her willingness to act as a witness".

32 Council Directive 2004/81/EC of 29 April 2004 on the Residence Permit Issued to Third-Country Nationals who are Victims of Trafficking in Human Beings or who have been the Subject of an Action to Facilitate Illegal Immigration, who Cooperate with the Competent Authorities [2004] OJ L261/19 (Residence Permit Directive).

even if the victim has withdrawn his or her statement. In that situation, the possibility to continue to stay in the respective state and benefitting from support and assistance is fundamental.

Even if sanctions are involving both individual and legal entities, the Directive provides for sanctions only against traffickers, without similar provisions against victims' exploiters; in fact, according to art. 18.4, a Member State only "shall consider taking measures to establish as a criminal offence the use of services which are the objects of exploitation", without compulsory provisions in that direction. It entails a clear gap in the victims' protection system, because the act of benefitting of their activity/services is a crucial element for the existence and the counteraction of the phenomenon.

The situation seems to be in conflict with the need not to leave dangerous loopholes that could be exploited by traffickers, which is the reason of the obligation for the States to provide for the prosecution of every type of crime related to human trafficking in the case they are committed, even if partially, in the national territory or, without any limitation, in the case they are committed by their own citizens.[33]

Finally, despite the human rights and gender approaches, and a – generally speaking – victims oriented approach, the EU legal framework still continues to have gaps of legislation or difficulties in implementation and actual application, with concrete possibilities of differential treatment. All these types of situations look like more oriented to a State security approach; they are jeopardising the real protection of victims and in turn their human security, in case they are refused the assistance they need to live and to escape their terrible conditions.

4 Gaps in the Anti-Trafficking Legislation and Impact on Human Security

In line with the abovementioned aim of the chapter, in this part I will address the question of access to victims' rights, also from an equality perspective, as well as the lack of legislation on the exploitation of victims by

---

33 Trafficking Directive 2011/36/EU (n 25) Art 10(1); in addiction, every member State has the possibility to extend the jurisdiction to different situations, as in the case in which the victim (TCN) is someone who habitually resides on the territory; if the benefit is for a legal person based on the territory; if the offender (TCN) habitually dwells on its territory (Art 10(2)).

persons that are not involved in trafficking activities. In both situations – as it will be explained below – the protection and guarantees of human security are jeopardised and put in danger.

4.1 *The Matter of Access to Victims' Rights*

To guarantee security, protection and access to victims' rights, the stay in the EU territory is crucial. However, according to the trafficking directive, permit is not a right; at the same time, the role of cooperation with competent authorities in the residence permit, employers' sanctions[34] and return[35] directives has to be considered. Generally speaking, the question is to understand how these implications are related to access to victims' rights and human security. Furthermore, the matter of staying is in connection to equality in law.

The concept of equality in the EU legal order is inclusive of equal rights to access to justice; the question is if people in irregular position, undocumented persons and third-country national victims of crime in the EU could be in a worse position to be assisted and protected. In practice, differences exist between citizens and non-citizens, as well as between irregular and regular migrants in access to victims' rights.

According to the residence permit directive, third country nationals (TCNs) that are victims of trafficking have the right to stay in a Member State getting a permit. However, the element of cooperation with national authorities has a relevant role, seeing as how the permit will guarantee first a period of reflection to cooperate, with a temporary and unconditional nature;[36] as a second step, the cooperation with the judiciary or

---

34 Directive 2009/52/EC of the European Parliament and of the Council of 18 June 2009 Providing for Minimum Standards on Sanctions and Measures Against Employers of Illegally Staying Third-Country Nationals [2009] OJ L168/24 (Employers' Sanctions Directive) (27) and Art 13(4).

35 Directive 2008/115/EC of the European Parliament and of the Council of 16 December 2008 on Common Standards and Procedures in Member States for Returning Illegally Staying Third-Country Nationals [2008] OJ L348/98; (Return Directive) Art 11(3).

36 Residence Permit Directive (n 32) Art 6. According to Art 6(1), "The duration and starting point of the period referred to in the first subparagraph shall be determined according to national law". In practice, "[t]hirteen MS provide for at least 30 days, in some cases extendable for vulnerable categories or in view of the victim's personal circumstances, while others opt directly for longer periods of 45, 60 or 90 days. There is considerable variation as to the maximum duration, which can range from one month with no anticipated extensions to several months, or may

the police authority. Given the connection between cooperation and the possibility to get the permit,[37] the right to stay is subject to conditions and it is of provisional nature.

The way victims of trafficking entered in the EU is not relevant. Once in, competent national authorities have to inform victims about the reflection period, during which expulsion and return cannot be implemented. At the same time, basic needs have to be satisfied: of sufficient resources; emergency medical care and safety and protection needs; furthermore, the possibility to gain access to translation and interpreting services or of the right to understand and to be understood in the normal life (arts. 6-7).

After the reflection period, the duration of which is fixed by national laws, in the case of permit non-renewal, the return directive will apply (art. 13). However, article 15 of the residence permit directive established the possibility to have more favourable conditions in the national legislation for staying in the territory. In this hypothesis, the right to stay is recognised by national legislation and it is not under the umbrella of the directive.[38] It is clear that linking the permit to cooperation has a positive effect in pushing the victims to cooperate with the police. However, a somewhat short period of stay for the reflection period can be an obstacle to achieving the expected results of this provision, considering not only the individuals, but also their family situation, in the country of origin or – in case – in countries of transit or of destination.[39]

The fact that being issued with a permit is not a right arises also from the trafficking directive that expressly underlines the importance of action "without prejudice" of dir. 2004/81;[40] the lack of further details in

---

even be extended on a case-by-case basis, and as to the type of residence status granted" – European Commission, 'Communication from the Commission to the Council and the European Parliament: On the application of Directive 2004/81 on the Residence Permit Issued to Third-Country Nationals who are Victims of Trafficking in Human Beings or who have been the Subject of an Action to Facilitate Illegal Immigration, who Cooperate with the Competent Authorities (COM/2014 635 final, 17 October 2014).

37 Residence Permit Directive 2004/81/EC (n 32) Art 8(b).

38 According to ibid Art 15, without cooperation, residence could be an issue only following local legislation, without being in connection to directive rules.

39 If one of the more critical points is the short period of staying for reflection, and the clear link between cooperation and the possibility to stay longer, another critical point is the fact that this cannot apply to family members.

40 Trafficking Directive 2011/36/EU (n 25) Art 11(3); Residence Permit Directive (n 32).

Directive 2011/36/EU on this provision, apart from recital 18, cited above, could result in arbitrary interpretation by competent national authorities.

As pointed out earlier, the main objectives of the trafficking directive are a more rigorous prevention, prosecution and protection of victims' rights, recognizing the gender-specific phenomenon of trafficking. To achieve one of its aims, the directive obliges the States to guarantee that prosecution is not dependent on the report or on the accusation by the victim; in theory, it establishes specific protective measures for any victims of trafficking in human beings and it does not deal with the conditions of the residence of the victims of THB in the territory of the M. States. However, in practice, cooperation is a fundamental element for TCNs hosted in the EU territory and this situation puts them in a different position compared to the one of European citizens: in fact, dir. 2004/38 – the so-called 'citizens directive' – guarantee the protection from expulsion, which cannot be effected.[41] So, if European citizens are victims of this crime, there are no differences between the ones that decide to cooperate or not.

In the case of TCNs, the residence permit directive recognizes the possibility to issue a residence permit to victims that are cooperating. In the opposite case, with the exception of the case of a national permit outside its remit, victims will not have the possibility to continue to stay in the Member State, with the high risk to be returned to the country of origin or transit.[42]

The situation is clearly calling into question the respect of equality among victims of trafficking.

The theoretical approach is different from real and practical situations where the effective exercise of their rights (assistance, support, resources) does not have the same implications. In cases where the victims do not reside lawfully, assistance and support should be provided unconditionally at least during the reflection period. It is not the same for European citizens that – in any case – benefit from the right to move freely inside the EU. If not eligible for a residence permit or a lawful residence, the Member State is not obliged to continue support; this type

41 Directive 2004/38/EC of the European Parliament and the Council of 29 April 2004 on the Right of Citizens of the Union and their Family Members to Move and Reside Freely within the Territory of the Member States [2004] OJ L158/77 (Citizens' Directive) (16), (17), (23), (24).

42 In that situation the Return Directive 2008/115/EC (n 35) will apply.

of situation means that a TCN must cooperate with authorities to have a residence permit[43] and to have access to support.[44] In this respect, in cases where victims are not in a position to cooperate with the authorities, they are left unprotected and possibly subject to expulsion. This places in jeopardy their physical integrity and puts them at heightened risk of being re-trafficked; in that case, their individual security will be seriously threatened.

In a more general framework, the victims' rights directive[45] is also stressing the importance of the respect of the principle of equality as a means to guarantee and to aim at the goal of the human security approach. This directive does not address the conditions of the residence of victims of crime and the rights are not made conditional on their residence status or on the victims' citizenship or nationality. However, the question related to permits is supporting the doubts of full effectiveness of protection. Effectiveness means the protection of the concerned persons; the protection of their family members; and, finally, the importance to guarantee their protection once victims – or their families – are living abroad. Guaranteeing this type of protection would represent one of the pillars of the directive.

The victims' rights directive applies to criminal offences committed in the EU and to criminal proceedings that take place in the EU; from a *ratione personae* perspective, it applies to the victims of crime. It contributes to realize a complete legal framework with dir. 2011/99 on the European protection order[46] and dir. 2011/93 on the sexual abuse and sexual exploitation of children and child pornography[47] that applies to specific categories of victims. In particular, according to the latter, vic-

---

43 Residence Permit Directive 2004/81/EC (n 32) Art. 8.

44 According to the Trafficking Directive 2011/36/EU (n 25), in particular recital 18, if "the victim is not considered eligible for a residence permit or does not otherwise have lawful residence in that Member State", competent authorities are not obliged "to continue providing assistance and support to that person on the basis of this Directive".

45 Victims Directive 2012/29/EU (n 30) establishing minimum standards on the rights, support and protection of victims of crime.

46 Directive 2011/99/EU of the European Parliament and of the Council of 13 December 2011 on the European Protection Order [2011] OJ L338/2.

47 Directive 2011/93/EU of the European Parliament and of the Council of 13 December 2011 on Combating Sexual Abuse and Sexual Exploitation of Children, and Child Pornography, Replacing the Council Framework-Decision 2004/68/JHA [2011] OJ L335/1.

tims of crime have to be treated without discrimination and they have to be protected from secondary and repeated victimization,[48] intimidation and retaliation.

Protection for victims and their family members from secondary and repeated victimization, intimidation, retaliation, such as interim injunctions or protection or restraining orders, are the instruments needed to concretely realize and implement a human security approach, giving victims the possibility to be protected from traffickers and to have the guarantee that the latter will be prosecuted and form no threat to them in the future. However, given that there are no provisions on the right to stay or on the way or procedures to get a permit, the conditions to have a permit are related to the trafficking directive and to the residence permit directive.

The application of the victims' rights directive – to everybody who is a victim of a crime – irrespective of the residence status (art. 1), is a rule of incredible importance for undocumented people, above all in the case of first assistance. The only risk is that, after this particular moment, they will not be supported by the State in a moment crucial for restoring their physical and psychological condition. The access to victim support services is not dependent on a formal complaint with regard to a criminal offence; it is a confirmation of the general rule according to which a victim's positive action (art. 8) is not necessary. At the same time, art.17 obliges competent national authorities to take appropriate measures to minimize the difficulties faced where the victim is a resident of a Member State (art. 17).

Again, the gaps in cases where victims are TCNs and not resident in the EU must be pointed out; it means not having an equality approach to persons that are living in a similar situation, putting non-Europeans in a weaker and more dangerous situation: the need of a regular position to benefit from State assistance and the need to cooperate to be in a regular position and to get a residence permit could put the victims in a condition of illegality, with the high risk of falling prey to criminal networks of trafficking and being re-trafficked and re-victimised. Only a modification of the legal provisions explained above will guarantee the full respect of the principle of equality and above all a full human security approach.

---

48 See ibid. (24).

4.2 *The Matter of Exploitation*

A second focus has to be put on the lack of legislation in the fight against exploiters, who are not necessarily traffickers or members of the criminal organizations involved in this 'dark-side oriented' activity, but 'only' persons that benefit from the victims' services. In this context, it is important to be aware that from a legal perspective, there is not a definition of exploitation *per se*. International law itself does not contain a general definition of exploitation: "certain practices commonly identified as 'exploitative' are indeed defined. However, other practices, such as the exploitation of the prostitution of others, and economic or sexual exploitation in relation to children, are not".[49] It has to be assumed that, for the reasoning in this paper and in this paragraph, we can consider a general meaning of "one person taking unfair advantage of another person, their vulnerability or their situation".[50]

As mentioned above, the trafficking directive stipulated the meaning of exploitation, "as a minimum, the exploitation of the prostitution of others or other forms of sexual exploitation, forced labour or services, including begging, slavery or practices similar to slavery, servitude, or the exploitation of criminal activities, or the removal of organs".[51]

Despite the fact that the directive provides for sanctions against traffickers, there are no similar provisions against victims' exploiters and users. Furthermore, art. 18.4 only asks the Member States to "consider taking measures to establish as a criminal offence the use of services, which are the objects of exploitation". Therefore, there are no compulsory provisions to take measures against external exploiters, but the question has

49 UN Office on Drugs and Crime, 'The Concept of "Exploitation" in the Trafficking in Persons Protocol' (Issue Paper, 2015) – The paper points out that there are different national approaches to exploitation: States that closely follow the Protocol's approach (Malaysia or UAE); States that stipulate additional forms of exploitation (Bulgaria or Colombia); States with a different approach to exploitation (Australia or Canada).

50 Ibid. 39.

51 It should be noted that the 'European' definition of exploitation is more inclusive that the one in the Palermo Protocol (n 18) according to which, Art 3, "Exploitation shall include, at a minimum, the exploitation of the prostitution of others or other forms of sexual exploitation, forced labour or services, slavery or practices similar to slavery, servitude or the removal of organs". In fact, in the Trafficking Directive 2011/36/EU (n 25) Art 2(3), 'begging' is expressly included in the part of "forced labour or services".

only to be 'taken into consideration' by the Member State. This means that there is no required regulatory final result.

In this context, the question is how to manage the situation, finding a way to sanction the exploiters; the fact that the 65% of registered victims are European citizens and the fact that 16% of registered victims of sexual exploitation are children lead us to a make a distinction on the rules applicable in the concerned legal framework.[52]

In the case victims are TCN, national authorities have the possibility to use dir. 2009/52, recognizing a secondary effect in the light of its primary goal, the fight against irregular migration through the punishment of those who employ irregular migrants as workforce. In fact, if a trafficked person in irregular position is working in a Member State, the employers that benefit from their activities would be punished by fine or sentence, although not as serious as the gravity of the crime would merit.

However, this solution could not have application to the hypothesis of victims in regular position and to the one of sexual exploitation *per se*; except in cases where the victim is in an employment relation with the employer, sexual exploitation could not be punished.[53] In addition, for the countries where prostitution is legal and a form of work, the instances of self-employed victims are not covered by the employers sanctions directive, because they are not in a formal dependent employment relationship with the employer, as required by the scope of the directive. Instead, prevention and criminalization of sexual exploitation – as, more in general, of all the forms of exploitation – have to be the core of a human security oriented legal framework.

Nevertheless, in the case of EU citizens' involvement, dir. 2009/52 cannot be applied to employers of 'European' victims because it only deals with "third country nationals illegally staying".

For that reason, it is important to examine the possibility of having a similar rule in the case where EU citizens are concerned.

It seems difficult to declare a EU citizen 'irregular', because of the pillar of the freedom of movement of persons, according to the Charter, the Treaties and the legal order provisions.

---

52 According to the EUROSTAT Report on Trafficking in Human Beings – EUROSTAT, 'Trafficking in Human Beings' (February 2015) – the 80% of registered victims were female; the 69% of victims were trafficked for sexual exploitation and the 95% of them were female; the 71% of victims trafficked for labour exploitation were male; the 65% of registered victims are EU citizens.

53 69% of trafficked registered persons are victims of sexual exploitation, ibid.

On one hand, there is no irregularity in case the citizen is on the territory of a Member State for a period of less than three months. On the other hand, for a period of more than 3 months, the Citizens Directive – in particular art. 7 – requires the fulfilment of certain conditions[54] and – until today – the evaluation of the fulfilment happened only the first time or in the case of "reasonable doubt as to weather a Union citizen satisfies the conditions"; but, a systematic verification, i.e. in regular intervals, is forbidden.[55] Only the failure to comply with these certain conditions probably creates a situation of irregularity, even if the Court of Justice has not yet decided upon the irregular position of a EU citizen, rather giving judgments on the possibility to benefit social and health care assistance.[56] Also the possibility to return victims to their European country of origin for public security, public and health policy has to be excluded:[57] the effect would provoke the victims' criminalisation, in an opposite direction to their protection that is the aim pursued by the trafficking directive.

---

54 According to Art. 7 of the Citizens' Directive 2004/38/EC (n 41), EU citizens "shall have" the right to reside for more than three months in another Member States, if they: "a) are workers or self-employed persons in the host Member State; or b) have sufficient resources for themselves not to become a burden on the social assistance system of the host Member State during their period of residence and have comprehensive sickness insurance cover in the host Member State; or (c) – are enrolled at a private or public establishment, accredited or financed by the host Member State on the basis of its legislation or administrative practice, for the principal purpose of following a course of study, including vocational training; and – have comprehensive sickness insurance cover in the host Member State and assure the relevant national authority, by means of a declaration or by such equivalent means as they may choose, that they have sufficient resources for themselves not to become a burden on the social assistance system of the host Member State during their period of residence; or (d) are family members accompanying or joining a Union citizen who satisfies the conditions referred to in points (a), (b) or (c)".

55 Ibid. Art 14(2). More in general, according to para. 11, "the fundamental and personal right of residence in another Member State is conferred directly on Union citizens by the Treaty and is not dependent upon their having fulfilled administrative procedures".

56 See, inter alia, Case C–67/14 *Jobcenter Berlin Neukölln v Nazifa Alimanovic and others* [2015] ECLI:EU:C:2015:597; Case C–299/14 *Vestische Arbeit Jobcenter Kreis Recklinghausen v García-Nieto and others* [2016] ECLI:EU:C:2016:114; Case C–333/13 *Elisabeta Dano and Florin Dano v Jobcenter Leipzig* [2014] ECLI:EU:C:2014:2358.

57 Citizens' Directive 2004/38/EC (n 41) Art 27.

The idea to link users' sanctions to irregularity could be wrong not only because of the fact that EU citizens in conditions of irregularity are a numerical minority; but also because it is quite simple for them to attain a situation of regularity: in that case, criminal networks surely have the power to create the conditions to exploit victims in full respect of Union laws. Finally, the matter of sexual exploitation could continue to exist, above all in the countries where prostitution is legal[58] and considered as a 'normal' job;[59] in addition, following an ideal path similar to the employers sanctions directive, it has to be considered that not all victims have an employer and that not all employers are using their services. In that case, some of the people that should be criminalised – because of an exploiting or benefiting situation – are in the condition to continue to act in full respect of the law.[60]

Therefore, the problem still continues, given the gap in the EU legal order due to the absence of a provision affecting the exploiters, and in particular in the case where victims are citizens of the EU. The legislation could be better and more comprehensive on punishing people benefitting from victims and use their services, focusing on the exploitation of the victims and not on the victims' country of origin. Any other parameter, such as the employment relationship with the exploiter or the user of the services of victims or the nature of the provision of the services as such, runs the risk of disregarding the actual focus on the exploitation of victims and misrepresenting such exploitation as actual and legitimate work. In addition, in this way, it would overcome any distinction between EU citizens and TCNs, thus over-passing any distinction in the

58 According to Europol Situation Report 2016 on Trafficking in Human Beings in the EU – EUROPOL, 'Situation Report: Trafficking in Human Beings in the EU' (Doc Ref No 765175, 2016) 11-12 – 'in countries where prostitution is legal and regulated, it is possible that sex work is affected by the demand for cheap labour' and in those countries 'it is much easier for traffickers who wish to use a legal environment in order to exploit their victims'.

59 The first judgment of the Court of Justice of the European union on prostitution was Case C-268/99 *Aldona Malgorzata Jany and others v Staatssecretaris van Justitie* [2001] ECLI:EU:C:2001:616. In this case, the Court linked the legal nature of prostitution to the legislation of the concerned Member State.

60 The fact that Art 32(2) of the EU Charter of Fundamental Rights – EU, Charter of Fundamental Rights of the EU (26 October 2012) 2012/C 326/02 – expressly forbids the economic exploitation of children does not modify the substance of the approach, because of the number of the exploited persons not covered by it, i.e. adult victims.

legal framework and offering a real solution to fight against any type of exploitation.

For this purpose, art. 83(2) TFEU could be the appropriate legal basis. This provision gives the EU – in an area which has been subject to harmonization measures – the power to issue directives establishing minimum rules with regard to the definition of criminal offences and sanctions in the area concerned. In that case, the area of freedom, security and justice has been subject to harmonization; in particular, the fight against THB has been subject of a framework decision and now of a directive, but it is not enough. Although according to art. 18.4 of the trafficking directive Member States shall consider taking measures to establish as a criminal offence the use of services, which are the objects of exploitation; there are no compulsory provisions in that direction. This is evidence, as elaborated above, of the need of a directive accomplishing and consolidating the existing legal framework.[61]

5 Final Remarks

A lacuna has been found in the EU legislation on trafficking in human beings in the inconsistent framework between victims, who come from EU- or non-EU countries, respectively, especially as in relation to the right to stay and to the punishment of victims' exploiters. This lacuna can have adverse effects on the human security of victims, affecting their freedoms from fear and from want. What is more, an approach that focuses on state security is still predominant in the implementation of national policies to counter trafficking, even if the opposite intention arises from the European legal framework.

In fact, the Trafficking directive establishes protective measures for any victim without dealing with the conditions of residence and the investigation and prosecution of offences are not depending on victims' consent or cooperation. However, the directive applies without prejudice to the residence permit directive that links the right to stay (getting a per-

61 According to ibid. Art 23(2), the Commission will "submit a report to the European Parliament and the Council, assessing the impact of existing national law, establishing as a criminal offence the use of services which are the objects of exploitation of trafficking in human beings, on the prevention of trafficking in human beings, accompanied, if necessary, by adequate proposals".

mit) with victims' cooperation after a period of reflection whose length is fixed by national legislations and not at the EU level.

The possibility that without a permit the State will guarantee only basic assistance and at the beginning of the period is real; the serious risk is to put the victims in the condition to have to choose between cooperation and deportation, with a high level of risk not only for them but also for their families in countries of transit or of origin. The idea to decouple cooperation and residence could be a practical solution to guarantee safer conditions for victims and an effective fight against human trafficking at the same time. From a second perspective, despite dir. 2011/36 is always applicable, a difference arises in the case of exploitation. Given the absence of a specific legal act sanctioning exploiters in case victims are TCNs, the application of the employers sanctions directive has to be considered.

The same could not happen in the case of European victims of trafficking because, first, the employers' sanctions directive applies only in the case for the employment of TCN; second, in the European legal framework there is not a similar rule that applies in the case of EU citizens' employment; third, the idea to have a similar one is far from reality, because of the difficult application of a concept of irregularity to EU citizens.[62] The importance of putting the exploitation factor in the core of the legislation brings about the need of a new directive on sanctions against the exploiters.

What would this entail? Firstly, it would highlight that there are no differences between the origin of the victims and, secondly that a common framework against all the exploiters, for any type of exploitation, is in place. The provision of sanctions against them would certainly contribute to the fight against human trafficking. Sanctioning exploiters will have also the effect of creating a safer framework and a normative effect, in the name of respect of human dignity and fundamental rights.

Only in this way can the human security paradigm be considered a real goal of the EU legal and policy framework to address THB and, above all, in the protection of the victims: on the one hand, the fact of guaranteeing a real access to victims' rights taking into consideration more their personal needs and their personal position as victim, instead of the importance to cooperate with the national authorities; on the other, the idea to put any type of victims' of trafficking exploitation at the core of

62 In that situation, it has also to be considered that there is no irregularity if workers are staying for a short period of up to three months.

the European legal framework, to counteract and to fight against this serious form of crime. If not, human security will be at serious risk because of the conditions of vulnerability with a climate that fosters trafficking in persons, impunity for exploiters and – above all – insecurity for victims.

Index